HAITI STRONGMAN

The Life and Times of Jean Pierre Boyer

Nancy Dubosse

For information contact :
Nancy Dubosse, email: dubossebooks@gmail.com

Book Formatting by Derek Murphy@Creativindie
Cover design by Michael Rehder
ISBN: 979-8-9997056-0-0

First Edition: September 2025

Acknowledgments

The conception and form of this biography benefited greatly from the references consulted in the Theodore family library in Port-au-Prince, Haiti.

Though these references are freely accessible by anyone with internet access, the writer is appreciative of the initiative of the French government to digitize its collections. The tremendous cost of making these resources widely available is counterbalanced by the global social benefit of universal access to the archives of what was a formidable empire.[1]

"All successful revolutions, however idealistic, probably betray themselves in time."

- Graham Greene

CONTENTS

Preface

Wondering why no biography had yet been written on Jean Pierre Boyer—the president for twenty-five years of a black republic during the nineteenth century, in a sea of slave colonies—I googled "longest-serving heads of state." My search was partly to see if Boyer's tenure was considered long relative to other world leaders, and partly to see how the world had interpreted this period in American history.

Unsurprisingly, there were numerous websites dedicated to ridiculing long-serving (current and former) African leaders like Museveni, Kagame, and Mugabe, as well as the more infamous (from a North American perspective) current world leaders like Putin. But there was no mention of Boyer. I did find several sites which mentioned long-serving non-monarchs, but they mostly focused on Castro, who presided over Cuba for some forty-nine years.

After scrolling through several pages of search results without seeing any mention of Boyer, I refined the google search by adding "Latin America" and encountered many sites on Bolivia's Morales and Nicaragua's Ortega. Still no mention of Boyer. I then further refined the search to "Head of State - Caribbean - 19th century," knowing full well that the only sovereign nation at the time of Boyer's election was the Republic of Haiti. There, I saw pages debating the more recent question of Puerto Rican statehood versus its independence, the even-more recent election of a female president and prime minister in Barbados, the extent to which the British Commonwealth would be preserved consequent to the passing of Queen Elizabeth II, and lots on the United States' invasion of Haiti, which actually occurred in the twentieth century.

How can it be—considering the palpable hostility between Haiti and the Dominican Republic; the recent media coverage of the multinational involvement of the assassination of President Jovenel Moïse and the persistent political and social turmoil that Haiti has endured; the unexpectedly lengthy coverage afforded by The New York Times on Haiti's indemnity payment to France in exchange for recognition of its independence, negotiated during Boyer's presidency; not to mention the numerous natural disasters Haiti has suffered—that no book has highlighted the life and times of a man who consolidated the island of Hispaniola and governed it for twenty-five years, even in the face of European and American hostility?

Although it is obviously too late to interview any of Boyer's contemporaries for their personal perspectives, it is never too late to add to the general knowledge of the island, to improve the understanding of the statecraft employed to ensure the sovereignty of the Republic of Haiti during the height of the transatlantic slave trade, and to dissolve any doubts that people of African origin are capable of effective self-governance. Thus, I offer this biography of Jean Pierre Boyer (1776–1850), president of the Republic of Haiti from 1818 to 1843.

Nancy Dubosse
Port-au-Prince, Haïti
August 2025

Author's Note on the Evolution of the Island of Hispaniola's Nomenclature

Hispaniola is widely recognized as the name given to the entire island upon which we find the two modern nations of the Republic of Haiti and the Dominican Republic. The literal translation of Hispaniola is "diminutive" or "off-shoot" of Spain. When Spain invaded the island, it was inhabited by the Taino people, who themselves had named the island Ayiti.

Spain and Portugal, two great naval powers of the fifteenth and sixteenth centuries, had expanded their empires to the American hemisphere. Increasing dispute of territory led to the Treaty of Tordesillas (1494), which set the demarcations of their possessions in the New World. Spain would retain Hispaniola. A 1598 map by Johannes Matalius Mettelus referred to the entire island as Hispaniola, indicating its Spanish possession, and included the Taino names of its various localities.[2]

However, because ownership claims over the island and its parts changed many times, the various names that appear in literature are largely dependent on the time period under discussion. This section will discuss briefly the evolution of this island's nomenclature since Spain's initial possession of it.

The name of the administrative capital on the island of Hispaniola, Santo Domingo, eventually became the name for the entire eastern portion of the island when Spain lost the western part of the island to France in 1697. France named this possession Saint-Domingue. These two regions coexisted for almost a century with their respective names, Santo Domingo and Saint-Domingue, even throughout intensive British incursions in the southern part of Saint-Domingue and Spanish perturbations in the northeastern part of Saint-Domingue during the latter half of the eighteenth century. Spain eventually lost possession of Santo Domingo in the 1795 Treaty of Basel. However, the two crowns being close relatives, France asked Spain to maintain a military presence until it could send administrators.

The entire island was then referred to as Saint-Domingue—or as Santo (or San) Domingo by the English. Even though Toussaint Louverture, then a general in the French army, would conquer the eastern side and abolish slavery in 1801, he did not change the name. He instead claimed the entire island of Saint-Domingue as an autonomously governed island in the French Empire. A sea chart commissioned by the French Ministry of the Navy and Colonies in 1802 confirmed this appellation[3], as did an English map by John Luffman in the same year.[4]

Napoleon did manage to retake the eastern part from Louverture in what Haitians refer to as the War of Independence, which began in 1791 and ended in 1804. Indeed, the armistice to end that war was technically negotiated for the western part of the island only, which appears to have been an oversight by Jean-Jacques Dessalines, the general who succeeded after Louverture's arrest and deportation. Nevertheless, the Indigenous Army considered the entire island liberated, as evidenced by its proclamation of independence. Under the leadership of Dessalines in 1804, the occupants of the island reverted to the original Taino name for the island, Ayiti—or in French orthography, Haïti. It is important to note that the French made it clear in writing that the eastern part, which was colloquially referred to as the "Spanish side" because its inhabitants were largely iberophone, remained a French possession. Consequently, Dessalines attempted to conquer it in 1805 but failed.

In the same year of Haitian independence, 1804, a map published by the Weimar Geographisches Institut continued to refer to the entire island as "San Domingo or Hispaniola," without recognition of any transfer of power, signaling Europe's refusal to recognize the newly formed nation of Haiti.[5]

Politically divided, among other things, the revolutionaries were unable to hold the western part together. It was subsequently divided into two countries: the Kingdom of Northern Haiti, ruled by King Christophe I, and the Republic of Haiti, presided over by Alexandre Pétion. A map dated 1814, published in Philadelphia by Matthew Carey, presented the area occupied by both the Northern and Southern regimes, without specifically naming them, as well as the "Spanish part" in the east.[6]

The eastern side of the island remained in a state of flux, still officially a French territory but administered and protected by Spain. An attempt to reinstate slavery by the Europeans and to put pressure on inhabitants to increase agricultural production (the principal activity of the eastern part was livestock), created conflict among Santo Domingo's social classes. One segment of civil society wanted to join the Bolivarian Republic, another wanted to join with the Republic of Haiti and named itself the Republic of Spanish Haiti, and still others wanted to remain with Spain. The Boyer camp emerged as the stronger, backed by two considerable military columns that invaded the eastern side at a most opportune moment. In 1822, the eastern part and the adjacent smaller islands were annexed, constituting the entirety of the Republic of Haiti, and presided over by Boyer until 1843, the year in which he was deposed. The Dominican Republic would come into being in 1844.

American maps continued to refer to the island as Santo Domingo or Hispaniola, because the United States of

America also had not yet officially recognized the Republic of Haiti. For example, an 1822 map published in Philadelphia by American cartographers Henry Charles Carey (Matthew Carey's son) and Isaac Lea depicted the geographical division between the Republic of Haiti (or Hayti in the old American spelling) from the eastern side of the island but did not recognize Boyer's presidency nor his occupation of the entire island at that point.[7] Actually, the United States' recognition of the Republic of Haiti didn't come until 1862, during the presidency of Abraham Lincoln, when the former was itself engaged in a civil war precisely on the issue of whether member states had the right to absolute autonomy, which implicated the right to decide on the question of slavery for themselves.

While modern cartographic practice has been to refer to the island as Hispaniola, as the Spanish had done in the sixteenth century, this author believes that nomenclature is critical to understanding the impact of European and American power struggles, the racism engrained in geopolitics (including cartography), and the Haitian revolutionaries' need for recognition in order to attract investment and to participate in international commerce. Hence, in this narrative, references to the island and its respective regions adhere strictly to the nomenclature appropriate to the chronology of events under discussion rather than to its modern appellation.

Significant Events of Boyer's Life

YEAR	EVENT
1776	Born in Saint Domingue (28 February)
1791	Witnessed the organization of the mulatto revolt but left soon after for studies in France.
1793	Returned to Saint Domingue as adjutant captain with French commissioner Polverel but deserted the French army to join Rigaud's Legion of Equality of the Sud
1800	Fled Saint Domingue for France and was captured by US Naval cruiser Trumbell
1801	Napoleon's armada arrived at Saint Domingue
1802	Sentenced to die
1803	The French surrendered Saint Domingue to the Indigenous Army
1806	Named colonel and Petion's aide-de-camp
1807	Became Petion's personal secretary
1808	Named head of the presidential guard
1810	Named commander of the capital of Port-au-Prince
1812	Led the defense of Port-au-Prince against King Christophe's attack
1818	Took the oath of office as President of the Republic of Haiti (01 April)
1819	Put an end to the Goman rebellion
1820	Annexed the Kingdom of Northern Haiti
1822	Annexed Santo Domingo
1825	France recognized Haiti's independence in exchange for indemnification of lost property

1826	Introduced paper money
1838	Renegotiated the French indemnity
1842	Expelled one-third of those elected to the Chamber of Communal Representatives
1843	Resigned and fled to Jamaica where Joutte, his companion of 25 years, died
1844	Traveled to France and was received by King Louis-Phillippe d'Orléans
1850	Died in Paris, France (09 July)

About Boyer, in Their Words...[8]

He believes nothing to be the result of chance, or the effect of time and misrule; and arrogates to himself the capacity of accomplishing any thing which he may design and wish to execute.

FRANKLIN, James (1828)

Doué d'une intelligence supérieure, Boyer s'était perfectionné par la lecture, qu'il aimait passionnément. Avec des formes gracieuses, une élocution facile, il cherchait toujours, dans ses audiences du dimanche, à capter son auditoire. Aux tièdes, à ceux qu'il savait animés d'une certaine ambition, il adressait des paroles affectueuses en leur donnant congé. 'Ménagez-vous pour la patrie ; la patrie a besoin de vos services ; la patrie compte sur vous' et chacun se retirait le cœur plein de joie.

BONNET, Edmond (1864)

Lorsque nous envisageons sa carrière et le haut rang où il se trouve placé, nous serions tentés de croire, avec les anciens, qu'il existe une fatalité injuste, aveugle et bizarre, qui préside à la destinée des humains ; si d'ailleurs nous n'étions entièrement convaincus que Dieu gouverne le monde par une providence juste et par des voies impénétrables aux faibles mortels.

de VASTEY, Pompée Valentin (1819)

The manners of the ruler of Hayti are simple and

unaffected; to republican plainness, he adds the polish of France, and preserves a quiet independent dignity suited to his rank and station.

MACKENZIE, Charles (1830)

Il établit partout une surveillance paternelle, remarquable par sa vigueur. Déjà, sous son commandement militaire, la police du Port-au-Prince avait déployé une extrême activité. Dès qu'il se vit placé à la tête de l'État, il prit des mesures encore plus efficaces. Les mœurs devinrent moins relâchées dans la capitale ; et cet exemple influa bientôt sur les autres villes de la république.

WALLEZ, Jean Baptiste Guislain (1826)

Le calme gouvernement de Boyer, ses talens élevés, sa justice, sa douceur, ont déjà fermé quelqu'une de ces plaies ; les autres disparaitront avec le temps.

d'ORBIGNY, Alcide (1836)

Le président Boyer et la plupart de ses contemporains de couleur, comme lui anciens affranchis, pensaient que les masses avant tout devaient être maintenues dans une complète tranquillité, dans la docilité ; ils craignaient que la propagation des lumières n'introduisît chez eux l'esprit d'agitation et ne les portât à des excès qui eussent empiré la situation.

MADIOU fils, Thomas (1988)

Boyer manquait d'initiative ; mais les révolutionnaires s'exagéraient singulièrement les torts du président et la valeur de leurs propres théories. Ils en tardèrent pas à en faire la cruelle expérience. La nation en supporta malheureusement les déplorables conséquences, dont la première fut la scission de l'ancienne colonie espagnole....

BONNEAU, Alexandre (1862)

Quoique naturellement doux, il a beaucoup d'énergie guerrière... Le général Boyer est aujourd'hui à la force de l'âge. On l'aime et on l'estime, parce qu'il commande avec modération et énergie.

de LACROIX, Pamphile (1819)

Personne n'avait plus que lui le sentiment de la justice envers tous ses concitoyens ; la plupart de ses actes le prouvent, et cependant, dans l'application particulière qu'il en faisait, il lui est arrivé souvent d'être injuste par ce sentiment même. Mais, s'il était prompt à l'être par la vivacité de son caractère, signe ordinaire d'un bon cœur, il était aussi prompt à revenir sur une décision injuste, tant sa juste raison savait l'emporter à la fin sur ses passions du moment. Il avait l'amour de l'ordre à un degré supérieur, et l'organisation successive de toute gouvernement de notre pays n'a obtenu autant de régulation civile et militaire ; et il a dû ce succès par les exigences de son caractère qu'ils connaissaient.

ARDOUIN, Beaubrun (1856)

MAP OF HISPANIOLA[9]

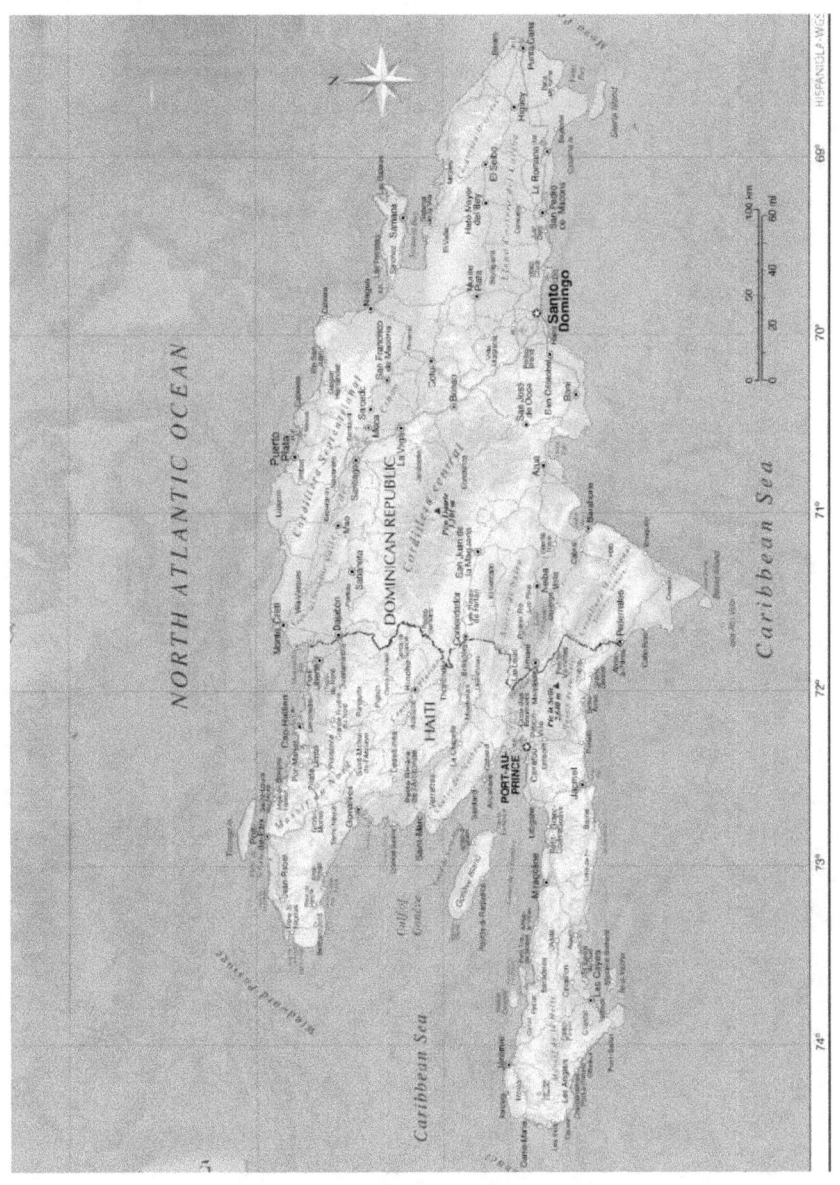

Haiti Strongman

Jean Pierre Boyer[10]

(1776-1850)

BOYER,
Président de la République d'Haïti

1

Rendezvous with Destiny

THE REGIMENTS OF THE NORD, less the several thousand who had defected to attempt to mount a rebellion in the forests surrounding Cap-Haïtien, stood shoulder to shoulder for inspection. The aroma of boot polish flooded the nostrils. Most of King Christophe's commanding officers had surrendered in writing to Boyer and stood in front of their respective units to welcome the president of the Republic of Haiti. The Kingdom of Northern Haiti and the Republic of Haiti had been at war for thirteen years. Virtually no one from the southern country had traveled north since the War of Independence against France had ended. This moment could have gone awry in many ways, yet the only speck of blood spilled was from the shaving razors of soldiers getting ready for the ceremonial transition of power.

Boyer cantered his horse through the *barrière Bouteille* - the entrance to Cap-Haïtien fashioned into two prominent concrete bottles - alone. He had intentionally created some distance with his carriage and accompanying regiments. Boyer was overcome with emotion. The last time he had been there was eighteen years earlier, in 1802, when French General Rochambeau had sentenced him to die by drowning. He was, in fact, already in the queue on the ship when a fellow Freemason spotted him and intervened. *Not my time*, he probably thought to himself then, as he ran off to rejoin his commanding officer Pétion.

Despite his shortcomings, King Christophe had taken good care of the city, and it was lovelier than Boyer remembered. Its charm is partially owed to its natural setting; the city was – and still is– wedged between the sea and mountains. Manicured trees on both sides of the main road shaded the visitor to Cap as soon as they entered through the gate. Considered a large city, its streets were formed at right angles, paved, and spacious. Boyer rode past a military hospital, a school and a printing press. The stone houses were sufficiently enchanting, but Christophe added public squares with water fountains. This dramatic setting was accompanied by a soft tourbillon of sea breeze in the mornings. Above all, the city was clean.

Léocand[11] stood with his company. He dared to look into the president's eyes as Boyer passed on his horse. He first saw the large rimmed, feathered hat that was part of the formal regalia for Haitian division generals. And then he saw the baby-faced Boyer and immediately felt unsteady. But it wasn't the boot polish; he knew that face— it was the face of the boy whose life he had spared on the battlefield in March 1812.

"That can't be *him*," Léocand said to himself. He realized that he had changed the fate of the country with one humanitarian act.

The year was 1812. Brigadier General Boyer was in a bind. He had just been promoted from the rank of colonel by his childhood friend, commanding officer, and mentor, but his peers did not think that the promotion was merited—no one could attest to ever having seen Boyer in battle. He was Pétion's aide-de-camp, which meant that the two were close. (Their contemporaries later learned that the two men shared a lover.) Pétion had named Boyer commander of the presidential guard—which came with a battalion of grenadiers, an elite infantry unit—and commander of the military arrondissement of Port-au-Prince, the capital, all while holding the rank of colonel. This recent promotion to brigadier general could only mean one thing: He was well-positioned to succeed Pétion as president.

Christophe's attack was perfectly timed but far from serendipitous. Pétion had chosen the month of March to travel to the Sud region for troop inspection. Christophe probably had several spies in the republic who informed him of the latter's departure. Likely the best battle architect the country had ever seen, Pétion left Boyer with plans to defend the capital, in case of need. The need arose, and Boyer followed the plan to its punctuation.

His fellow generals and their regiments were positioned as commanded but took a dismissive posture. "Indifferent," "calm," and "cold" are the words historians have used to describe their disposition on that day. Their message couldn't have been clearer than if they had spoken it: Boyer's military career would progress no further; they would not allow him to be president.

Compared to previous attacks, Christophe's offensive was particularly virulent. This time, he meant to take Port-au-Prince. From the capital he could stage the invasion of the island's central plateau and expand his kingdom all the way to Santo Domingo. As the body count increased in Christophe's favor, the infantry posted to defend the capital observed the generals' hostility against Boyer and despair set in among them. They began to retreat. Boyer soon found himself alone with his battalion and a few other officers who reasoned that the power struggle came second to preserving the geographical integrity of the country.

He needed a moment, a memory that could be attributed only to him, validation that he belonged there, that he could lead. He dismounted and walked to the front line. His tongue and throat were cotton—January through March are dry months in Port-au-Prince, with March being particularly windy.

"Grenadiers, I promised you that you would die the way you wanted. I have held my promise. Advance!" Boyer rallied them.

He remained with the grenadiers, on foot, and on the front line. Eyewitness accounts attested to the arrowhead form that began to emerge on the field, with Boyer at its point, piercing through Christophe's dense line of soldiers. Remarkably, Boyer and his grenadiers left dozens of bodies behind them. Christophe's army of fifteen thousand men recovered quickly, but the moment provided sufficient exhilaration to the entire corps to defend the capital for nearly three months.

Somehow in the melee, Boyer was separated from his battalion and found himself alone, behind enemy lines.

He had gone too far ahead. One of Christophe's horsemen spotted him and galloped towards him. It was Léocand. Described by another general as colossal,[12] Léocand had already drawn his sword, with the singular intention of killing the general. Impossible to say if the vents de Carême, strong winds typically marking the spring season, were giving him headwind or tailwind, but the permanent whistle blowing through the trees framed the encounter. Nature dominates this island, on the farm as well as on the battlefield. Boyer began to run but stumbled when he tried to hurdle over a hedge. As Léocand approached for the kill, he saw the puerile features of the scrambling soldier and felt the same unsteadiness. Compassion for whom he thought was a boy wearing an officer's uniform prevented him from making the final thrust. He rode away.

Boyer didn't even take the time to exhale. He hurried back to claim the partial victory and accolades; Pétion promoted him to division general.

2

1776

JEAN PIERRE BOYER WAS BORN IN 1776, but that year is better known as when Great Britain and a cluster of its colonies in the Americas parted ways, marked by the adoption of the American Declaration of Independence on July 4. Somewhat less understood is that this discrete event was a consequence of a larger and older conflict—a European war for overseas territories in the New World. Over eight years, these nations sacrificed tens of thousands of men in a struggle for control of land in the Antilles and on the South American continent. This gives more context to the opening paragraph of the American Declaration of Independence: "It becomes necessary for one People ... to assume among the Powers of the Earth." Europe, the center of the civilized world and where the most formidable of forces could be found, was about to change considerably.

The outcome of the American Revolution would determine the repartition of the Caribbean colonies, particularly the adjacent islands of Cuba, Hispaniola, and Puerto Rico. Yet, this wasn't the first global conflict. The Seven Years' War, which initially took the form of a border dispute between France and Great Britian of their North American possessions in 1754, morphed into a global melee in 1756, which included even Russia and Sweden. Great Britain had declared war on France for encroaching on its territory in the American colonies. The kingdoms of Prussia and Russia chose separate camps: Great Britain and France, respectively. Prussia invaded parts of France, on behalf of its ally—who was no doubt distracted by its struggle for influence in the Americas—shifting borders considerably. In the peace treaty that put an end to that war, Spain gained the port of Louisiana, Cuba, and the Philippines; and Great Britain acquired Canada, the territory along the Mississippi River, and Florida. France was left with debts, and debt inspires initiative.

It was these territorial changes that set the scene for the American conflict. In response to a series of taxes imposed on them by Great Britain, no doubt to pay for the Seven Years' War and to compensate its allies, the American colonies declared their independence. This declaration, however sensational and symbolic of the civil liberties movement that would shortly thereafter result in a regime change (and reversion) in France, was only the start of the war. Rather than being an internal conflict in the British Empire, as is largely perceived, the American rebellion escalated to implicate many countries, including France, who, still smarting from its losses in the preceding conflict, aligned itself with the American colonies, even enlisting Spain and the Netherlands to support them.

Under the guise of liberating other British colonies from oppression, the French invaded Dominica, Guadeloupe, Martinique, and St. Lucia, all in 1778. The British reconquered St. Lucia but then also lost St. Vincent and Grenada to the French in 1779. In solidarity with France, but also perhaps because it recognized that Great Britain was entirely on the defensive, Spain (the Royal House of Bourbon ruled both France and Spain) opened the port of New Orleans to French and American warships, who used the port as a staging area to attack British vessels.

Great Britain did not back down. In 1780, she declared war on the Dutch Republic (later the Kingdom of the Netherlands), who allowed American merchants to trade in St. Eustatius despite the British ban on extra-colonial trade, a widespread practice among "mother" countries vis a vis their colonies with a view to protecting the value chains of certain commodities from competition. By 1781, it had retaken the islands of St. Eustatius, St. Martin, Saba, and St. Barthélemy. These trading posts, in turn, were re-seized by the French later that year; in 1782, the French also took St. Kitts, Montserrat, and Nevis. Likewise, the islands of the western Caribbean, Leeward and Windward Islands, would change hands many times.

It was only in 1783 that Great Britain, France, Spain, and the recently formed United States of America signed the Treaty of Paris to end the American Revolution, with most colonies returned to their original colonizers. However, this peace was short-lived because, despite having contributed greatly to the Battle of Yorktown under the leadership of Count Rochambeau in the American Revolution, France would anew be short-changed, losing all territory acquired in the war.

The main consequence for Hispaniola island was that the ports of Cap-Français, Môle St.-Nicolas, and Port-au-Prince, all located in Saint-Domingue (the western side of the island), became centers of trade for American, Spanish, and French goods. This colony had suffered in the years leading up to and during the American Revolution, as Britain had imposed a tax on sugar and molasses coming from non-British colonies to eliminate competition, which sharply reduced trade with the French West Indies. Spain, for its part, remained in possession of many of the colonies surrounding Saint-Domingue, including the eastern side of the island (Santo Domingo), Puerto Rico, Colombia, and Panama.

News of the American Declaration of Independence eventually made its way across the ocean, and the French also realized that they too were "endowed by their Creator with certain unalienable rights." The French National Assembly drafted in 1789 the Declaration of the Rights of Man and of the Citizen. France was, at the same time, overwhelmed by burgeoning debt. However, amidst increasing public debates on civil rights and representation, the Bourbon royal family was unable to impose any new taxes without having to implement radical political reform in exchange. To pay off its creditors, France intensified production in Saint-Domingue, which necessitated the increased importation of slaves. At the start of the American Revolution, there were just over 260,000 African slaves in Saint-Domingue. By 1786, they numbered 340,000, climbing to over 465,000 just two years later in 1788.[13] France also authorized merchants to sell freely, liberating the ports of Cap-Français, Port-au-Prince, and Les Cayes from the monopsonistic mercantilist system.

However, this time it would not be able to count on its star colony of Saint-Domingue to settle its war debt. The black inhabitants were also infected with the notions of freedom and human rights and began to assert themselves accordingly. Sensing imminent change in its northern neighbor and, in the hopes of regaining control of Saint-Domingue, Spain decided to support the black antislavery movement there.

***

Yet it was not all about military aggression. The implacable appetite for colonies and natural resources accompanied significant human losses from smallpox. In fact, inoculation against smallpox proved to be a determining factor in many of the battles fought between the British and the American Continental army.

Smallpox was the disease du jour—an old disease, first recorded during the Roman Empire—which came to the Caribbean via its explorers. [14] Smallpox was first registered on the island of Hispaniola in 1518 via a Portuguese vessel carrying slaves, and within twenty-five years of the first European contact, the native populations of Hispaniola, Jamaica, Puerto Rico, Antigua, Martinique, Barbados, Cuba, and Mexico were decimated by smallpox. The years 1647, 1659, 1666, 1673, and 1689 all saw epidemics of smallpox killing thousands of people, enslaved and free, of Puerto Rico and Hispaniola (present-day Republic of Haiti and Dominican Republic). Shortly before Boyer's birth in 1771, a smallpox epidemic killed many slaves in Saint-Domingue, amounting to a significant loss of investment. Experts estimated the case fatality rate to be around 18.5 percent. What was estimated to be a pre-colonial regional population of 54 million was reduced to around eight hundred thousand by 1800.

However, Boyer and his generation would be spared this recurrent viral massacre. Saint-Domingue was one of the first testing places for the smallpox vaccine, as slave owners were anxious about losing additional stocks of human capital. Dr. Simeon Worlock, after terminating a vaccination campaign in the city of Paris, arrived in Cap-Français (Saint-Domingue) in 1774 to administer the vaccine to thousands of slaves.[15] By the 1780s, inoculation against smallpox was systematically undertaken throughout the colony. With mortality averted, the black population rebounded, and, by 1789, the number of slaves was approximately five hundred thousand, in contrast to eight thousand whites and people of color[16]

A disease as calamitous as smallpox incentivized both European migration and the importation of slaves for labor. In mitigation, the importation of slaves to Saint-Domingue reached a peak of forty thousand per year. This considerable investment was more than covered, as the colony produced 40 percent of the world's sugar supply, 60 percent of the world's coffee, and 40 percent of France's foreign trade.

Furthermore, disease was not the only check on human populations. The Caribbean – its built environment, language and customs – are set against the backdrop of recurring natural disasters. There was an earthquake on 3 June 1770 which destroyed Port-au-Prince and the surrounding localities. While only two hundred deaths were recorded, these towns were flattened—churches, houses, government buildings, even brick and clay ovens. The tremors were felt for as long as fifteen days afterwards, several times per day. "An earthquake comes with a general terror, felt by all living things. And in this horrific moment when the earth opens up, it is often preceded by a moment of calm, a change in the atmosphere imperceptible," described Guillaume Pierre François de la Mardelle, who was procurer general in Saint-Domingue at the time.[17]

Extreme weather events, as well, repeatedly and mercilessly destroyed whole harvests, valuable fruit trees, livestock, and tens of thousands of lives throughout the Caribbean. A hurricane in 1780, baptized the "Great Hurricane," decimated much of the Caribbean, with thousands of deaths recorded on every island and damage to maritime infrastructure. France suffered considerable losses: forty ships and four thousand men stationed off Martinique. There were equally devastating hurricanes that affected the entire island in 1781, 1784, 1785, 1786, and 1788. The hurricane that struck Port-au-Prince and its environs on 16 August 1788 was also eloquently described by de la Mardelle as "a unification of the forces of nature—lightning, thunder, water, and wind—for a terrifying display of its strength, with death as the inevitable consequence."

In an act impermissible under the current

mercantilist trade regime, in which the colonial power was a unique buyer of the colony's production, American merchants brought provisions for the inhabitants of Saint-Domingue out of sympathy for their repetitive misfortune. However, the ports were abruptly closed by François Barbé de Marbois, the governor-general of Saint-Domingue in 1785. Despite the devastation, one of de Marbois' responsibilities was to protect French business interests, and, in doing so, he created a shortage of food. Thus, the combination of natural disasters and an oppressive trade regime contributed to growing local hostility among Saint-Domingue residents with the French metropole. They felt neglected.

Shortly thereafter, inspired by the American Revolution, France experienced a change of government, sparked by a July 1789 spectacular storming of the Bastille, a weapons depot, in response to increased taxation and lack of representation in the National Assembly. Yet, the new governing council found itself crippled by the previous monarch's debt incurred during both the Seven Years' War and the American Revolution and, in 1792, declared war on Great Britain, the Dutch Republic, Spain, Austria, Prussia, and Sardinia, rupturing the Treaty of Paris. War is generally an effective way to get people's minds off what they need and what is owed to them.

Furthermore, the social stratification and resulting class grievances observed in France were also present in its colonies. Broadly speaking, there were white plantation owners (*grands blancs*) and white colonists (*petits blancs*), who were commonly artisans, tradesmen, and craftsmen, as well as clergy. But there was a high incidence of plantation owner absenteeism; French aristocracy had largely chosen to remain in France with their families and instead sent trusted agents to manage the plantations. These and the other petits blancs found themselves with fewer rights than their aristocratic counterparts. There were also Creoles, whites born in the colony who had relatively little social standing in France. Then, as a direct consequence of slavery, there were mulattos or *mulatres*. Mulattos were of mixed race, and most were born free, inheriting their freedom from their white parents. Finally, there were blacks, both free and enslaved, the majority obviously falling into the latter category. Any free mulattos or blacks were known as *les affranchis*, "the freedmen"; although they had no civil recognition, meaning that they were not considered French citizens, they did have the economic freedom to pursue skilled trades, and many were jewelers, tailors, tutors, etc.

However, the internal political chaos made it impossible for France to properly conduct war. There were now several political factions vying for power: agriculturalists, royalists, Jacobins, and the military. One of the many points of conflict was regarding how to treat the residents of the colonies, who had now evolved into a variety of social classes and political persuasions: landholding and non-landholding whites, free and enslaved blacks, and mulattos of various categories. As early as September 1789, the affranchis had already hired a lawyer in France, Monsieur de Joly, to present their claim of French citizenship to the National Assembly. Local representatives from the colony, the deputies, and the National Assembly exchanged many letters on the issue. [18] Some representatives from the National Assembly supported the claim, arguing that it would appease tensions and counter the insurrections. The affranchis were quite literally referred to as the "best defense against the slaves." Although they were born free, the current legal framework did not address their rights and responsibilities. Ignoring them would push them to align with blacks. By October 1791, an agreement was reached in which the French accorded citizenship to free and land-holding mulattos and blacks in Saint-Domingue, with the rights to vote and run for public office. However, its revocation mere months later was one of many catalytic actions that incited the revolt of 1791, mainly in the northern region, where the slaves left the plantations, demanding their personal freedom. In what is surely a reflection and consequence of the political turmoil in France in the 1780s, the colony had eleven different governors under French rule.

In some ways, the colony had become a victim of its own success. The volume of production required slaves, whose productivity was linked to their nutrition. However, the colony didn't produce its own food, and the annual hurricanes impacted their harvests. Also in 1789, Saint-Domingue's deputies wrote to the French National Assembly pleading for more bread flour. Although they required 400,000 *barils* (barrels) annually just to feed the slaves, they'd only been sent 150,000 barils the previous year (1788); and, by the end of the first quarter of 1789, they had only received 5,600 barils.[19] The hurricane of 1788 had also sharply reduced harvests and hence revenue from exports. Duchilleau, a former governor of the colony, reported to the National Assembly that the shortage of food had resulted in the increase in prices: a baril of bread flour doubled from 70 to 140 British pounds.[20]

The shortage of food and the resulting inflationary pressure was aggravated by declining export revenues. In the cases of both tobacco and indigo, world prices dropped with the unanticipated volumes placed on the market by Saint-Domingue's productivity. Colonial officials complained that indigo dye prices had fallen 40 percent with Saint-Domingue's entry into production.

The petits blancs and mulattos began to write to the

English officials in Jamaica for assistance, and British vessels could be seen in the waters around Saint-Domingue as early as August 1789. Other factions—despite their professed allegiance to the deposed Bourbon King Louis XVI and ambitions to retake the island—directed their calls for assistance to the Spanish on the eastern part of the island. The Spanish also generously financed attacks led by former slaves, with a view to expelling the French from the island. What was evident, through the diverse calls for various forms of self-governance and independence, was that stability was a necessary condition for white and mulatto inhabitants to return to their commercial enterprises.

The British did not lose any time and landed in the Sud region of Saint-Domingue in 1793, where the number of French soldiers numbered less than eight hundred. This region had social and cultural ties to the English, particularly those from Jamaica, and some British families had even settled there. The year prior to British arrival, in 1792, the commanding officer in Jérémie, then the regional capital, sent an official request for British respite. This region had already been self-governing for two years and had renounced the authority of the successive French commissioners and boasted of the management of their "docile" slaves. The British stayed for five years, until 1798, taking over nearly all the major ports in Saint-Domingue, including Grande Anse, Môle Saint-Nicolas, Saint-Marc,

Arcahaie, Croix-de-Bouquets, and Léogâne.

By 1793, Saint-Domingue, the western part of Hispaniola, was occupied by several European powers: the English occupied the Sud region and ports throughout, the Spanish were in the east and along the border with Santo Domingo, and the French were in the Nord (the northern part of the island). Both free blacks and slaves, because of their numerical advantage, were being courted by all parties.

In looking to improve his odds and keep the colony under French rule, the governor at the time, Léger Félicité Sonthonax, abolished slavery in August 1793 in an attempt to win over the black insurgents. It worked; the number of black and mulatto soldiers fighting for England and Spain was effectively reduced, weakening their fronts. One of the blacks who deserted the Spanish Army was Toussaint Louverture.

Louverture was a former slave who had learned to read and write. When France refused to recognize the rights of the residents of Saint-Domingue or assist in calamity, Louverture joined the Spanish army. He led successful incursions on Saint-Domingue's eastern front and was duly promoted. However, Sonthonax could not uphold his declaration; he had made it unilaterally and could not find enough support from the French National Assembly.

Louverture formed the Legion of Equality in the North, along with the thousands of blacks who had returned with him.

Also in 1793, Boyer, age seventeen, returned to Saint-Domingue from France, where he had attended a military academy. Though he was officially part of the French Republican Army, he also defected—along with a whole cohort of young mulattos who felt betrayed by Sonthonax's lack of sincerity—and formed the Legion of Equality of the Sud, under the command of Andre Rigaud, who, incidentally, had fought in the Battle of Savannah, Georgia.

Disease intervened in favor of the affranchis and slaves. A yellow fever outbreak in British garrisons resulted in an estimated mortality rate of 20 percent per month. By 1794, just one year after landing, only half of British troops on the island were considered fit. Feeling less protected, white plantation owners began to emigrate to the United States and to Jamaica, a lucrative British colony.

Étienne Lavaux, Sonthonax's replacement, had another idea. In place of equality, he offered Louverture the equivalent rank that he held in the Spanish army in exchange for the re-annexation of territories taken by Spain under his leadership. Louverture accepted and enthusiastically reverted the northern part of Saint-

Domingue to French control. Lavaux made the same offer to Rigaud if he could deliver on territories taken by the British. To reward their valiant efforts to maintain French authority over the colony, both Louverture and Rigaud were promoted to the rank of brigadier general in 1795.

These were the events and people that shaped Jean Pierre Boyer's formative years.

3

Rigaud and Pétion, *soon* Boyer

THE IMPORTATION OF AFRICAN SLAVES to work the Saint-Domingue plantations resulted in the creation of a new social class, les mulatres or mulattos. The mulattos of held no political or civil standing in France, which was the object of their political advocacy. They were inspired by the human rights arguments of the French peasants in the 1789 revolution. The mulattos were literate and read voraciously the literature of the times, including the Declaration of the Rights of Man and of the Citizen, advocating adequate representation, universal suffrage, and equality, with Maximilien Robespierre as one of its most prolific advocates. More tangibly, he contributed the motto "Liberté, Égalité, Fraternité," which would appear on all

French regalia and army materials. *Amis des noirs*, an abolitionist organization which included Robespierre, communicated regularly with mulattos in Saint-Domingue and is credited with having sent assistance in the form of arms.

The mulatres were united on their primary objective: to receive legal recognition and French nationality. Most were born free, typically because their fathers were white. Most were sent to France for education and had learned a trade. Nearly all had initially joined the French Royal Army to suppress the initial slave rebellions, ostensibly to preserve their social stature, which was based on the existence of slavery. As a result, not all mulattos were abolitionists. However, French recognition of their civil status was inconsistent. French nationality had been conferred and revoked several times, which revealed the insincerity of the Jacobin movement in France, which seeded skepticism among the mulatto community in Saint-Domingue.

There was also the issue of representation of the petits blancs. They called for regular elections in the colony and a space at policy forums in France, calls which predated the French Revolution. In 1788, taking matters into their own hands after repeated requests to the French metropole had been ignored, the plantation owners held their own elections for eighteen deputies. They also designated municipal and parochial boundaries and created provincial assemblies of Nord Ouest, and Sud. However, these acts went unrecognized, both by the Bourbon royal family and by the new Republican government.

One principal motivation for this parallel government was the perception of the unfairness of the mercantilist regime. Mercantilism was essentially bilateral trade between the mother country and its colonies with a view to establishing control over resources not found in Europe. It was enforced by creating a disincentive to trade outside the colonial network in the form of tariff barriers. Tariffs were the principal source of income for European royal families, as trade lines were privatized. With mercantilism widely practiced at the time, each European power secured primary commodities from their own colonies, at the lowest prices. As a result, the emerging industries in these metropoles were assured of getting the best price for these products and were insulated from foreign competition. In 1789, France's supply network included Saint-Domingue, Martinique, Guadeloupe, and Saint Lucia (Sainte Lucie under French possession). Great Britain's network included Jamaica, Saint Vincent, Barbados, Grenada, and Dominica, among others. Spain, Portugal, the Dutch Republic, and Denmark all practiced colonial mercantilism. Primary commodities were pre-ordered by European manufacturers, essentially pre-financing planting seasons. This would enable them to control the cost of each phase of the value chain, from seedling to the final product consumed by households.

Yet, one could say mercantilism was its own worst enemy by incentivizing smuggling. The same government agents whose responsibility was to inspect cargo and levy tariffs were abed with *contrebandiers,* or smugglers. Ironically, it was the repeated raids on Hispaniola by French and British pirates that originally caused the Spanish to retreat to the eastern side of the island. Smugglers knew no national boundaries and sold to the most willing buyers: timber and cattle from Spanish colonies, wheat from the United States, and molasses and rum from Saint-Domingue. The immediate consequence of the intensified smuggling was the drop in tariff revenues, and the French crown designating certain ports as "free trade" ports throughout Saint-Domingue, where anything could be traded, from anywhere, at a 1 percent duty. Though the intention was to increase the volume of trade, preferably within the network, it appears that trade increased considerably with the United States and British and Spanish colonies.

While European financiers were driven by interest payments and industrialists, by profits, the revenues of plantation owners depended on many factors, not all under their control. The tariff reduction didn't address their concerns or needs. War, natural disasters, the unforgiving extreme weather patterns of the Caribbean, and oversupply of commodities lowered planters' profit margins to around

5 percent on average, whereas those of slave traders were upwards of 50 percent.[21]

These three issues of economic governance, French citizenship, and slavery were the basis of the emergence of various factions in Saint-Domingue, and the divisions were not along color lines. Among the mulattos there were both abolitionists and those who desired independence from France to continue with the slavery mode of production and the freedom to trade. Likewise, among the whites there were abolitionists and also those who pushed for the independence of the colony from the monarchy and from the mercantilist structure. Even among some blacks, the concept of forced labor by itself wasn't as offensive as the fact that only blacks were being forced to work.

By 1789, several attempts by whites, largely petits blancs and creoles, to petition the local assemblies for inclusion and recognition of the mulattos were met with assassinations. The first casualty in the representation movement was a white man named Ferand de Baudières in the city of Petit-Goâve who drafted a formal petition. In Aquin, a man named Labadie, a mulatto, was tied to a horse and dragged through several towns for his advocacy of racial inclusion.

The initial reaction of French loyalists was too cruel, and public opinion in the colony began to turn towards alternative governance models. Parallel assemblies were organized in the Ouest and Sud regions. This mobilization coincided with France's approval to allow the colony to hold elections for representatives to the National Assembly.

The French plantation owners eventually received recognition of their assembly of deputies, which was formally constituted as the General Assembly of Saint-Domingue and supported by provincial assemblies of Ouest, Nord, and Sud in April 1790. This recognition temporarily muted demands for independence, as the colony was now considered part of the confederation of the French Empire. Participation in the assembly was restricted to property holders over the age of twenty-five. Noting that blacks far outnumbered whites in the colony, the white residents found it advantageous to align with mulattos, whose numbers were growing and who would be defenders of the colony. So the mulattos were invited to attend parochial and departmental assemblies and were accorded the opportunity to select a white colonist to present and make arguments at such assemblies on their behalf. However, they were excluded from direct participation, meaning that they could not be representatives themselves. Mulattos also didn't have the right to carry arms and were often stopped in public and asked to recite a vow of respect and obedience to the white race.

There was widespread, categorical refusal to take this vow among mulattos throughout the country. They began to migrate towards the Sud region. As the white planters also militarized, creating a colonial militia of twelve hundred, not including their slaves, a number of skirmishes ensued in which mulattos were repeatedly massacred and mutilated. The issues of race and slavery began to take up more space in the mixture of the different ideologies that existed in the colony, and rising to the top was the simple issue of whether the affranchis, a largely mulatto class, could continue to remain on the island.

✳✳✳

The white planters of the Sud region, namely those in Les Cayes and in Jérémie, opposed the civil recognition of the affranchis, and the incidence of violence against mulattos intensified, giving rise to the formation of brigades. They began to assemble clandestinely to discuss the situation. One of the leaders who emerged from this movement was André Rigaud. He and other mulatres had accompanied Admiral d'Estaing to fight on the side of the American colonists at the Battle of Savannah. Witnessing a war of independence imbued Rigaud with the desire for freedom for all and the courage to advocate for it.

Rigaud was born on 17 January 1761, in Les Cayes, which was and remains the largest city in the Sud region. Described by his contemporaries as energetic, virtuous, courageous, and zealous where it concerned the subject of freedom, Rigaud was both a French Republican *and* an abolitionist. Since the National Assembly had granted all slaves their freedom, he had elected to continue to fight for France against the British, Spanish, and colonial separatists. He had several siblings, including two brothers who fought alongside him, Augustin and Joseph.

Rigaud was almost immediately captured by a French colonel named Mauduit, who burst into their Les Cayes meeting, arrested Rigaud and company, and took them to Port-au-Prince, where they remained imprisoned. That's how Rigaud met Anne-Alexandre Pétion, who was stationed in Port-au-Prince under Mauduit's command.

Pétion was born in Port Républicain (Port-au-Prince) on 2 April 1770 to Pascal Sabes and Ursule. Mixed race people and blacks were often identified by only a first name and the name of the plantation to which they belonged. Thus, Pétion's mother was known as Ursule of Sabes. He would get the nickname Pétion from a neighboring couple with whom he studied the art of *bijouterie* (jewelry making). He took the name as his family name, having been rejected by his father. He was working as a jeweler when the revolution began in 1789. Recognizing that certain colonial factions were still pushing for independence, the French began actively recruiting mulattos into the French army in 1790, and Pétion was among them. He handled the cannons with such distinction that within two months he was promoted to sergeant. Personality-wise, he was described as being prone to raillery, caustic even, and a peoples' man.[22]

The affranchis in the city began to riot when they saw Rigaud and his crew walked into the city and led straight to prison. Mauduit was killed, and in the chaos, Rigaud and the others escaped. Pétion, although known for his reserve, changed camps to join the movement. He was placed under the command of Louis Jacques Beauvais, who had also fought at the Battle of Savannah.

On 24 August 1791, a group of young Haitians (mostly mulattos but all freedmen) dissatisfied with the lack of recognition by the French National Assembly decided to set up base camp at the Diegue plantation in the hills of Port-au-Prince. Boyer, at the impressionable age of fifteen, was brought there by his childhood friend Pétion. He was too young to join the army and left soon thereafter to conclude his studies in France. However, rather than merely reading about human rights and race and governance in the newspapers that came to the colony, Boyer witnessed these live debates; he took note of the various ideological differences. At this meeting at Diegue, the decision was made to formalize the brigades, and military assignments were given. Rigaud was recognized as the ranking colonel among them, and Pétion received the rank of captain and was placed in charge of an artillery battery, which in those days were comprised mostly of cannons. Haitian historians would refer to this regrouping as "the Confederation." This confederation was divided into two: the Confederation of Equality in the Ouest department, headed by Beauvais, and that of the Sud, headed by Rigaud.

In response, the armed plantation owners began to strategize and even arm slaves. When the Confederate Army realized that they would soon be outnumbered if slaves were enlisted to fight with their masters, they also began to recruit slaves and maroons. Maroons are escaped slaves and freedmen living in remote areas, which are numerous in Haiti given its mountain ranges. These recruits would come to be called *les Suisses*. Approximately fifteen hundred men in total, they won their first battle against the colonial army at Nerette.

Coincidentally, the Nord region was already in full rebellion. Vincent Oge, who had witnessed the storming of the Bastille and was inspired by Robespierre, found himself at the head of a slave revolt. There were many ebbs and flows, but the Nord region remained in resistance to French rule for the next thirteen years. And it was particularly bloody, marked by the burning down of plantations and the killing of their owners. Oge was joined by legends Dutty Boukman, Jean-François, and Georges Biassou. Their cause was more straightforward because they were blacks—they were only interested in abolition. It was from this movement Toussaint Louverture emerged.

The colonial army recognized that it could not fight a war on two fronts, with the Nord wanting the abolition of slavery and the Sud desiring recognition and peace. So on 11 September 1791, as part of a peace accord, French nationality was granted to the affranchis, freed mulattos, and blacks.[23] The Confederate Army eagerly surrendered, given their inferior numbers. But what to do with les Suisses, the blacks that had joined the Confederate Army? The French had not abolished slavery, and the French Assembly had ordered them to return to their respective plantations. Permitting them to live as free men would set a dangerous precedent, given the ongoing insurrection in the Nord.

Unable to arrive at a consensus, the high-ranking mulatto soldiers of the Confederation decided to put les Suisses, numbering 213 men, to La Baie de Mosquitos (now Nicaragua), with provisions, on two merchant ships, the *Philippine* and the *Emmanuel,* to live out the rest of their days in isolation. The *Emmanuel* carried all the Suisses; the *Philippine* carried the four officers sent to accompany them and get them settled. The *Philippine* arrived at its destination, as planned. However, the *Emmanuel* was nowhere to be found, so the officers decided to make a tour of the Caribbean Sea looking for it. When they arrived at Port Royal in Jamaica, they learned that the captain of the *Emmanuel* had unsuccessfully attempted to sell les Suisses back into slavery and abandoned them on an adjacent, deserted island, known at the time as English Key. The governor of Jamaica, a British colony, collected them and sent them back to Saint-Domingue, via Cap-Haïtien in the Nord. Some died of smallpox; some were executed by the French.

Although the main advocacy point of the Confederate Army was the recognition of affranchis, there were also affranchis who were abolitionists and had vehemently protested the exile of les Suisses. This ideological schism would widen shortly after the les Suisses affair when a black drummer named Scarpin attacked a French soldier who was berating him. Scarpin was immediately tried by the colonial assembly and hung. All pleas by the Confederate leaders fell on deaf ears, and Pétion, without even waiting for orders from Beauvais or Jean Pierre Lambert, the other commanding general of the Confederate Army, attacked the colonial army with his artillery battery. This act of disobedience revitalized the Confederate Army, with even petits blancs enlisting.

4

France Wins at Diplomacy

FRANCE DECIDED TO SEND a colonial commission of three members to pacify the colony. These were civilians who would be supported by General-in-chief Étienne Lavaux. One of the members, Philippe Rose Roume, would play a prominent role in the events to come. Roume was a Creole (a European born in a colony) from Grenada but grew up in France. The commission appears to have been given a particular mission, for which Roume would take the lead: to pit the blacks against the mulattos. The French were betting that the former would win easily with their greater numbers. They would then sow seeds of discontent between blacks born in the colony (Creoles) and those who emigrated from the African continent. The final objective was to reestablish slavery. General Lavaux had his role to play as well: He withheld reinforcements to Rigaud, now the commanding officer of the Sud.

Roume remained at Cap-Français in the Nord, attempting to reestablish French control, but the problem there was as black and white as its combatants: The slaves simply wanted their freedom. There was nothing he could use as leverage. The concentration of mulattos in the Sud also slowed progress; he needed to find a way to physically disperse them. The Sud department pushed forward by establishing their own provincial assembly and eventually independence. Furthermore, despite resistance by some of the large plantation owners, particularly in the Grand'Anse region, to liberating the blacks, Rigaud liberated approximately seven hundred, as per his communication to Roume in September 1792, to whom he planned to give military training.[24]

Perceived to have failed, Roume and the other commissioners were replaced within months by a new colonial commission in October 1792: Sonthonax, Étienne Polverel, and Jean-Antoine Ailhaud. This time, they were accompanied by four thousand French national guards, two thousand troops, and four generals. While we don't know much about Ailhaud,[25] the first two commissioners were Jacobins, members of a populist party in France promoting the social and political rights of all men; and yet both declared themselves anti-abolitionists, assuring those at their investiture ceremony in Cap-Français (Cap-Haïtien) that they had no intention of facilitating such an outcome.

In fact, upon arrival, the commissioners issued a proclamation confirming that slavery was a necessary institution to preserve both the culture and economy of the colony, and, declaring that they respected the principle of private property (and that slaves were "property"), they recognized only two classes of men: free (without discrimination against color) and slaves.

> *Que l'esclavage est nécessaire à la culture et à la prospérité des colonies; qui n'est ni dans les principes, ni dans la volonté de la nation de toucher à cet égard aux propriétés des colons. nous mourrons plutôt que de souffrir l'exécution d'un projet antipopulaire.... Les commissaires ne reconnaitraient désormais que deux classes d'hommes dans la colonie, les libres sans aucune distinction de couleur et les esclaves.*[26]

The commissioners' definitive pro-slavery sentiments impelled the leaders of the rebellion in the Nord—Louverture, Biassou, and Jean François—in June 1793, to write to Joachim Garcia, the governor of Santo Domingo, the eastern part of the island. They pledged loyalty to the Spanish crown in return for recognition of their freedom and homologation in the Spanish army. Spain accepted their request to be integrated at their current military ranks.

Commissioner Polverel was dispatched to Port-au-Prince, where he received the pledge of fealty from the

Confederates there, led by General Beauvais. However, he would not get the same outcome in Jacmel and Les Cayes. The Sud Confederates insisted on self-governance. Nevertheless, in a bid to win them over, the commission dissolved the segregated colonial assembly that had been created, created an interim assembly, and replaced many of the municipal representatives with mulattos.

Meanwhile in France, the new Republican National Assembly abolished the monarchy in October 1792 and then executed Louis XVI along with many royalists and aristocratic families in January 1793. In fact, royalists were arrested, persecuted, and assassinated both in France and throughout its colonies. The Assembly also granted the affranchis of Saint-Domingue the long-awaited political recognition for which they had been advocating and fighting—news that would be brought to the colony by two new commissioners, Blanchelande and Roume (again) around March or April 1793. As a further show of support for the affranchis, Blanchelande promoted both Beauvais and Rigaud to the rank of brigadier general. The Confederates remodeled themselves under General Beauvais, taking on the name the *Legion de l'Égalité de l'Ouest* (Legion of Equality in the Ouest); with Pétion as captain of artillery. Still aligned with the French Republican Army, they carried out several incursions in municipalities where plantation owners remained loyal to the French royal family.

Further south, Rigaud fell into line—fortunately so, because Rigaud's Legion de l'Égalité du Sud now numbered four thousand. However, the two principal communes in the extreme southwest and southeastern points, Jérémie and Jacmel, were experiencing slightly different social dynamics. Although accessible by sea, they were relatively isolated from inland incursion, as the two cities are surrounded by mountain ranges; Jérémie also enjoys natural protection from the formidable Voldrogue River, which runs north-south. The municipalities of Jérémie and Jacmel were colonial strongholds, and the affranchis had been driven from the cities for their autonomy and abolition rhetoric. These cities, in open conflict with France's Republican National Assembly, the colonial commissioners, and the affranchis, declared autonomy from the rest of the colony and established their own administrative assembly. Their unwavering position on the questions of democracy, representation, livelihoods, and human rights incited them to seek a new military sponsor, which they did by formally reaching out to England.

In response to the pleas of the southern plantation owners, and because they recognized this as an opportunity to annex what was a profitable colony, the English invaded Saint-Domingue at Jérémie on 20 September 1793. They occupied most of the commercial ports of Saint-Domingue (Môle Saint-Nicolas, Léogane, Saint-Marc, and even Port-au-Prince) for five years. Having deposed Louis XVI, a relative of the Spanish crown, the Jacobins were in direct conflict with the Spanish-owned Santo Domingo, which had now enlisted Louverture, Biassou, and Jean François, who occupied its eastern border and the plains of Artibonite. Finally, the Nord was still experiencing slave resistance.

For having now created three battlefronts and nearly losing the colony to England, the old commission was replaced with Polverel, Sonthonax, and Ailhaud (who would soon be replaced by Delpech) in late 1793. At their installation ceremony they promised to protect the institution of slavery *and* respect the civil rights of affranchis, who they hoped could co-exist with slave-based plantations. In fact, many affranchis had slaves themselves. Boyer, who had been in France completing his studies, returned to Haiti on the same vessel and became a soldier in the French Republican Army and Polverel's aide.

But it was a *jeu de dupes:* the (insincere) promise of French recognition had the objective of reducing the number of battlefronts. Abraham Lincoln used this same tactic during the American Civil War. There were slave states (like Delaware and Maryland) that did not wish to secede from the Union, and they were allowed to maintain the slave system. In order to leverage their support and to decrease the number of insurgents in the South, President Lincoln liberated the slaves in the states that had already seceded with the Emancipation Proclamation of 1863.

Entirely inapplicable, it gave the appearance of moral superiority and consolidated support, while allowing some Union states to continue with their slave systems. Likewise, the French commissioners were betting that having French citizenship would appeal to more people than abolitionist ideals would.

This time, given the racial dynamics, the three commissioners decided that it would be best if there was a republican presence in all the regions: Sonthonax in the Nord, Polverel in the Ouest, and Delpech in the Sud. Ailhaud was not battle ready and fled to France instead of taking a post. However, countercurrents in France worked to change their disposition. The National Assembly was a largely abolitionist legislature. They dissolved Saint-Domingue's colonial assembly, replacing them with twelve new members (evenly divided between white and affranchis), unseated many of the colonial administrators loyal to the royal family, and ended slavery on 13 October 1793.

As commander of the Sud and a Frenchman, Rigaud valiantly fought against the royalists and the English, often supported by Pétion and his artillery battery. However, Rigaud's men needed arms, food, and uniforms, so he wrote frequently and desperately to General-in-chief Lavaux. Lavaux, whose own supplies had diminished in fighting both the Spanish and the slaves, challenged Rigaud to use his zealousness to acquire what he could. Rigaud emerged as an elite commander of remarkable ingenuity: He sent his father, a white man, to the United States to lobby for munitions to support their fight against the British.[27]

Having won over the mulattos, the French Republican Army and the Legions of the Ouest and Sud concentrated on retaking territory from the British and Spanish. Yellow fever would again tip the scales, this time in favor of the French Republican Army. The British were so diminished in number, they began recruiting among the local population, specifically focusing on the formation of black legions headed by black commanders. They managed to raise twelve thousand men and placed these legions in Saint-Marc, Arcahaie, Port-au-Prince, and Jérémie.[28]

Rigaud organized a four-column formation of six thousand men, one of which was headed by Pétion. They retook Léogâne in October 1794, Tiburon in December 1794, and Port-au-Prince in March 1795. Impressed with his leadership skills, the British offered Rigaud three million pounds, British citizenship, the rank of general in the British army, and the equivalent ranking of his officers that chose to accompany him. He declined, and they would continue to fight each other, gaining and losing territory for another three years. As recompense, Polverel promoted Pétion to lieutenant colonel and put him at the head of all artillery batteries. His base camp was at Jacmel, under the command of General Beauvais.

At about the same time, a peace treaty was concluded between France and Spain, effectively reducing the number of fronts to two: the northern pro-French imperialists against the abolitionists, and the clusters of English-supported autonomists in the Sud. But Louverture was fickle, and Spain underestimated his reach. He marched his army of twelve thousand men back to the French, offering them control of the Nord, the Nord'est (North-east), and the plains of Artibonite.[29] England and the unruly slaves were now the only things standing in the way of France's former glory.

5

Louverture's Very Short Learning Curve

RIGAUD AND LOUVERTURE had been promoted to the rank of brigadier general in recognition of their efforts to preserve the territorial integrity of Saint-Domingue. However, the English were still there, and the Spanish were inciting insurrection on the eastern border. The unsatisfied French National Assembly appointed a new set of civil commissioners, which included the return of Sonthonax and Roume in April 1796.

The French expertly used a number of "divide and rule" tactics to sow discord among the inhabitants. To further this agenda, Sonthonax distributed firearms to blacks and encouraged them to kill anti-abolitionists of all races.[30] He also established several schools in Cap-Haïtien for general education; successful graduates were sent to France to complete their studies. Even Louverture's children benefited from this program. Sonthonax also promoted Louverture to general-in-chief of the Republican Army of Saint-Domingue, making him the highest-ranking military officer in the colony. Roume, for his part, invalidated the elections of the Sud representatives, mostly mulattos, to the colonial assembly and sent administrators to manage Rigaud. There was a campaign of disinformation designed to foment racial tension launched in the region—anti-mulatto propaganda—which took such a violent turn that as many as eight thousand blacks attacked the city of Les Cayes in August 1795. However, the concentration of mulattos in the Sud was such that they were able to retake Les Cayes. This caused an exodus of blacks from the Sud region to join Louverture's army in the Nord.[31] In reaction to these events, the cities of the Sud, not occupied by the British, formally placed themselves under Rigaud's authority.

Sonthonax soon emerged as the dominant personality of the commission. Not seeing the desired results of his attempts to create division among the various groups, in December 1796 he declared the officers of the Legion du Sud as traitors and urged residents of the Sud to reject their leadership. Furthermore, in an attempt to isolate Rigaud from his allies, Sonthonax removed Pétion from Rigaud's command and promoted him to adjutant general in the Ouest department, under the command of General Laplume, a black general. Boyer, now twenty-one, was also placed under Pétion's command as adjutant captain. Sonthonax also removed several localities under Rigaud's jurisdiction and gave them to his fellow generals, including the municipality of Léogâne, which was a blow to his ego as he had personally led the unit that had retaken it from the British. Léogâne, a lucrative port city, was now also conferred to Laplume. These actions, rather than isolate Rigaud, only put mulatto soldiers on the defensive; some intentionally sought rebellion.

Louverture realized that Sonthonax had sown the seeds of racism and jealousy into the army, but he had larger ambitions: He wanted to govern the entire colony, rather than just the Nord region. His first challenge was the three commissioners—three too many. He asked Sonthonax to depart the colony in August 1797, and by then, Louverture could not be resisted; tens of thousands of blacks had left their plantations to join him, thanks to Sonthonax. Back in France, Sonthonax had appeared before the assembly to explain how Louverture was able to remove him from his post.[32] While Sonthonax was censured for having freed the slaves and advocating their autonomy, the abrupt rise of Louverture and the self-declared autonomy of the Sud was disturbing.[33] Along with other testimonies, a clear picture emerged of the power that both Rigaud and

Louverture wielded. Republican France chose Louverture because, even though he was black, he professed a desire to remain part of the French Empire.

In early 1798, France sent General Joseph d'Hédouville to Saint-Domingue as the new governor, with explicit instructions to arrest Rigaud. When he raised the issue with Louverture, the latter feigned indignation. This incident is mentioned in a letter written by General Leclerc, the man who would lead the last French expedition to reclaim Saint-Domingue. According to that letter, Louverture responded ironically, «Arrêter Rigaud !...., autant vaut m'arrêter moi-même ! Vous ne savez donc pas qu'il est un des zélés défenseurs de la cause pour laquelle nous combattons, et que je le regarde comme mon digne fils?». (Translation: "Arrest Rigaud! You might as well arrest me, as he defends our cause with such zeal, and I regard him like a son.")[34]

In addition, there was still the matter of the British occupation in five communes. Pétion helped Louverture with that at the Battle of Port-au-Prince. Boyer, who was his adjutant, recounted the details years later to Beaubrun Ardouin, who would go on to be a senator and prominent historian. The glory of this battle belonged to Pétion. In February 1798, he received orders from Louverture via General Laplume, his commanding officer, to blockade the city, thereby cutting the British off from all communications and reinforcements. Instead, he led a full-on assault and took the city in only four hours. Port-au-Prince was his native city and Pétion couldn't bear to see the foreign occupation. But he also defied orders to partially vindicate Rigaud. He had been placed under General Laplume's command against his will and regarded Rigaud's treatment as unjust. Rigaud was fiercely patriotic.

That demonstration of force so thoroughly convinced the British that they would lose significant footing and would need to save face by initiating negotiations, that the British sent Brigadier General Thomas Maitland to negotiate their withdrawal. But after being briefed on recent events, Maitland saw the situation differently. He didn't write to d'Hédouville or any French administrator; rather, he wrote to Louverture on 28 April 1798 with an offer to withdraw all military from the environs of Port-au-Prince, as well as the communes of Arcahaie and Saint-Marc in exchange for amnesty for British settlers and permission to let them stay and continue farming. Louverture accepted this offer and also offered amnesty to all those who had fought *against* the French Republic during the five years of British occupation. He invited refugees on the Spanish side as well as in neighboring islands to return and resume their commercial interests, including British nationals. He even allowed English, American, and other countries' commercial vessels to trade, despite the continued French mercantilist policy of monopsonistic control of the colony's commodities.

Incredulous as to the degree of autonomy with which Louverture acted, d'Hédouville observed but said nothing. In May 1798, as agreed, Maitland evacuated Port-au-Prince, and Pétion, the city's hero, went to take possession of the commune with his artillery company. However, Louverture had already anticipated that move and had sent battalions ahead. He reassigned Pétion to Léogâne.

The renowned British navy still occupied the ports of Môle St.-Nicolas and Jérémie. Unexpectedly, one month later, in June 1798, Louverture received correspondence from Rigaud asking for reinforcements because the British had attacked the surrounding communes of Cavaillon, Camp-Perrin, and Tiburon. This is when Louverture began to understand that Maitland had shrewdly negotiated an interior position to reinforce the British presence along the coast.

Nevertheless, the British, seeing their hold on the island as tenuous and perhaps dated, attempted to negotiate new terms with Louverture, for the northern port of Môle Saint-Nicolas, and with Rigaud, for the southern port of Jérémie. To Louverture, they promised to recognize his authority and even name him king of Saint-Domingue. To Rigaud, they promised to recognize the autonomy of the Sud. Louverture put them on ice.

There were two remaining hurdles: Consul General d'Hédouville and Rigaud. Without any invitation, on 13

July, Louverture wrote to notify d'Hédouville that both he and Rigaud were traveling to Cap-Haïtien to meet him. D'Hédouville hurriedly summoned General Kerverseau, the governor of the Spanish side, to join him for these talks—a fortuitous decision, since Kerverseau's observations provide a more nuanced view of the forthcoming events.[35]

There appears to be some discrepancy among historians about who initiated this "summit of generals," but we do know that this is the first recorded meeting of the two generals. We know that d'Hédouville met separately with the generals, and we also know that Louverture and Rigaud met separately. Finally, we know that the two traveled back together from Cap-Haïtien to Saint-Marc, then to Port-au-Prince. Unfortunately, we don't know what was said but only what was written, and the communication arising from these meetings unveils a master of political craftiness.

Louverture had never met Rigaud and apparently had never heard how physically appealing he was. Haitian historian Ardouin described him as having a visibly military stature, open mannerisms, and a smile "that captivated hearts."[36] To Louverture's displeasure, Rigaud charmed Kerverseau and d'Hédouville. Kerverseau wrote that Louverture was unable to mask his displeasure and jealousy. Whatever was said, Rigaud returned from the summit with the intention of liberating Jérémie, on the condition that Pétion be reassigned to him. Together, they effectively took command of the remaining British forts there. But d'Hédouville had had no idea of the plan and did not appreciate the initiative demonstrated by the generals. He wrote to Louverture to express his displeasure and remind him of the colonial hierarchy. In response, the latter replied to d'Hédouville, in a letter dated 13 October 1798, renewing his loyalty to the French Republic, while, on the same day, ordering his nephew, Moyse Louverture, to lead an insurrection of black soldiers in Fort-Liberté, a city in the Nord'est region of the colony.

Now that Rigaud had retaken control of the southern peninsula, Louverture calculated that this was the opportune moment to remove him. Just four days later, on 17 October 1798, Louverture wrote to him intimating that d'Hédouville had a hidden agenda to destroy the blacks of Saint-Domingue. Rigaud expressed disbelief at such an allegation, arguing that any accusations against him in this regard were likely fabricated. Not having obtained the bellicose response desired from Rigaud, Louverture wrote again to Rigaud accusing d'Hédouville of wanting to suppress the blacks. The incredulous Rigaud responded that such a move would go against the Republican values and that Louverture should not trust the English settlers who actively sowed discord between them, if indeed they were his source of information.

A few weeks later, on 22 October 1798, d'Hédouville wrote to both Beauvais and Rigaud to denounce Louverture, accusing him of treachery with the English and Americans. In an astonishing move, even though he was initially dispatched to Saint-Domingue with orders to arrest him, the consul general gave Rigaud absolute command of the Sud department, pitting him against Louverture, who had already been named general-in-chief by Sonthonax. Evidently, d'Hedouville sensed that Louverture was the greater menace. This was his last act. Less than a week later, militarily outnumbered and feeling threatened by Louverture's Nord army, d'Hédouville boarded the French frigate *La Bravoure* and left the island for France. However, per Louverture's request, the vessel was detained for some time by an English cruiser patrolling the coasts of Cap-Haïtien. But they couldn't hold him forever, and France soon learned of Louverture's emerging power. They sent former commissioner Roume, who was an administrator on the other side of the island, Santo Domingo, to try to reign him in.

In replacement, Roume was transferred back to Saint-Domingue from the eastern side in January 1799. He organized a second summit,[37] in February 1799, this time with all generals: Rigaud, Beauvais, Louverture, and Laplume. This did not go well, and on 6 February Rigaud resigned his commission, which was not accepted by Roume. Shrewdly, Roume believed, given Rigaud's popularity in the Sud, it would be better to keep him in the French army, where the empire would have more control over him; at the very least, Roume could maintain regular communication with him. However, desiring to diminish Rigaud's sphere of power and influence, Roume removed again certain municipalities under his command, reassigning Miragoâne to Beauvais and the cities of Léogâne, Petit-Goâve, and Grand-Goâve to Laplume.[38]

According to General Kerverseau, who was still on the island, the civil war began immediately. As early as three days after Rigaud's departure, Louverture spoke at a church in Port-au-Prince, delivering an incendiary indictment against the mulattos, which was duly followed by arrests and killings of the latter. Kerverseau recounted that the killings ended as abruptly as they had begun, which indicated that they were not spontaneous, but rather a coded message to mulattos, which they understood. Consequently, the island witnessed another migration of mulattos both to the Sud and to the Spanish side.[39]

But Roume had erred; the ambitions about which Louverture wrote were his own. Roume had weakened Rigaud's authority in favor of the man who really did have aspirations to govern autonomously. His regret was palpable. In a bizarre report to France on 22 January 1799, Roume described that the island was running smoothly under Louverture's authority but that he was not able to leave Louverture's side, sensing the need to watch his every move.

In an unprecedented break with mercantilist trade policy of the previous two hundred years, in April 1799, Louverture unilaterally negotiated a commercial treaty with the United States of America. Further, in May 1799, Maitland returned with the approval of the King of England to permit trade between Jamaica and Saint-Domingue. Now both England and the USA had unofficially recognized the sovereignty of Saint-Domingue and the leadership of Louverture. *Echec et mat*: Louverture delivered a masterclass in politicking, while Rigaud was simply being patriotic.

On 19 May 1799, two incredible, isochronous communications took place. Louverture published an eight-page pamphlet accusing Rigaud of treason and racism.[40] He used adjectives such as perfidious, tyrannical, prideful, ambitious, and despotic to describe Rigaud. He accused him of not wanting to serve under a black commander-in-chief; and, judging him to be a menace to the French republic, Louverture called on the Northern armies to assemble in Port-au-Prince with the objective of marching to take the Sud. Meanwhile, Rigaud sent Louverture a letter congratulating him for the negotiation of the treaties. Louverture promptly moved his base camp south to Port-au-Prince; Rigaud to Miragoâne. Louverture drew first blood, sending his nephew to the head of the army.

The caustic combination of Louverture's ambitions, Rigaud's capacity to seduce and lead, and the shenanigans of the previous commissioners caused a rapid degeneration in the relationship between the generals. Further, the gradual agglomeration of mulatto soldiers in the Sud and blacks in the Nord provided the necessary conditions for civil war.[41]

The other generals and brigadier generals had to choose a side. Unsurprisingly, General Laplume sided with Louverture and imprisoned Captain Boyer, among many officers. Pétion managed to secure their release, and together they deserted Louverture's army and headed south to join Rigaud.

The first battle in the civil war was at Petit-Goâve, one of the jurisdictions Commissioner Roume had removed from under Rigaud's authority. Rigaud was victorious, even though no historians estimated his army at more than three thousand men. Rigaud was vastly outnumbered and needed the psychological win. However, Louverture divided his army in two divisions, keeping Moyse at the head of the northern division and placed Jean-Jacques Dessalines at the head of the southern division. Dessalines, a former slave, was, by many accounts, brutish, "quick to violence," incapable of reasoning if it meant not following orders, and generally angry at the world. His intrepidity was terrifying, scaring his own soldiers into submission, making him a formidable adversary on the battlefield. Dessalines would change the tone of the civil war.

What happened to General Beauvais? He was delegated the jurisdiction of Jacmel, an area naturally defended by its surrounding mountain ranges, rendering a terrestrial attack impossible. He commanded 4,500 soldiers but refused to take part in the civil war and kept his colonels from doing so as well. However, they desired to fight for the Sud and, unknown to Beauvais, planned a surprise attack on the eastern wing of the Army of the Nord. Beauvais, older and with no longer the stomach for warfare, fled Saint-Domingue for Curaçao. Several of his officers did the same. Pétion assumed command of Jacmel after Beauvais, rallying some hope as his reputation for valiancy had spread. Boyer, again, duly accompanied his childhood friend.[42] But no amount of courage or skill could stop Dessalines. He pushed them back from Jacmel to Aquin and eventually to Les Cayes, Rigaud's base.

Louverture graciously offered the Army of the Sud amnesty, with the exception of four officers, including Pétion, who had defected from his army to join Rigaud. Notice of the amnesty arrived in Les Cayes in July 1799, as well as the news that they were surrounded by the Nord Army by land and the British and American patrols, by sea. Some took the amnesty; hundreds, including Rigaud, Pétion, and Boyer, hopped on vessels destined to other countries.

There was still the matter of Roume. Louverture did not want the French to send yet another replacement, as he had cultivated a dysfunctional relationship with Roume in which the latter was mollified by his assertiveness. Louverture wrote to Roume; he suggested that the departure of d'Hédouville was the fault of Rigaud, who had also intimated a desire to get rid of Roume, eliminate the white colonists, and declare the island's independence. "I tried my best to discourage him from these horrible aspirations," he concluded in his letter of 23 August 1799.

Louverture only had one thing left to do: He annexed the Spanish side, Santo Domingo. Annexation is not entirely accurate, as the "Spanish" side already belonged to France, conceded by Spain in the Treaty of Basel (1795). Nonetheless, Spain kept a presence there, having been asked by the French government to administer the eastern side until such time that they could effectively take over. Louverture, invoking that treaty, assumed command of the entire island in January 1801.

6

Saved by the Square and Compasses

LOUVERTURE'S OFFICERS WERE SHOWING little mercy to the inhabitants of the Sud. The war for equality and recognition had morphed into a race war of blacks against mulattos, Nord against Sud, Louverture against Rigaud. As early as 1799, Louverture had negotiated with the United States' President John Adams preferential access to Haitian merchandise, despite a French ban on its colonies trading outside of its network. In return, the American navy patrolled the perimeter of the Saint-Domingue coast, on the pretext that it had to protect its own commercial vessels. Louverture, who didn't want to lose the Sud region to secession, arranged with the American navy to blockade the ports in the region, with a view to starving the residents. It worked; the soldiers could no longer receive their daily rations of bread. They ate the horses of the cavalry and had even begun to eat soldiers fallen in battle.

There were reports of assassinations and arrests throughout the region. Rigaud wanted to launch a last offensive from Les Cayes, but the people of the Sud Department were starving and tired. They urged him to accept the amnesty that Louverture was offering, which a considerable number of his officers had already accepted. Ultimately, he accepted and left the island from the port of Les Cayes on a Danish ship in July 1800. He was accompanied by his brothers François and Augustin and eighty-four other officers, heading to the island of Saint Thomas.

Rigaud's lieutenant, Alexandre Pétion, was also in Les Cayes, ill with fever, as he often was. Pétion learned of Louverture's order to arrest him—he had defected from Louverture's division to join Rigaud—and realized that he did not have sufficient resources to emigrate. He sent Boyer, his captain, to Jérémie, where the Sud's treasury was kept, to withdraw enough species to finance their exile. However, while waiting for Boyer to return with the money, Pétion learned that they were out of time; Louverture's army had entered Les Cayes. His arrest was imminent. Unable to wait for Boyer, Pétion managed to hop on a ship at the harbor, ironically called *Le Bonaparte,* bound for Curaçao, a Dutch colony, where he arrived around August 1800, after a stop in Aruba. In September 1800, he arrived in Guadeloupe (still a French colony), where a number of soldiers from the Army of the Sud had also landed, including his commanding general Rigaud. They both booked passage to France and were immediately reintegrated into the French army.

By the time Boyer reached Jérémie, the treasury had already been emptied. On his way back to his childhood friend, Boyer learned that Les Cayes had fallen and he and several remaining mulatto officers negotiated passage on *La Vengeance*, which was destined for Cuba. But the US naval cruiser *Trumbull*, navigated by Captain David Jewett, captured the ship in the Mona Passage and escorted it to the port of Charleston, South Carolina. Boyer was painfully aware that this was a slave state where there was no distinction between mulatto and black. Likely, he would be sold and sent to work on some plantation. Doubting that his military uniform would be enough to rescue him from that fate, he discretely slipped on some jewelry and prayed that the Masonic Square and Compasses would save him from life on a tobacco plantation. Never leaving the ship, Boyer and his fellow captives only remained a few days in Charleston, until Jewett steered the ship to the New London harbor in Connecticut. Boyer and the 149 other soldiers were relieved; Connecticut was a free state. The worst that could happen was a prolonged imprisonment.

Captain Jewett was a Freemason and noticed that Boyer was sporting the same two silver captain's bars *and* Masonic jewelry. After a search, he found various Masonic documents from Boyer's lodge, the Grand Orient of France in Jacmel.[43] Among the documents were certificates of his progression through the order from Apprentice to Perfect Master, written communication from the Grand Orient at Paris, and a charter for the Masonic lodge in Jacmel, Haiti, the *Loge Frères Choisis*, issued in 1774. The charter was signed by a S. Morin. Captain Jewett recognized this name and what it meant: Boyer had been initiated into the Scottish Rite, a branch founded in France in the 1760s. Within a decade, Stephen Morin had established the first lodge in the French Caribbean. Boyer was perhaps introduced to Freemasonry by a French commissioner named Étienne Polverel, who had been sent to co-govern with Sonthonax and with whom Boyer had traveled in 1793 on his way back from studying in France. Upon arrival, Boyer served as his adjutant before defecting to join Rigaud. However, once in New London, Jewett, a member of Wooster Lodge in Colchester, Connecticut, shared these items with his uncle, Eliphalet Bulkeley, Master Freemason of Wooster. They seized these articles, perhaps believing that no black man should have been integrated into the Masonic Order. Worse still, the documents revealed that Boyer, in fact, was a higher degree Freemason in a state in which the Masonic rite was still new; members in other countries believed that the brotherhood should be reserved for descendants of the Knights Templar. Even worse, Boyer had achieved Master, which meant that he had been studying for many years. All attempts to recuperate these effects from the resentful Bulkeley and Jewett failed.

Boyer nonetheless made an impact on the Freemason community during his short stay in Connecticut. He was hosted by a number of aristocratic families of Norwich, Connecticut, and housed with the Manning family, headed by Diah Manning. Described by one Connecticut contemporary as "a young mulatto of manly and dignified deportment," Boyer kept in touch with the Manning family and, as a show of gratitude, sent a gift of $400 of support to the widow of Diah Manning when he died in 1815. He did the same for Consider Sterry, a scientist and mathematician who also warmly hosted Boyer.[44] Boyer was apparently treated humanely in the small Norwich community; he attended lodge meetings regularly and was free to socialize with residents until his deportation one year later, in April 1801.[45] Boyer arrived in Bordeaux, France, on 4 September 1801. He eventually made his way to Paris, where he reunited with his buddies Rigaud and Pétion.

7

Madagascar

NAPOLEON WAS PENSIVE: What was he supposed to do with the hundreds of mulatto soldiers in his army—and on his payroll? He understood how they came to be part of the army—France needed to align itself with a segment of Saint-Domingue society to retain control of the colony. The British had taken control of their ports; the Spanish, who had also enlisted blacks, were attacking from the east. The mulattos in the Sud had created their own militia and declared autonomy. The French made the only choice available to them, because liberating their productive African slaves was not an option. They had to win over the mulattos, so this people group was granted French nationality and integrated into the French army.

The mulatto refugees had integrated not only into

the army, but into French society. For two years, hundreds of them were parading around Paris, in respectable military uniforms, awaiting their next assignment. This was not representative of the new French identity that Napoleon was trying to build. He definitely could not send them to any other part of Europe. But he did have plans for conquest beyond the Mediterranean Sea. He would send them to accompany the expedition - in case they could be of any assistance – and then continue to Madagascar.

Rigaud, Pétion, Boyer, and dozens of other mulattos left France in the middle of winter in December 1801, on board the war vessel *La Vertu,* along with Poles, Austrians, and Germans—all conquests of the French consul general and soon-to-be-named emperor. Poles weren't considered the most elite of soldiers, largely derided for their lack of intelligence, causing the mulattos to be apprehensive—why were they, a part of the conquering army, traveling on a ship with soldiers from conquered regions?

The month-long traverse across the Atlantic was tense for other reasons as well. They had retained their military ranks but had not received any instructions nor assignments to report to commanding officers. Rigaud was particularly worried, as he held the rank of brigadier general—his brevet signed by Napoleon himself. But he had no unit assigned to him. They were aware of Napoleon's expansionist plans, but they were also excited to be returning to their homeland. The news was all over the world: Louverture had taken control of the entire island and abolished slavery. He had signed treaties with both the Americans and the British. Could they bring themselves to fight against Louverture? His blackness aside, he was the object of their admiration. Could they somehow convince Napoleon to accept Louverture's governorship *and* remain French citizens? The fact was that not all mulattos were anti-slavery; but they knew that, in order to get off that ship alive in Saint-Domingue, they needed to arrive at a consensus. As the climate improved with the ship's approach to the Caribbean Sea, the various options were endlessly and heatedly debated.

But when the French armada arrived at Cap-Haïtien in January 1802, they were unable to disembark. One of Louverture's generals, Henri Christophe, who had command of the port and the city, declined their entry and refused to send tender boats. There followed an incendiary exchange of letters with General Charles Victor Emmanuel Leclerc, the head of the expedition—and also Napoleon's brother-in-law. Leclerc made alternative arrangements to disembark anyway; so, Christophe set fire to the city. The mulatto soldiers observed all of this from the ship's deck. As they watched recognizable Cap-Haïtien landmarks dematerialize, Pétion realized that Christophe had summarily put an end to their own deliberations. He turned to Rigaud and Boyer beside him. "We are no longer going to Madagascar."

8

Louverture's Unconquerable Mind

NAPOLEON TRIED ONE LAST diplomatic maneuver: In April 1802, he sent three new commissioners with a special communication for Louverture, which had to be delivered to him personally. In the letter, Napoleon complemented his leadership and expressed gratitude that such a formidable soldier was loyal to France. He assured Louverture that the liberty and rights of blacks were recognized by their mother country and offered that the weapons and soldiers that had accompanied the commissioners were meant to be used against foreign enemies, namely the English. Napoleon asked him to employ moderation in bringing an end to the civil war. Finally, he asked Louverture to print and disseminate widely the new French Constitution, which was applicable in its overseas territories.[46] In response, Louverture ordered the arrest of two of the commissioners, leaving one free to communicate with France.

Napoleon was too late. Having annihilated his largely mulatto opposition, Louverture had made several power moves between November 1800 and January 1801. For one, he had massacred large numbers of affranchis, who were aligned with Rigaud. Though some communities had been spared, their movements were closely monitored, and they required authorization to travel, even internally. He also negotiated a trade treaty with the United States of America, offering them preferential tariffs for their exports to Saint-Domingue. He arranged for Roume's arrest, for refusing to sanction his annexation of Saint-Domingue, and held him for eight months, until August 1801, when he was allowed to board a frigate to the United States. Finally, on 27 January 1801, he had assumed command of the entire island, declaring administrative and commercial independence.

The broad strokes of Louverture's administration of the island are notable, even if short-lived. It was the first time in the history of Hispaniola that it had been effectively governed as one administrative entity. The second and only other time in the island's history was the unification later realized by Boyer. Louverture's government lasted two years against Boyer's twenty-two years. Nonetheless, Louverture's administrative accomplishments cannot be ignored, and one can't help but consider that they served as models for Boyer.

As early as March 1801, he divided Hispaniola into six departments (Sud, Ouest, Nord, Cibao, Ozama, and Louverture), all with departmental capitals. He established a general assembly and organized elections, allocating two representatives from each department. He also established municipal administrations, equipped with their own gendarmerie. The highest authority would be a governor, with a mandate of five years. However, since he was the founder of this new nation, he named himself governor-for-life with the power to choose his successor. The island would remain part of the French Empire, and all those born in the colony were French citizens, regardless of color. Roman Catholicism was the official religion. On 13 July 1801, Louverture published these and many other laws under the new constitution of Saint-Domingue. He even printed species for internal exchange.

Naturally, slavery was prohibited, and Louverture proclaimed that agriculture would receive "special attention" from his administration, given it was the main source of wealth creation during its colonial period. This attention, however, came in the form of forced labor. Even before the annexation, Louverture had been implementing a system of forced labor, converting a portion of the army into a policing force. When communicating to the workers, he placed great emphasis on the fact that a high level of productivity was needed to maintain the army and finance military operations. It is important to note that this system already was widely practiced in the Sud and Ouest provinces, which is also how Rigaud financed his campaigns against the British. "If degradation accompanied labor, the cultivators under Toussaint were the most abject people in existence, for they were driven to it under the strong arm of military power, and for any offense which they committed they were liable to be brought before a military tribunal," observed Englishman James Franklin in an account of his several visits to the island.[47]

Obviously, these measures met with much resistance. Even his nephew, General Moyse Louverture, responsible for agriculture in the Nord department, led an insurrection of farmers in October 1801, which killed hundreds of whites. This is the same area where the revolt against slavery was violently initiated in 1791, and the blacks in this region were loath to farm only to see the proceeds of their efforts go back to white plantation owners, who were still present among them. Moyse rejected Louverture's use of force and consequently the harvests in the Nord were markedly lower. In an attempt to find a compromise, Moyse proposed an alternative: to subdivide the large plantations and sell them to army officers. However, Louverture rejected this plan, and historians have put forth a variety of reasons ranging from the need to consolidate his wealth to the refusal to renounce the previous dominance of Saint-Domingue in world trade, via the plantation/slavery mode of production. Whatever the motivation, practically the Moyse proposal implied dispossessing white plantation owners. Accused of fomenting the insurrection, Moyse was executed in November 1801, along with thousands of farm workers in Cap-Haïtien and Fort Liberté. In one northern city called Plaisance, one quarter of the population was massacred, an act of deterrence to dissuade the remaining residents from following Moyse. Henri Christophe, who would later vie for absolute power over Haiti against Pétion, was promoted in Moyse's place.[48]

Recognizing that this was a radical change of lifestyle and economy for the districts in the East (Santo Domingo), Louverture lowered tariffs on both imports and exports to 6 percent, with a view to stimulating commerce at the ports, as well as allowing the residents to keep a larger percentage of revenue. To this end, he allowed the ports on the Spanish side—Puerto Plata, Monte Christi, Santo Domingo, and Samaná, among others—to trade freely. He also created a structure dedicated to commercial arbitration. This new economic and political order was maintained throughout the island with an army of approximately twenty thousand men.[49]

Louverture also realized that the large plantations were being subdivided through sale to farmers, who didn't have the capital or labor to farm large tracts of land, as had been done under the slavery mode of production. He thus limited subdivisions to 50 *carreaux de terre* (64,650 hectares), with the condition that ownership could only be transferred provided the buyer demonstrated the means to farm the land in its entirety. This created a source of tension with the Spanish residents, because they were not traditionally farmers. They specialized in logging and livestock. However, Louverture was particularly interested in boosting exports, and he perceived the most value to be in sugar cane, coffee, cacao, and cotton. Furthermore, he outlawed the sale of lumber for export and mandated that trees could be cut only for internal construction projects.

By many accounts, from both Europeans and Americans, Louverture was an effective leader and negotiator. True, he governed autocratically, but he was also known to seek counsel in areas in which he felt relatively uninformed. "The end of the year 1801 placed the whole island once more in some degree of tranquility, and in submission to the authority of the negro chief, rapidly advancing in wealth and increasing its intercourse with those countries which sought to establish with it the friendly relations of commerce," concluded Franklin.[50]

Meanwhile across the ocean, Napoleon Bonaparte was simply embarrassed. A black man had not only taken control of the most lucrative island in the Caribbean, but negotiated commercial treaties as a sovereign country, though he claimed to be part of the French Empire. Napoleon had sent a constitution for Louverture, and instead the latter printed his own. Although the documents were largely identical, there was one essential difference: Saint-Domingue would no longer participate in the mercantilist regime but instead take part in free trade. Louverture also had humiliated France by arresting and deporting Commissioners d'Hédouville and Roume, referring to them as "inadequate" in his correspondence.[51]

In a world where a demonstration of force was a commonly applied and accepted diplomatic tool, on 23 November 1801, Napoleon issued a proclamation ordering a military expedition—which had actually set sail two days prior—of considerable size to rectify what he described as "actes irréguliers" and to retake control of Saint-Domingue. On 14 December 1801, the expedition, which was headed by General-in-chief Leclerc, landed at Samaná Bay on 28 January 1802. Napoleon assigned 56,000 men to the task.[52]

Leclerc was armed with a letter to Louverture from Bonaparte dated 18 November 1801. Affirming his rank of general in the salutation, Bonapart informed Louverture that he had named Leclerc as the chief administrator of the colony and had sent a force of "appropriate size" to ensure he could undertake his responsibilities. He wrote also of his expectation that Louverture would assure Leclerc of the sincerity of his allegiance to France, as he had in past communications. He also acknowledged Louverture's military accomplishments, stating that if the French flag was still flying in Saint-Domingue, it was because of Louverture's efforts during what Bonaparte described as a "period of anarchy" for France. To summarize: Bonaparte masterfully validated Louverture's actions, including his constitution, as necessary to secure Saint-Domingue from foreign invasion, as the government had not been able to send reinforcements nor guidance in time.

One may ask why it took France so long to react to Louverture's aggressions. During this time France, in addition to experiencing internal political instability, had been at war, yet again, with England. Also, its resources were concentrated elsewhere: The French Republican Army was busy conquering Italy and Egypt, under the leadership of General Napoleon Bonaparte. With these successes under his belt, he staged a coup in France and was elected to the highest office, known then as Premier Consul. Bonaparte sent an invitation to negotiate an armistice to England, the only country that had not accepted integration into the French Empire. Of course, one of the motivating factors to negotiate was the continued blockade of French ports. Rather than negotiate, Britain decided to take Egypt and succeeded. However, Britain had a series of poor harvests, resulting in severe food price inflation, which diverted resources and attention away from their military activities. Then, on 25 March 1802, they announced a peace treaty at Amiens (France), known as the Treaty of Amiens. The historical enmity between the two countries, momentarily put to sleep, freed up resources for Bonaparte. Among other things, Britain agreed to restore all possessions of France, Spain, and the Dutch Republic. For France, this included the Saint-Domingue ports and the nearby islands of Guadeloupe, St. Lucia, and Martinique that the British annexed in 1794. As they had done in Saint-Domingue, Great Britain gained a foothold in these countries by supporting plantation owners, who desired autonomy from what was, at the time, a chaotic France.

There is some evidence that the rise of Louverture gave the British and French a common objective: to squash any semblance of the beginnings of a black republic. Correspondence in November 1801 from the British secretary of state, Lord Hobart, to the governor of Jamaica, General Nugent, just before the sailing of Leclerc's expedition, brought to light the possible additional motivations for the Treaty of Amiens.

> *Whatever may be the consequence of the Reestablishment of the Government of France in the Island of St. Domingo, I think there can be no doubt, that the Eventual danger from the Continuance of the power of Toussaint [sic], or a Black Empire there in any hands,*

must be the subject of more real and well-founded alarm to the Jamaica planters, than any that can be apprehended from its being restored to the Authority of the Mother Country; and therefore, that at all hazards, it is not fit that we should throw any obstacle in the way of the Accomplishment of that Object.[53]

Although Britain had initially thought that the size of the armada was exaggerated considering the meager resources of the colony and wondered if Bonaparte had a larger design in the Caribbean, Hobart informed the governor that they would send the appropriate reinforcements to protect Jamaica, writing, "Toussaint's [sic] Black Empire is one, amongst many evils, that have grown out of the War; and it is by no means our interest to prevent its Annihilation."[54]

Louverture did not submit to Leclerc's authority. He chose to fight. However, the French scored early wins against the Indigenous Army (aka the Army of Saint-Domingue). As early as February 1802, the French took Port-de-Paix and Port-au-Prince. Twice, in March 1802, Louverture tried to take control of Cap-Haïtien and was pushed back by Leclerc's forces. Leclerc's early and decisive victories were enough to knock the winds out of the sails of independence of the Indigenous Army.

The sheer size of the French fleet was enough to make any soldier reevaluate their motivations. Understandably, defections occurred. Leclerc also had announced that he would reintegrate these soldiers into the French army, preserving their current ranks, and that he would extend the French constitutional guarantee of "liberty for all" to the inhabitants of Saint-Domingue. General Laplume, whom Louverture had placed as commander of the Sud Region after Rigaud's departure, accepted the offer, and several high-ranking officers in the Indigenous Army surrendered, including Paul Louverture, Toussaint's brother. Christophe also surrendered, along with several thousand men, in late March 1802.

When Louverture heard the news that the last of his brigadier generals had given up the fight, he himself inquired about the terms of surrender. Finding them fair, he went to Cap-Haïtien, where Leclerc was based. The outcome of their negotiations was that Louverture agreed to remain at a plantation in Gonaïves. The bellicose Dessalines followed suit and was sent to Saint-Marc. They were asked not to communicate with each other nor with anyone else and not to leave while Leclerc restored order, which he did. Black soldiers were duly integrated into the French army; the French inventoried the island for artillery and other weapons; farmers were allowed to return to their plantations; and Leclerc organized the reconstruction of Cap-Haïtien.

Alexandre Paul Marie de Laujon, a French commercial agent who had persuaded Leclerc to allow him to sail in the armada, described in his memoirs the extent to which normalcy was restored, once the indigenous generals capitulated. "Cafes and restaurants reopened, and commercial exchanges in Cap-Haïtien recommenced, with boats arriving from the Ouest and Sud departments with merchandise for sale."[55] However, this calm lasted only a few months.

Leclerc wrote to Louverture again to give him an update on the stabilization efforts and offered him amnesty—he could remain on the island but would have to retire from the army. Unfortunately, the taste of power that Louverture had during the year or so that he was in absolute control of the island had rendered him feverish for more. Leclerc then learned that the Americans had been selling arms to Louverture, which raised suspicions that Louverture's long game was to secede from the empire. In June 1802, Louverture was arrested after intercepted correspondence revealed that he had attempted to rally the population for independence. On 29 May 1802, Louverture was deported to France, where he would perish in prison. This brought a definitive end to his role in Haitian history.

There's not a breathing of the common wind
That will forget thee; thou hast great allies;
Thy friends are exultations, agonies,
And love, and Man's unconquerable mind.
"To Toussaint L'Ouverture," by William Wordsworth[56]

9

By Dog or By Drowning?

AMONG THE DIVISION GENERALS who accompanied Leclerc was General Donatien Rochambeau. He had previously been posted to the island colony of Martinique, which he surrendered to the British in 1794. This wasn't his first assignment to Saint-Domingue; he had been promoted to general-in-chief of the eastern part, while the British occupied many of the ports on the western side of the island. He even claimed to have given Louverture the plan to attack Saint-Marc, one of the occupied ports.[57] He was relieved of that position—"*destitué* " and "*déporté* " in his words—for having spoken out about the mismanagement of the colony by Polverel and Sonthonax, who had armed the blacks that were now killing plantation owners. They, in return, accused him of insubordination and uncivilized behavior.

Haitians remember Rochambeau for his intense dislike of blacks and his sadistic punishments. He regularly organized public spectacles in which black- or black-sympathizer prisoners were hung, drowned, or devoured by dogs. The English had used dogs as well to hold the various port cities that they had seized. He imported several hundred Spanish bulldogs from Cuba, which he had hoped would devour recalcitrant blacks; at the very least, they could be unleashed as an advance team to weed out soldiers in hidden positions.[58]

Many in the Indigenous Army went into hiding in the mountains and remote areas of the island, adopting a guerilla fighting strategy. But the dogs' arrival and deployment also coincided with a number of key losses to the Indigenous Army, and Rochambeau began summarily executing officers by drowning them.

The word circulated among officers to go into hiding. Boyer, who was in Cap-Haïtien at the time, was ordered by Pétion to move south. However, Boyer was slow to relocate because of a social entanglement, and he was captured and bound. The vessel assigned to drowning duty was called the *Duguay-Trouin*. Both the dock and the boat were crowded, soldiers and civilians – boot shiners, vendors, prostitutes - milling about. Boyer scanned the boat, looking for clues about his fate. Was he going back to France? He didn't see flour rations or barrels of potable water nor did he see fresh carcasses drying in the sun for the voyage. Suddenly, through the medley of activities, he saw clearly: He was in a queue to be drowned.

Jacques Boyé, a French general, was on the dock watching the drownings. As he looked at the men in line, he recognized Boyer. The two knew each other. Boyé had had a heated confrontation with Pétion over an earlier conflict between Beauvais and another officer, which culminated in a duel. Boyé had been injured, fortunately not mortally, because he intervened immediately on Boyer's behalf when he spotted him. Boyé was also a Freemason.[59] A young French officer who wrote a memoir about his experiences in the French army, in particular the expedition to Saint-Domingue, witnessed the incident, without using any names. Boyer's social entanglement involved Rochambeau's mistress. Boyer and Boyé apparently exchanged signals of Masonic affiliation, and Boyé saw to his release.

The Square and Compasses are not just symbols of masonic affiliation; they are emblematic of its sacred principles of morality, brotherhood, and virtuous comportment. Boyer would integrate these same principles in his government.

Jacques Boyé arrived in Saint-Domingue in 1791. He had a stellar military career and had served as aide-de-camp to General Antoine Lasalle. General Lasalle, considered exceptionally brave, was blindly loyal to Napoleon and had participated in many of the emperor's conquests. In 1793, Boyé was placed in command of Port-au-Prince. In 1794, he was promoted to lieutenant colonel and assigned to Polverel and Sonthonax's Legion of the Ouest. In 1795, he served under the command of General Beauvais, stationed in Jacmel, along with Boyer. In 1800, he was promoted to adjutant general and reassigned to the eastern part of Saint-Domingue. Shortly thereafter, he was sent on a mission to the western part and was captured by the British. He remained in their custody in Jamaica until his escape in 1802. Boyé was promoted by Bonaparte to brigadier general the following year. Sent on a mission to Europe, he was again captured by the British and imprisoned until 1811. Boyé died in Saint Petersburg, Russia, in 1838. However, this isn't the last time we encounter Boyé in Boyer's story. Despite the ten-year age gap, the two were intimate and communicated frequently. In fact, President Boyer sent Boyé on several diplomatic missions before his death, including the infamous indemnity negotiation for Haiti to pay France in exchange for recognition of its independence.

10

Rigaud and Pétion, *soon* Boyer, Part II

THE VICTORIES OVER THE Indigenous Army were a placebo against the hostile tropical environment. From June to November is the hurricane season, and with the rain comes malaria and yellow fever. In a letter dated 6 July 1802, Leclerc estimated the number of daily deaths to be as high as 160. By the end of November 1802, of the thirty-five thousand that had been sent to Saint-Domingue to that date, fifteen thousand had died, a mortality rate of 43 percent.[60] At final count, based on reports from French officers in the expedition, the total death toll was twenty thousand infantry, nine thousand sailors, fourteen generals of various ranks, and seven hundred medical personnel.[61] Leclerc also died from yellow fever in November 1802, but not before deporting Rigaud.

Despite retaining his rank of brigadier general, Rigaud had received no command since disembarking *La Vertu*. Upon disembarkation, he wrote a letter dated 11 March 1802 to the commander of the Sud division, none other than General Laplume, the man who had replaced him, to inform him that his rank in the French army had been preserved and that he had been exonerated of all charges of treason. He went on to write that once the insurgency had been dealt with, he had every intention of returning to the Sud, his native land, to be with his family. He also seized the occasion to direct transfer of his property to his sister. Laplume sent the letter to Leclerc, who rapidly devised a plan to have Rigaud arrested without much fuss. To that effect, Rigaud was asked to accompany another general on a tour of the Sud, presumably to make sure that things were in order. Who could refuse a trip home? Rigaud joyously boarded the ship *La Cornelie* at Saint-Marc. But, once on board, he was arrested and asked to hand over his sword. He refused and dropped it into the sea, where it presumably lies to this day. Rigaud was taken back to France and imprisoned at Fort-de-Joux.[62]

Whereas Rigaud had stayed in Cap-Haïtien under Leclerc's command, Pétion and Boyer were sent to Port-au-Prince to serve under General Boudet. Pétion was given and humbly accepted command of an infantry battalion, even though he had risen to the rank of adjutant general of all artillery batteries. Nevertheless, it was with this battalion that Pétion joined Dessalines and twelve thousand other soldiers in the siege of the fort at Crête-à-Pierrot. Pétion heard his soldiers' rumblings about being on the front line of the advance. Then, with the bravura for which he became well-known, he admonished them, "Why aren't you all proud to be at the front? Shut up and follow me!"[63] They were pushed back and would make a second attempt to take the fort one month later.

Haitian historians uniformly characterize Pétion as a brave and highly skilled artillerist. Artillery in eighteenth-century Saint-Domingue was the cannon, which weighed twelve to sixteen pounds, with eight- to twelve-inch mortars. France's success with cannons is largely attributed to the innovations of Jean-Baptiste Vaquette de Gribeauval (1715–1789), who fashioned the cast iron mortar shorter, making it lighter, and then mounted it on wheels for improved mobility. He also introduced tangent sights and the interchangeability of parts. The French frequently mounted them on ships. Preferably placed in an elevated position, the artillery battery was meant to protect the front infantry battalion by blasting through the opponent's formation or decimating their cavalry. Requiring talent as much as training, assignment to an artillery battery was not left to volunteer recruits or even soldiers from lower social castes. Pétion would have required a mastery in geometry to adjust for windage and distance, and he did not study in France.[64] To this day, forgotten and obsolete Gribeauval cannons can be found throughout the Haitian countryside.

An example of Pétion's engineering brilliance was observed and described by Jean-Baptiste Lemmonier-Delafosse, a retired lieutenant-colonel, who had survived the Leclerc expedition, and the same memoirist who had witnessed Boyer's near-drowning. In preparing for battle with the French at Crête-à-Pierrot, Pétion had constructed ramparts—essentially gabion steps (metal cages filled with rocks)—in all the streets so that they formed strict right angles, making it difficult to take cover. Pétion had already mounted and camouflaged his cannons on higher ground. In addition, they built fortifications of split bamboo, five feet in diameter. All of this work was done in one night, with two thousand men, while the French were asleep. "No French engineer could have done better," Lemmonier-Delafosse concluded.[65]

With their leaders gone and the humiliation of consecutive defeats, the rest of the Indigenous Army was on the verge of capitulation, but then they got word that the expedition's genuine purpose was to reinstate slavery, as had just occurred in Guadeloupe in July 1802. Though often overlooked, probably because they were reintegrated into the French Republic, the island of nearby Guadeloupe had declared their independence and abolished slavery in 1794. *La Restauration*, the restoration of the former glory of France, which included the reinstatement of slavery as a mode of production, began to circulate as the strategic objective of Napoleon Bonaparte. Indeed, on 7 July 1802, France issued a proclamation of the reestablishment of slavery and the expulsion of mulattos and blacks from the French army.

But the potential reinstatement of slavery and Rochambeau's unmatched viciousness was not enough to rally everyone. There was still the issue of color, the devastation and loss of life from the civil war, borne principally by those in the Sud—the mulattos—and the exile of their revered leader, Rigaud. Leclerc had tasked both Dessalines and Christophe to disarm the population, a task which was accomplished so deftly that together they collected more than thirty thousand weapons. But they were met with formidable resistance in the municipality of Plaisance, led by three African-born leaders: Sylla, Macaya, and Mathieu. It was only after nineteen days of battle that Dessalines was able to retake Plaisance for the French. Pétion was serving under his command, heading up one of three columns of attack.

It may have been during the joint effort to take Plaisance for the French that some meeting of the minds occurred between Pétion and Dessalines. They were both repulsed by the comportment of Rochambeau and his officers and inspired by the African resistance. There is no written communication, but it is not unlikely that during the nineteen-day siege of Plaisance the two had several conversations.[66] This is as it should have been, since they shared the same ideology: independence *and* abolition. However, given what had transpired during the civil war, trust was something that would need time to take root.

News of Guadeloupe had reached Saint-Domingue. Soon after Plaisance, rebellions against the French ignited almost simultaneously in Sainte-Suzanne, Dondon, and Saint-Raphaël, again in the Nord department—with the rebels using the mountains as cover—and spread all the way down to Arcahaie, in the Ouest department.

We do know that on 13 October 1802, Pétion called a meeting with his captains and advised them that he would join the renewed resistance. Not all were immediately persuaded to defect yet again from the French army, but he managed to convince approximately five hundred soldiers from three companies. Together they would take the armory guarded by French soldiers at Haut-du-Cap.

Guided by their military training, they instinctively organized themselves by rank, which meant that since Henry Christophe was the highest-ranking officer among the rebels (Dessalines had not yet deserted his post) he was their general-in-chief. Then Leclerc died of yellow fever in November 1802, and the most despised of his officers, Rochambeau, assumed authority over the expedition forces. This Dessalines could not stomach, and he also defected. His defection was like the scent of rain on earth that has been baking under a tropical sun. A natural and calming scent, it was a relief that the resistance welcomed: Christophe was so unliked that the other officers, and he would have no choice but to submit to Dessalines' authority.

Pétion marched his brigade to Petite Rivière, where Dessalines was camped. Together they took Mirebalais, Arcahaie, Gonaïves, Léogâne, and Anse-à-Veau, but Rochambeau, back up north, would retake Fort Liberté and Port-de-Paix. One understated aspect of this latest rebellion against the French is that it was fractional. Dessalines led the Indigenous Army; however, there were other armed paramilitary groups, led by people like Makaya and Goman. The latter we will meet again, as his resistance was not just to slavery but to any authority. Anarchist to the grave, he kept the Grand'Anse region in the Sud department from joining the Republic of Haiti until 1819.

The Indigenous Army would gradually win territory, and by October 1803, the French were left with only Cap-Haïtien and Môle St.-Nicolas. Pétion, frequently unwell, remained in Port-au-Prince as Dessalines marched north with fifteen thousand men. After what is known as the

Battle at Vertières, Rochambeau surrendered on 19 November 1803 and departed with the remaining French army, a mere 8,200 men.

How Rochambeau departed Saint-Domingue is as important as the French defeat. The general was escorted on a British ship, interred in Jamaica as a prisoner of war, and then later sent to England. Correspondence between Governor-General Nugent and Lord Hobart revealed a *volte-face* regarding the black republic. "If you can secure the proposed commercial intercourse, and restrain the Brigands from getting upon the Water, the establishment of a Black Government at St. Domingo will be less dangerous to Jamaica than that of the French," Hobart wrote to Nugent. Thus, the British navy returned to blockading what would once again become lucrative ports.

This is how yellow fever, French imperial ambitions, the American and French Revolutions, the African slave resistance, and English commercial interests conspired to make real an idea that was just notional up until 1804: the idea that *all* men are born free and endowed with certain rights, including the right to self-governance.

Where was Boyer, now age twenty-eight, during this final surge for independence? Historian and biographer

Joseph Saint-Remy mentioned that Pétion left Boyer at his house during the battle of Plaisance. There is no record of Boyer's participation at the meeting in Arcahaie. He was not present at the battles at Miragoâne and Port-au-Prince, nor the final battle of the revolution at Vertières. At the summit of generals at Gonaïves, where all regions of Saint-Domingue were represented, the Indigenous Army declared their definite independence from France in January 1804, naming the new country the Republic of Haiti. There is no record of Boyer's presence or participation at this assembly. He remained inconspicuous, a close friend and ally of Pétion, and a Freemason with formal military training. Not the obvious profile of a strongman; yet, it was Boyer, despite the successive governments of Dessalines, Pétion, and Christophe, that operationalized the foundational principles of freedom, territorial integrity, and equality in the Haitian Declaration of Independence.

11

Tug of War

RACIAL CLEANSING AND DESPOTISM marked the next few years. Dessalines inherited a country in a markedly worse state of affairs, compared to Louverture. In his observations about Haiti during this period, Englishman James Franklin wrote: "Every operation of agriculture was therefore in a very languid state, and the apprehension under which people laboured was so great that they thought not of any productions beyond what they required for their own sustenance: having no inducement to look forward, they only guarded against present wants."[67]

Dessalines crowned himself emperor and, with an army of thirty-seven thousand, instituted many repressive policies, including communal taxes to support the state, forced labor and expropriation of land, and violence against political dissidents. His policies were a natural continuation of Louverture's; however, Dessalines exhibited little restraint where it related to punishment. He ordered the massacre of whites, prisoners of war, and Creoles who had allied themselves with France during the Haitian Revolution. General Guy Joseph Bonnet, who was Dessalines' aide-de-camp, mentioned in his memoirs that Pétion, who had since been promoted to division general, safeguarded many people during those dark years. Bonnet believed Dessalines knew, but the latter had so much respect for Pétion that he spared those whom he was protecting.[68] We do know that Boyer, Pétion's aide-de-camp, also actively assisted white residents to flee the country.[69]

Dessalines retained Louverture's plantation model of shared revenues. During the months of February and March 1805, he also tried to retake the eastern side but was met with formidable resistance. No one could forget the cruelty and rigidity with which he repressed his fellow Haitians under Leclerc. He was detested, and on 17 October 1806, he was assassinated by his fellow officers, black and mulatto.

Dessalines' death created a leadership vacuum. Christophe, who had been named general-in-chief of the Haitian army by Dessalines, was the obvious choice, but he was based and best known in the Nord, far away from the political machinations that were taking place in the rest of the country. Pétion, on the other hand, had been named division commander general in the Ouest department and was headquartered in Port-au-Prince, also his home.

Dessalines' death brought neither peace nor peaceful coexistence. By 21 October 1806, Pétion had already held a meeting with army officers from both the Sud and Ouest departments. He wrote to Christophe that the army was waiting for his instructions. He also alluded to the drafting of a new constitution, which was framed as one of the outcomes of the meeting. This letter was signed by all the officers, including Boyer, now a colonel.

In his response, Christophe instructed Pétion that a legislative assembly should first be established before the drafting of a constitution. Rather than send another letter, Pétion dispatched a commission of three officers to negotiate, including his own chief of staff and former aide-de-camp to Dessalines, General Bonnet. Christophe killed the emissaries but spared Bonnet, sending him back to Port-au-Prince with these prophetic sentiments: "You have shown indiscipline, which means you will never be able to govern, because those over whom you intend to govern, have witnessed your transgressions."

Realizing that he wasn't going to win the legislative battle—with two departments already against him—Christophe wrote to Pétion on 30 October 1806, calling for elections based on universal suffrage. In order to tilt the balance of power in his favor, he sent Philippe Sudre Dartiguenave, a Northern general, to Port-au-Prince with orders that Pétion should appoint the latter to replace Étienne-Élie Gérin, the commander of the Sud department. In fact, Dartiguenave is the one who delivered Christophe's proposition. In a more compromising tone, he proposed that Port-au-Prince be the capital and that the assembly should remain there. Finally, he ordered Pétion to come to Cap-Haïtien as soon as the affairs of state permitted.

Pétion didn't respond until December nor did he replace Gérin with Dartiguenave. There was no perceivable advantage to placing an ally of Christophe on his southern flank. He also never organized elections, and he certainly never traveled to Cap-Haïtien again. As a precaution, he ordered the battalions posted at Mirebalais to come to Port-au-Prince.

Christophe endeavored to have an alternative outcome than that of Louverture and Dessalines. However, despite making a formal plea for all participants in the coup to renounce their political ambitions for the sake of national unity, he suffered a political coup. Christophe had given orders to dissolve the assembly and hold elections for new representatives, providing one representative per *paroisse* (parish) who would, in turn, elect the president. The Ouest and Sud departments surpassed their allocations for representation in the legislative assembly by increasing the number of parishes. When word reached Christophe, during the month of December 1806, he marched his troops south in an effort to retain control.

Elections were held anyway. The newly formed Senate, largely composed of high-ranking military officers from the various departments, most of whom had signed the declaration of independence, hammered out a constitution during the month of December 1806. Once the legal framework was in place, they elected Christophe as president of the Republic of Haiti, for a renewable four-year term. Coincidentally, as they were preparing the formal notification to Christophe, the assembly learned that Christophe had marched his army south and was about to enter Arcahaie. Pétion and other newly elected senators, like Lys, Gérin, Magloire Ambroise, Yayou, David Troy, and Bonnet—also active military officers—immediately organized the defense of the capital. Other senators like Paul Romain and Magny sided with Christophe and traveled north.

Pétion sent orders to all regiments to defend the entries into the city of Port-au-Prince. Fortunately for Pétion and the inhabitants of the Ouest, there was no hesitation by Division General Gérin, commander of the Sud department: When the news arrived, he marched a column of soldiers from their base in Jacmel over the mountains to Port-au-Prince. While Christophe was certainly not outnumbered, he had not anticipated fighting on two fronts and had to withdraw and return to Cap-Haïtien. He would unsuccessfully attempt again to take the Ouest department during the summer and fall of 1808. So Christophe devised the next best alternative: He declared the independence of the Nord department, renaming it the Republic of Northern Haiti, setting the southern border at the city of Saint-Marc. He remained president-in-opposition from 1806 to 1811 and then crowned himself King Henry I for an additional nine years, from 1811 to 1820.

" *Pétion et sa bande orgueilleuse* [Pétion and his proud gang]," Christophe wrote. A prolific writer, he communicated with his fellow citizens consistently and frankly. [70] Christophe was understandably angry and embarrassed at the political maneuvering that had taken place, but there was some validity to his accusations. "Pétion was at the heart of the conspiracy," according to Frenchman Pompée-Valentin Baron de Vastey, a resident of the Nord department and secretary to Christophe.[71] Pétion was "making himself as likable by all parties, presenting himself as without ambition; a 'hypocrite,' who played on Dessalines' affection for him," wrote de Vastey.

Suspicions circulated about the prominence of Pétion's role in Dessalines' death. The ensemble of surviving correspondence reveals that his assassination was planned, and that the commanders of both the Ouest and Sud departments, Generals Pétion and Gérin respectively, had arrived at a consensus. Pétion's communication to

Dessalines' widow has also survived the years. He wrote to her on 19 October 1806, partially out of duty—as the assassination happened in his jurisdiction—and partly out of audacity. There is some arrogance that can be gleaned from his words: "All the sacred laws of nature were broken by him [Dessalines]. His excesses compelled people to take up arms. This sacrifice by the people on this memorable day was fate for their revenge. ... Forget that you were his wife, and you are now the wife to a nation."

He also wrote to Christophe: "We realized that the only way to preserve our nation was to rise up against him [Dessalines]. It was a spontaneous movement, but it was swift and coordinated." He ended the letter by reassuring Christophe that the army remained faithful and disciplined and invited him to take the reign of government.

Christophe wasn't born in the colony nor in Africa; he was born in Grenada. A French officer brought him to Cap-Haïtien, where he learned masonry. From there, he accompanied the French volunteers to fight against the British at the Battle of Savannah, in Georgia. He had fought alongside Rigaud and Beauvais. Upon returning to Cap-Haïtien, he was sold to a hotel matron, where he worked until he bought his freedom. He then became a butcher, traveling frequently to the Spanish side, Santo Domingo, to buy cattle. When he finally enlisted in the French army in 1793, well after the revolt in the Nord department had begun, he was integrated into the artillery service, like Pétion.

Historians have different and extreme perspectives on Christophe. Some paint him as a reasonable and restrained person, with good judgment, whereas others portray him as a psychopath. He was probably all these things, depending on with whom he was interacting. But it is also true that his cruelty and need to control even the most banal of daily tasks rendered him generally unpopular.

One thing is indisputable: The economic performance of the Republic of Northern Haiti surpassed the Republic of Haiti. Christophe's economic planning has been sufficiently documented, and what we know is impressive, given that he, too, was born a slave. By now, the Industrial Revolution had launched in the United Kingdom. Christophe had heard talk of an invention called the plough and invited several Englishmen to the Kingdom to offer technical support to local farmers. They planted tubers, indigo, cotton, cacao, and sugar, which products formed the basis for the commercial relations with the Netherlands, Great Britain, and the United States of America. The standing army was well-maintained and disciplined, and Christophe had impressive fortifications built, among which La Ferrière remains a tourist destination. It was a multilingual society, there was little crime, and everyone was encouraged to master a skill.[72]

Pétion's defense was formidable, and Christophe was obliged to retreat to Arcahaie, where he launched several assaults over the coming months. The Senate, in the meantime, had decided that, given the attack on his fellow countrymen, Christophe was unfit to be president. They also dismissed the four senator-generals that left to fight with Christophe, leaving the Nord department with no representation in Parliament.

Christophe reacted by creating his own legislative assembly for the Nord department. On 17 February 1807, this assembly promulgated a new constitution, naming Christophe president-for-life of the State of Haiti, essentially instituting a unimodal government in which the president had absolute power over the state's finances, military, and foreign relations.

Pétion was elected president of the Republic of Haiti on 9 March 1807. However, a number of black generals, like Yayou and Magloire Ambroise, were not happy with the outcome of the elections. They appreciated that Pétion, from the very start of the revolution in 1791, had never reversed himself on the principal issue of slavery, even when a peace offer of French nationality was on the table during the Suisses affair. Nevertheless, he was a mulatto and did not represent the majority of Haitians. And these weren't random officers—they had colluded with Pétion to kill Dessalines. Thus they organized another plot to unseat Pétion, which was uncovered at the last moment of planning, when officers were sent by Yayou, city commander of Port-au-Prince and Léogâne, to fetch gunpowder. The carriage of gunpowder was spotted on the dark road linking Léogâne and Port-au-Prince, and the alarm was sounded. Pétion, abed with an oft-recurring fever, needed assistance to mount his horse. But the desire for peace, after nearly seventeen years of warfare, prevailed, and sufficient numbers of Yayou's troops defected, forcing him to flee. Haitian historians differ on his fate, with reports ranging from him dying valiantly in battle to sneaking out of a window and disappearing.

Military reassignments were in order, and this is where Boyer's star began to rise. Pétion's cabinet consisted of Colonel Boyer, his personal secretary, now the head of the presidential guard. Joseph Balthazar Inginac, who was Yayou's personal secretary, was appointed as secretary of state, a position he would retain for the rest of Pétion's presidency as well as that of Boyer, a total of thirty-three years. Bonnet was initially his secretary of state finances but would soon be replaced by Jean Chrysostôme Imbert, as general administrator of finances (essentially the modern-day minister of finance), a position he held until 1843.

12

Everyone Wants to Be President

ACCOMPANIED BY BOYER, Pétion traveled to the Sud region in May 1808. There was a small insurrection led by Jean Baptiste du Perrier (aka Goman), an ambitious, Rigaud-trained African who began a campaign of guerilla warfare in the Grand'Anse region in 1807 and had obtained a certain popularity. President Pétion toured the military posts around the Grand'Anse region, Anse-d'Hainault, Les Anglais, and Tiburon. Observing that the region was vast, proving difficult for logistics, he opened the port of Tiburon to external commerce. He was adroitly giving the southern military units the opportunity to better provision themselves. It was only upon his return to Port-au-Prince that the president learned that he didn't have the constitutional discretion to create new administrative divisions or regulate external commerce; those were parliamentary powers.

In fact, the Senate was obliged to write an exceptionally long letter of censure to Pétion, dated 28 July 1808, for usurping their powers on more than one occasion. They had made several requests for information—including for the recurrent expenditures of the executive, the cadastral records of the country, and the financial state of the armed forces—and none had been addressed. He had named a new secretary of state without approval by the Senate. He had purchased ships without the Senate first appropriating the funds. And he offered amnesty to some soldiers who had been condemned for having participated in the recent insurrections, without notifying the Senate. *Un silence fâcheux* accused the Senate of Pétion's autocratic methods. Without legislative accountability, the Senate was just a decorative feature at the presidential palace.

Since the Senators from the Nord department had withdrawn and Senators Yayou and Magloire Ambroise died from leading an insurrection, the Senate was now an intimate group of war veterans. A few others would die, spawning the rumor that Pétion was working towards absolute power himself, under the cloak of republicanism. Blanchet Jeune died in May 1808; others resigned their seats, such as Depas-Medina in July 1808; and still others died in battle, including David Troy in 1809. Gérin died in January 1810, after having made several recommendations regarding strategy against Christophe, all of which were dismissed. Embarrassed, he retreated to the Sud department, his home. He was killed in an exchange of gunfire, while resisting the Pétion's order for arrest. Pétion announced the death of his division general with the words, "A new conspiracy has been unveiled and terminated like the others ... by a man who could not master his ambition." He warned other adversaries that the public's security was part of his mandate and anyone acting against this would meet with "the sword of justice." The convenient disappearance of political rivals and harsh words spoken of a war hero sparked resentment both in the Senate and across the army's rank and file. Pétion was the "one and only author of the war; the only one with the audacity and skill to manipulate everyone," accused de Vastey (1819), a Northerner and close ally of Christophe. Such sentiments were indeed shared by a number of contemporaries.

Meanwhile, England and France found new battlefronts. Napoleon's France invaded Spain in 1808, and this distraction cost it greatly. England did not waste time re-establishing itself in the Caribbean. Making an appeal to the English, the Spanish residents of Santo Domingo expelled the remaining French colonialists. In 1809, the English took Martinique; in 1810, Guadeloupe.

Rigaud, who was in France, perceived an opportunity to return to his homeland, which materialized on 7 April 1810. Some say he was dispatched on a mission; other assert that he escaped from prison.[73] Whichever was the case, his arrival in Haiti was unexpected but enthusiastically welcomed by the Southerners, who were mourning the loss of Gérin. The people were so excited that as his canoe approached the shore, they waded out to meet it and carried it to shore.[74] The celebration to welcome him has been described as extraordinary, with cannon fire, parades, and drums.

Rigaud wrote to President Pétion on the same day announcing his return: "The favorable reception that I have received fully recompenses what I was suffered these last ten years." Pétion invited him to Port-au-Prince, where he was honored with a promotion to division general. He spent several days at the National Palace, where Pétion briefed him on the events of the previous decade. Pétion, skeptical of his intentions, nevertheless gave him command of the Sud Legion with the mission to eliminate Goman, who was coincidentally his godson and now at the head of eighteen hundred men.[75]

By September 1810, it became obvious that there was a difference of opinion between Rigaud and Pétion on how to rid the Sud of Goman and his small band of rebels, whose guerilla-style of combat had begun to win over the local population. Rigaud preferred negotiation and infiltration as tactics, whereas Pétion urged him to take a more aggressive approach.

Thus, at Pétion's insistence, Rigaud proceeded with an assault. Coincidentally and without warning, a hurricane in late September bombarded the island for three days, giving Rigaud the strategic advantage, as Goman's militia had sought refuge in the forest and were trapped there. Rigaud waited out the storm and went in after them, taking many prisoners of those that had survived.[76]

Pétion was partially relieved with Rigaud's apparent success. Although Goman wasn't captured, he kept a low profile. On the other hand, Pétion perceived Rigaud to be a threat to the republic, as the latter had also mastered infiltration tactics and kept a steady correspondence with the high-ranking officers in the Sud. The president moved to station two companies in Aquin towards the end of November 1810, but they were met with local resistance. They received orders to retreat to Miragoâne, which became a de facto border between the Ouest and Sud departments.

Despite the stipulation in the 1807 constitution that senatorial elections be held every three years, there were no elections held in 1809. Moreover, the presidential term was limited to four years, and elections were meant to be organized in March 1810, but there was no movement on that either.

Rigaud took advantage of the government's indiscipline. In November 1810, the Sud department declared its autonomy from the Ouest. He was promptly joined by Generals (and Senators) Lys and Bonnet, who abandoned their posts in Port-au-Prince to return to their former allegiances—Bonnet still licking his wounds from having been removed from President Pétion's inner circle and (as he claimed in his memoirs) being the target of an assassination plot. As for Lys, his departure left vacant the command of the capital, which Boyer deftly slipped into. In fact, many mulattos migrated to the Sud during this period. In keeping with their political tradition, the people of the Sud sent up the *Assemblée départementale du Sud*, the Assembly of the Sud Department. With Rigaud's popularity clearly in evidence, along with the region's separatist tendencies, the Assembly elected him as general-in-chief and president of the Republic of the Sud Haiti, with wide-ranging administrative powers.

No one could have been more delighted than Jean Pierre Boyer. He was now head of the presidential guard, personal secretary to the president, and commander of the capital.

13

Rigaud, Pétion, *now* Boyer

MIRAGOANE IS A COASTAL CITY, parts of which are only 2 meters above sea level. It is partially encircled by mountains as high as 200 meters, where many winter vegetables are cultivated, including broccoli, carrots, cabbage, and beets. One is greeted with an unexpectedly spectacular view just after crossing the mountains.

Pétion and Rigaud met on the bridge over Lake Miragoâne, an inland lake approximately 2 kilometers from the coast. Lake Miragoâne is a freshwater lake; its visitors are hypnotized by its beautiful water lilies. On 2 December 1810, the men were greeted with a cool, swirling sea breeze, typically 25 degrees Celsius in that month. Pétion had come to retake the Sud and had invited Rigaud to come negotiate. However, while there, Goman had relaunched his attacks, and Pétion dispatched a fleet of vessels to the port of Jérémie to assist the soldiers there. And, not coincidentally nor unexpectedly, Christophe sent a delegation to Port-au-Prince, also under the guise of negotiations.

Pétion realized that he had no choice but to propose a truce with Rigaud, with whom he had more in common, so that they could together eliminate Christophe and Goman. Agreeing to put their hostilities aside for the time being, Pétion asked Rigaud to station two battalions to the west at Petit-Goâve, to be ready for a likely invasion by Christophe. In exchange, Pétion temporarily recognized Rigaud's authority in the Sud department.

Pétion precipitated to the capital, anxious to hear what Christophe's envoys had to say. Was there an army camped nearby ready to attack while they were distracted by negotiations? Why did Christophe choose this moment to send them? Perhaps he was aware of the events that had transpired between Rigaud and him? Perhaps Goman was an ally?

It turns out the delegates' only offer was surrender to Christophe's authority and claim to the presidency. After all, the Senate had originally voted for him. Pétion refused, citing his aggression against his fellow officers, the fact that he was foreign-born, and his (Pétion's) subsequent election as the basis of his legitimacy. Pétion maintained that he was not in rebellion; the people had chosen him. He would only consider granting Christophe and his army amnesty, should he request it.

The year 1811 began with the drawing of definitive borders. In January, the Assembly of the Sud published its own constitution. In February 1811, Pétion called the Senate, which was down to five members, into session to re-elect him as president; and the following month, Christophe declared himself king, Henry I, and established a royal house. What was a single glorious slave revolt against the formidable Napoleon, and the first attempt at statehood in modern times for African peoples, rapidly descended into rivalry for power over natural resources and commercial trade routes. There were now three countries in an area of just 27,750 square kilometers: the Kingdom of Northern Haiti under Henry I, the Republic of Haiti under President Pétion, and the Republic of Southern Haiti under President Rigaud.

Pétion had now lost more than half of his territory. The Sud department had sixteen communes against the seven of the Ouest. This meant that he would lose revenue from both land taxes and trade. Unwilling to let the Sud province detach itself, he launched a second assault on Rigaud in June 1811, to no avail. Pétion organized another assault in August, where Rigaud commanded the suppression from his balcony in the town center, with his telescope. Even though he was only fifty years old, Rigaud was weak and ailing; Pétion would not have to organize another attack.

Rigaud died of an unspecified illness on 18 September 1811.

The Sud Assembly named Brigadier General Jérôme-Maximilien Borgella as its president. Within a month, Borgella wrote to Pétion. He saw things differently: He was younger, just thirty-eight, and had a different vision for Haiti. He told Pétion that Christophe was their common enemy, and it was in their best interests to reunite the Ouest and Sud departments. Christophe had indeed locked arms with Goman, who now had his own royal title: the Count of Jérémie and Commander of the Sud Province. Munitions were sent regularly between the two self-proclaimed royals. Armed with Borgella's letter and sensing that he had sufficient support in the Sud, Pétion marched his army back to Miragoâne. Upon receiving word of Pétion's advance, Borgella's generals submitted to Pétion's authority. It was 22 March 1812, Palm Sunday.

At the same time as Pétion's march to recover the Sud department, and perhaps because of it, Christophe, at the head of an army of fourteen thousand, decided that an attack was opportune. Instead of approaching from the coastline plains, as he had done previously, Christophe was approaching from the plains of Mirebalais, east of Port-au-Prince.

Pétion had anticipated an attack by Christophe and had left a defense strategy with Boyer. He was to leave Port-au-Prince in the hands of one artillery battery and the national guard and take with him the grenadiers (elite soldiers who used grenades) on foot, as well as a cavalry squadron, an artillery battery, and four brigades to Habitation Bon Repos, just north of Port-au-Prince. Boyer sent the cavalry ahead on reconnaissance to alert them of Christophe's arrival. As hoped, on 24 March, the cavalry discovered that Christophe was approaching Port-au-Prince via the central plains of Mirebalais. They also discovered that their number was far inferior to Christophe's army.

Boyer was able to assemble four thousand infantrymen. After passing along instructions to weary and suspicious generals, he placed himself at the head of the grenadiers, who advanced on foot. The initial assault was encouraging; some of Christophe's frontline soldiers began to flee. But at almost the same moment, General Louis Laurent Bazelais and his brigade retreated; he was unwilling to engage. The grenadiers, though they didn't number more than three hundred, were not discouraged. They not only held the line but protected the retreat of Bazelais' brigade.

Nevertheless, they became encircled by Christophe's men and bullets were raining on them. When the munitions supply was depleted, the men fought with machetes and bayonets. In the melee, they broke formation and indiscipline set in, which quickly turned to despair. It was at this moment that Boyer addressed them, "Grenadiers, I promised you that you would die on the battlefield....". The soldiers fought valiantly, covering the other units as they retreated.

Boyer's battle experience is largely limited to this event. He was seconded by generals who were "unenthusiastic" about following his orders, both because of his youth (he was thirty-six) and because they didn't believe that he had merited this position of authority. Despite his French military training, he had graduated too quickly through the military hierarchy, without anyone ever having seen him on the battlefield. Most believed that he had risen through the ranks of the army largely as a result of his intimate relationship with Pétion.

But where did his courage come from on that day? Perhaps his friendship with Pétion prepared him for this moment. Perhaps being born and living in a constant state of war had given him the courage to lead. Whatever the origin, Boyer knew that he had it in him.

Christophe's siege on Port-au-Prince lasted until 14 June; there was no decisive win, as there were prisoners taken and high-ranking officers lost on both sides. Boyer never wrote of the insubordination that he experienced. Rather, in his letters to Pétion during the first days of the fighting, he commended the regiments under his command. "The officers and soldiers have fought with distinction. Rest assured that I have not neglected a single detail of the plan. Everyone remains engaged, and we will only be able to exhale with your return. You know how much we love you."

Pétion decided on another course of action against Christophe: infiltration and diplomacy. Though it was not for lack of effort, Pétion simply could not unseat his Northern rival. He tried offering the British concessionary tariffs to lure them away from Cap-Haïtien. He democratized land ownership, awarding titles to soldiers and their families. He initiated discussions on the payment of an indemnity to French plantation owners. However, the managed fury between the two men continued; the Republic of Haiti and the Kingdom of Northern Haiti would coexist for the next eight years, until Christophe's suicide in 1820, an attempt to escape the men wielding machetes en route to his castle, La Citadelle La Ferrière.

The War of 1812, between the United States and Great Britain, was tributary to the ongoing war between Great Britain and France. While the two colonial powers were blockading each other around the world, they also seized American ships destined for both French and British colonies. The impact on the United States, during the presidency of James Madison, was felt immediately by traders. Exports in 1811 were valued at $61 million and fell to $6.9 million by 1814; likewise, imports, which were valued at $58 million in 1811, fell to $1 million in 1814. Caribbean commodities could not reach their intended markets, nor could products reach them. Many were starving and had sent word to Pétion's Haiti about their circumstances. In response, he permitted grains and tubers to be bought by foreign merchants duty-free. In exchange, they were to bring cannon powder and other materials to sell to the Haitian government. Farmers who planted more to meet the growing demand from neighboring islands were instructed to first sell to the government stores the volume of produce needed before selling to merchants. This commerce lasted until August 1814, when the war ended.

During this period Pétion realized that foreign ships, even those from the United States, were coming to supply (informally) their own countries. Was Haiti excluded from doing so, despite not having been formally recognized by any of these countries? He sent *Le Coureur*, loaded with coffee and other merchandise, to the United States, under the consignment of Archibald Kane (1775–1817), an American living in Haiti. Whereas Great Britain had sent an agent, Robert Sutherland, to manage trade relations with Haiti, there were no official American commercial agents assigned to Haiti. Kane, sympathetic to Haiti and Pétion, was willing to test how far America's resistance to trading with a black country would go. Pétion attempted the same in sending *Le Conquérant* to London, which met with the same success. Neither the United States nor Great Britain officially recognized Haiti's sovereignty, but Haitian commercial vessels were welcomed nonetheless. By 1816, Pétion had reduced the tariffs of American merchant ships to the same level as those accorded to the United Kingdom.

By many accounts, Pétion was the right man for those times. He was described by Robert Sutherland, a British commercial agent, as being so kind that he wore it. Yet, his "mildness of temper," expressed in his gentleness and dedication to the preservation of individual liberty, did not see the expected return. Plot owners did not farm. Diplomats paraded to and from the National Palace with no definitive agreements. When the prices of certain commodities fell, he purchased large volumes, raising farmers' incomes but also driving away buyers to the Nord or Sud. He was nevertheless well liked, maybe for the sense of stability that he provided or maybe because he displayed no animosity or preference towards any group—whites, mulattos, or blacks. Whatever it was, Pétion was re-elected by the Senate, without contestation, in March 1815, for four additional years.

In 1814, France made yet another effort to retake Saint-Domingue. Named La Restoration, it was an attempt to restore the colony in some fashion under the authority of France. The Bourbon family had returned to the throne, and

Louis XVIII no doubt needed a way to pay his debts, so he immediately thought of his family's treasure of Saint-Domingue.

The King of France sent in the first instance a gentleman named Jean-François Dauxion-Lavaysse, who arrived via Jamaica on 24 October 1814 and whose presence had already been signaled by Haitian allies in Jamaica. However, ill with fever, he had to wait several days before meeting with President Pétion. His convalescence was undertaken in the Boyer household.

It wasn't until 6 November that he was able to present the king's proposition: In return for recognizing the authority of the crown, Haitians could elect representatives to the king's court. The king didn't want to spook Pétion, but he had already organized another expedition of thirty thousand men in case of any opposition. Fortuitously for Haiti, his plans were thwarted by the return of Napoleon, who ushered in the period known as The Hundred Days, March to July 1815. This gave President Pétion and his generals time to prepare.

Although Pétion declined the offer, he did gather his highest-ranking officers on 21 November to deliberate on the possibility of compensating former plantation owners for their confiscated property. Boyer was forcefully against the idea and left the palace before the vote could be taken. The generals agreed to the indemnity, provided that their independence was officially recognized by France. Lavaysse did not leave empty-handed; Pétion lowered the export tariffs of French commercial vessels to 5 percent, the same offered to the English. The impact was immediate: In 1816, 926,374 kilograms of coffee were exported to France from Haiti; by 1818, that amount grew to 1.4 million kilograms. Cotton and sugar saw more phenomenal increases of 274 percent and 812 percent, respectively. Having a need to satisfy local demand, Louis XVIII declared, in March 1816, that commerce between France and its "former colony Saint-Domingue" could recommence.

Pétion was open to the indemnity, provided France's recognition of Haiti's independence. Alexandre Paul Marie de Laujon, a commercial trade agent who made six voyages to Haiti between 1817 and 1822—and was widely suspected to be a spy, as evidenced by his unexplained access to men in high positions—was in Lavaysse's party and recounted not only how physically appealing he found Pétion but also how he was struck by the president's graciousness and douceur. Laujon wrote that he admired the Haitians' confidence. He traveled back to Haiti several times over the next few years as a trader and with the objective of reestablishing formal commercial ties between the two countries.

Pétion, in fact, had spent his entire life suffering from unexplainable episodes of fever. His frequent leaves of absence from military or public service were increasingly treated with the insouciant expectation that he merely needed time to convalesce, and then he would return to service with vigor. But he did not recover from a febrile episode in March 1818 and died.

In his memoirs, de Laujon describes the degree of anxiety experienced by whites in Haiti when Pétion died. They boarded up storefronts and safeguarded valuable merchandise on ships that were in harbor. Some even rented space to sleep aboard the ships, in fear that the transition of power would be violent. De Laujon recounted that he had gone to see Boyer immediately after the announcement of Pétion's death—which itself shows that he was a foreign agent looking for information—and was reassured that order would be maintained.

Pétion's constitution of 1807, which limited the president to a term of four years, was amended in 1816 to stipulate a life term for a president, with election by the Senate. Boyer had pressed for the creation of a vice presidency so that the succession of power would occur smoothly, but it got no traction. The Senate convened immediately after Pétion's funeral. There were fourteen senators in office, but only eleven in Port-au-Prince at the time of Pétion's death. There was much deliberation among them, as Pétion had not left written instructions nor a last testament concerning his successor, as provided for by the constitution. Those pushing for Boyer's election to the presidency forced a senate vote on the evening of the thirtieth, before the arrival of the other three which could have potentially upset the balance. Boyer was unanimously elected, at age forty-two, to the highest office in Haiti, on 1 April 1818. "Supreme power had been transferred easily, quickly, legally, and bloodlessly for the first time in Haitian history," wrote John Edward Baur in a biographical article of Boyer in 1947. It was also the last time.

14

From Obscurity to the National Palace

JEAN PIERRE BOYER WAS BORN on 28 February 1776. Though there is no archival evidence to support this, it is speculated that, Boyer was given the names of his grandfather, Jean Baptiste Boyer, and his godfather, Pierre Dupau.[77] The Catholic Church's baptismal registry of Port-au-Prince included the names of his mother and godparents. It was not possible for a Frenchman to recognize a mixed-race child, nor a child born out of wedlock; nor was it possible for colonial administrators to recognize mulattos and blacks born in the colony. However, surviving oral history identifies his father as Francois Louis Boyer.[78]

James Franklin, an English merchant who wrote a book of his observations on Haitian society during a visit, is the only historian to offer details on Boyer's parents, though his claims are unreferenced. He maintains that Boyer's father, "a man of good repute and possessed of some wealth," was a storekeeper and tailor in Port-au-Prince. The latter is the same claim repeated by John Edward Baur but not of Boyer's father—rather, of Boyer himself.[79] Neither would have had access, at the time, to the baptismal registry.

The Bourbon royal family of France was Roman Catholic; thus, Saint Domingue was a catholic colony. A common practice at the time in Saint Domingue was to celebrate one's birthday on the day corresponding to the patron saint. The date honoring Saint Pierre, which remains so to this day, is the twenty-ninth of June. There is archival evidence that Boyer and those around him celebrated this day in June. For example, a letter written to the president by his stepdaughter, Hersilie, included classic birthday sentiments: wishes for longevity, happiness, and prosperity.

Qu'il est agréable pour moi, mon cher Papa, de vous renouveler à l'occasion de votre fête l'expression de mes sentiments d'amour et de respect. Je supplie votre patron, saint Pierre, d'intercéder pour vous dans le ciel afin que le Tout-Puissant vous accorde de longues années pleines de bonheur et de prospérité. Croyez, mon cher Papa, que les vœux que je fais pour votre bonheur, partent d'un cœur sincère et reconnaissant.

Port-au-Prince, le 29 juin 1832[80]

There is no biographical depiction of Boyer that sheds light on his early life. We do know that he spent his early childhood in Port-au-Prince, having been a childhood friend of Pétion. We can only assume that he had a similar experience to his mulatto contemporaries: Some were acknowledged by their white fathers, others were not. With paternal recognition and the right social connections, the fortunate were offered the opportunity to travel to France to learn a trade. Boyer was, at some point, recognized by his father, who facilitated his military training in France. He returned to Saint-Domingue in 1793 as a soldier in the French army.

There is less ambiguity around Boyer's mother. We know that she was named Marie Francoise, a free *negresse*, as indicated in the Church's baptismal registry. Historical accounts are unified on the fact that she was African, and Boyer also made several such declarations. We also know that she was quite tall — "colossal" was how a French journalist described her— and lived into her nineties.[81]

There is marginally more information regarding his siblings and children. Archival evidence shows that he had at least two sisters, who both outlived him: Bonne (some refer to her as Françoise) Boyer (1773–1884) and Mariette

(1774–1861). Bonne married Antoine Moulut, with whom she had a daughter, Antoinette Moulut, who married Thomas Madiou, a doctor and the father of the reputed Haitian historian of the same name; but they had no children together. Bonne's second marriage, to Pierre Coquière, produced a son, Jean Pierre Edmond Coquière, who married Pétion's daughter Hersilie. By marrying his stepdaughter, Boyer's nephew became an integral part of the family. In fact, Coquière was with Boyer when he died. According to Haitian historians Thomas Madiou fils and Beaubrun Ardouin, Boyer also had a brother named Souverain Brun, who was allegedly killed by Christophe.[82]

Boyer is also alleged to have had a number of children, though only one survived childhood.[83] His last will and testament specifically mentioned his daughter, Azema (Jeanne Françoise Victoire) Boyer (1803–1890), who was the mother of Jean Pierre Boyer-Bazelais (1836–1884), who would later gain notoriety for leading a resistance movement in Miragoâne in 1883.[84] Azema may well have been named after her grandmother, Boyer's mother, in keeping with the tradition. Azema's husband was General Charles Bazelais, a Freemason and senator who would play a prominent role in Boyer's administration. His father, Louis Laurent Bazelais, also a military man, was the chief of staff of the Indigenous Army under General Dessalines and the same one who retreated against Boyer's orders during Christophe's siege of Port-au-Prince.

Also sparse are physical descriptions of Boyer. According to Franklin, Boyer is "darker than most mulattos, below the middle size, and very slender," with a constitution described as "weak." Franklin was clearly unimpressed with Boyer's appearance, writing that "his visage is far from being pleasing, but he has a quick eye, and makes a good use of it, for it is incessantly in motion." Franklin claimed that Boyer was sickly, which forced him to abstain from typical dietary pleasures, but this is the only source that makes this claim; and, since Boyer died at what would be considered an advanced age for his times and circumstances, seventy-seven years old, one would have to believe that perhaps what Franklin observed was a merely a bout of illness rather than a chronic condition. That said, Franklin used the word "abstemious" to describe Boyer, which, given other historical accounts, is coherent. From what we know, he possessed and consumed only what he needed.

Franklin's unfavorable opinion of Boyer cannot be overstated. He wrote that Boyer "possessed neither enlarged nor cultivated ideas and had no correct knowledge of the world." Franklin was also taken aback by the fact that Boyer only made public appearances on Sunday, when he reviewed the troops and then toured the capital of Port-au-Prince. Boyer used Sundays to receive public servants and elite families at the National Palace, followed by a military parade—a parade which was replicated in the main localities around the country. Basically, he found Boyer arrogant—"his vanity is too deeply ingrafted to be easily rooted out," similar to the chain of presidents preceding him—and concluded that this was to the detriment of the advancement of the country. Franklin wrote, "With such arrogance on the part of her rulers, it is not surprising that Hayti, instead of improving in her condition, should greatly decline, and that her advancement under such circumstances should be exceedingly slow." One can only imagine the indignation of traveling to Haiti with the expectations of seeing chaos and incompetence in all sectors. But instead what Franklin saw was a generation of Haitians still reveling in their freedom, curious, largely literate, and practicing a variety of trades such as jewelry design, masonry, carpentry, agroindustry, tobacco farming, and livestock management. Boyer, like Pétion, was wary of European and American emissaries and rarely received them, delegating this function to the state secretary.

Baur offered a more flattering perspective, writing that Boyer possessed a "republican plainness in a simple black suit and his 'quiet dignity.'" Several have written that when they met Boyer, he was dressed in a simple suit, without accoutrements. Baur was also charmed by Boyer's polish, which was no doubt accentuated by his pointy nose. Furthermore, contrary to Franklin's assessment of Boyer's health, Baur reported that Boyer's "robust health and evident activity made him appear much younger." He added that Boyer "is a mulatto with the physiognomy of the French. [Boyer] is rather under than over the average height and is neither thin nor corpulent; he has a keen expressive eye, and an expressive countenance. With strangers he converses only in French; though he has traveled in America and understands the English language."

General Bonnet, in the memoirs written by his son, also recounted that Boyer's youthful appearance saved him on the battlefield, as other soldiers hesitated to strike him with their machetes. Alcide d'Orbigny, a French naturalist who arrived in Haiti in May of 1826, also corroborated these observations with his description of Boyer including "a small frame, with expressive eyes." Rounding off the foreign descriptions of Boyer is Charles Mackenzie, a Scot who landed in Haiti in 1826 and served as British consul for approximately two years. Meeting the president just a few days after his arrival, Mackenzie also noticed Boyer's eyes. He described meeting a "little intelligent-looking man, with very keen black eyes, which he whirls about with extraordinary rapidity."[85]

There is no shortage of adjectives employed by Haitian historians to describe the man who governed for twenty-five years. As with any long-term relationship, Boyer was alternatively admired and respected and despised. Thomas Madiou fils, the historian, wrote that Boyer was agreeable, talented, ambitious, adroit, and sought to make peace. On the other hand, he "exercised great influence over Pétion" and "actively worked towards the ruin of any potential political adversaries." Beaubrun Ardouin, who knew Boyer personally, commented that he had a fiery temperament that made him prone to animated outbursts, during which he was known to be acidulous. Ardouin maintained that this was a widely shared characterization of Boyer, who gesticulated often while speaking, which was balanced by the fact that people also knew him to be a straight arrow, rigid when it came to administrative affairs.

Other sources present comparable profiles. The *Niles' Weekly Register* was a Maryland periodical which ran from 1811 to 1849, covering the entirety of Boyer's presidency. Various editions described Boyer as intelligent, brave, and worthy. Jean-François Dauxion-Lavaysse, the first representative of France sent by Louis XVIII to negotiate with Haiti, said of Boyer that he was "pretentious and ambitious" but also "capable." In 1926, Pierre-Eugène de Lespinasse, archivist of the Society of History and Geography of Haiti, wrote a book including Boyer's intimate correspondence, hoping to convince his readers that "despite twenty-five years of reign" Boyer was not "the ogre that historians have depicted him and that he was a man ahead of his times." Still, de Lespinasse conceded that Boyer's authoritarian nature tempered this aspect of his personality.[86]

Assembling his personal correspondence, de Lespinasse revealed a tender side of Boyer, assiduous in his communications to his family, despite the demands of his position. In these intimate letters, one discovers an affectionate man who was most productive and happy when near his family. If we take him at his word, Boyer loved his partner (Pétion's former partner), Joutte (Marie-Madeleine) Lachenais, and her children unequivocally. A letter dated December 1819, written while he was inspecting military posts in Jacmel and Marigot, exposed his affection for them. We also get a glimpse of the various degrees in his moral compass as he urged them to follow his advice and to remain on the moral trajectory on which they had been placed by their elders: "One who remains faithful to his principles wins the respect of honest people." The following letter unveiled a special attachment to Hersilie, born after Pétion's death, though assumed to be Pétion's daughter. That Hersilie may have been Boyer's daughter is not an incredible proposition; in any case, Boyer raised her as his own, and, as a testament to his devotion, Hersilie named her first child Boyer.

Je dois partir pour Marigot vendredi matin. Je voudrais avoir déjà fait cette tournée pour être à même de retourner près de vous. Je m'ennuie déjà ici et je sens plus que jamais qu'il n'y a que le devoir qui peut me retenir éloigné des personnes qui font le charme de ma vie. Conservez votre santé, vous savez combien elle m'intéresse. Embrassez Fine et Célie pour lesquelles vous connaissez toute ma tendresse et dites leur de toujours songer à leur éducation, que la douceur, la vertu, les principes de morale doivent former la base de cette éducation et que ce n'est qu'en observant ces principes que l'on acquiert les droits à l'estime et à la considération des honnêtes gens. Dites-leur enfin que mon attachement pour elles m'oblige à leur conseiller sans cesse de suivre la vraie route qui conduit au bonheur.

Jacmel, 1er décembre 1819

In a display of devotion, Boyer wrote to Joutte regularly and at what would be critical moments in Haitian history. And Boyer's attachment to Joutte was reciprocated in her responses. She wrote to him about the children, local happenings, and even the most banal of events, like spanking her youngest, Hersilie. Yet no detail was too trivial for Boyer, who had something to say on that matter as well and sided with Hersilie in his reply.

While on the same trip, in another example of his attention to detail and attachment to family, Boyer wrote to his niece, Antoinette Moulut, a letter dated 2 December 1819. Antoinette was apparently ill with fever when he left, and he counseled her to take *quina*, Cinchona officinalis, a medicinal plant from South America used to treat malarial fever. He again expressed his desire to be with his family. He sent greetings to his sister and the whole family, in particular his only daughter, Azema, and ended the letter with "your affectionate uncle, Boyer."

We also learned from his personal correspondence that his favorite place in the world was Volant-le-Thort, Pétion's plantation, located on the road to Léogâne. Although the house was unremarkable, as described by Scottish writer Michael Scott, it had an exceptionally decorative terrace overlooking the bay of Port-au-Prince.[87]

> *Je suis fatigué à l'excès de mes occupations ; il me tarde d'être de retour à Volant pour me reposer; j'en ai bien besoin, je t'assure.*
>
> Cap, 29 octobre 1820

As was required by law and perhaps also to avoid familial disputes, after Boyer's death, his nephew and the husband of his step-daughter Hersilie, Jean Pierre Edmond Coquière, solicited a notary and lawyer to take inventory of Boyer's belongings. Boyer was living in Paris, France, at the time of his death. The notary's report, which can be found in the French national archives, listed his most prized possessions and gave some insight into his social network.[88] Among his possessions was a gold snuffbox, offered to him by King Charles X of France. Set with twenty-eight large diamonds, it was appraised at twelve thousand francs. Three family portraits with gold insets, hair necklaces, and gold clasps, belonging to Joutte, were valued at two hundred francs. There was a modest amount of gold currency (American, French, Spanish) valued at

6,611 francs, and three French treasury bonds valued at 52,200 francs.

Also found were a number of property deeds. Many were gifts from promotions. For example, when he was named division general, he was given a sugar plantation called Drouillard, at Varreux. Another example is when the Senate, in 1823, gifted him two sugar plantations in the Nord department for the reunification of the island.

> *Citoyen Président, le Sénat a la faveur de vous adresser sous ce pli le décret rendu dans sa séance d'hier relatif à deux habitations établies en sucrerie qui vous sont accordées en toute propriété au nom de la nation : veuillez agréer, l'assurance de la très haute considération, le Président du Sénat (Signé) Hogue.*
>
> *Port-au-Prince, 15 juillet 1823*

Other properties that he had acquired—such as Vaudreuil, a sugar plantation located in the plains of Cul de Sac—were accompanied by a bill of sale. He had plantations throughout the country, including in Arcahaie, Limonade, and Grande-Rivière-du-Nord.

He also had in his possession a Latin manuscript by Pope Gregory XVI, who presided over the Vatican from 1831 to 1846. He was a contemporary, though they likely never met, unless they had crossed paths in France in Boyer's youth or during his brief exile with Rigaud and

Pétion. However, Boyer had received the Pope's envoy, Bishop John England, several times in Haiti, when he came to negotiate a concordat between the Haitian republic and the Roman Catholic Church.

Finally, the notary found his memoirs, consisting of four notebooks, his handwriting confirmed by Coquière. They were historical notes, from 1789, predating the War of Independence, up to his presidency. They have since been lost.

Boyer's last will and testament also revealed a great deal about his personal doctrine.[89] He identified as Roman Catholic. He considered himself a loyal public servant. He did not believe himself to be indebted to anyone; but if there were any debts, he was sure that his family would settle them. Coquière, Hersilie's husband, declared to the notary that indeed Boyer had the habit of paying for everything at the time of purchase. He left half of his estate to the children of Hersilie (who died prematurely, leaving four children), and the other half to his daughter, Azema.

Boyer is not considered one of the leading revolutionaries of the War of Independence. A junior officer, he held the rank of captain adjutant in the Indigenous Army. He was not a signatory to the 1804 Haitian Declaration of Independence, which was signed by all division and brigadier generals, as well as several adjutant generals, division chiefs, and other officers. But he was *present* and apparently learned a great deal, leaving behind a lesson of how strategic obscurity and humility of conduct can effectively mask ambition.

It was Pétion's ascendency to the presidency which propelled his military and political career. He was swiftly promoted to battalion chief, then colonel, brigadier general, and then division general. In April 1808, Pétion decided to create a presidential guard, a corps of five hundred men, which included infantry, cavalry, and an artillery battery, and gave the command of this guard to Boyer, who was already his personal secretary.

It is commonly asserted by Haitian historians that Boyer's promotions were closely linked to an intimate relationship with Pétion's partner, Joutte Lachenais, which may or may not be true. She is described as having been exceptionally beautiful, which, in Haiti, can be a liability for an intelligent woman. Nevertheless, what is evident is that with the rank of division general, the command of the capital of Port-au-Prince, the role of chief of staff, and finally the head of the presidential guard, Boyer was strategically positioned. He could at any time have an audience with President Pétion and he could take power at any time, if necessary.

On 30 March 1818, he was elected to the presidency by the Senate. His investiture was held on 1 April 1818 at Volant-le-Thort, probably on the gallery, alongside its splendid gardens, as attested to by many visitors. At noon, Casimir Panayoty, president of the Senate, spoke first, addressing the president, explaining that the nation had high expectations of him because of his proximity to Pétion. Boyer responded that Pétion was indeed his benefactor and that his laws would be respected, and that he intended to walk the path that was already traced by Pétion. He would be frugal with the state's resources, and he would ensure an efficient public administration. He vowed, "I make this sacred promise before God, I promise to the nation, to the Senate, on the remains of Pétion, that I will faithfully meet my obligations as president of Haiti, to uphold the constitution, to respect and defend the rights and independence of the Haitian people. I promise it."

As was and remains the custom at solemn political events, a mass was celebrated with a performance of Te Deum and followed by a reception at the National Palace. There were many kites visible on the horizon as children seized the opportunity of the Carême season after their classes. Boyer addressed the nation again, saying, "In a popular government, it is the confidence and trust from the people that give them authority. I ask the people for their trust, the Senate for their guidance, the army for their support ... [These are] the arms that would assure peace and tranquility to our families."

His first popular act was to free all prisoners not already serving a life sentence. Though he was not endowed with the power of pardon, the Senate did not object. It was an instrument that had been used liberally by Pétion. He also gifted the army with meat, biscuits, and rum. However, the generosity displayed just after his inauguration was not typical of Boyer's conduct during his presidency. Boyer was frugal, and he saw himself as more of an auditor than a chief administrator. He audited every government unit. When he felt like things were getting out of control, he habitually suspended all ministerial expenditures pending review. He stayed civil and military promotions until convinced that the state could afford them. He was obsessed with repairing military equipment and installations instead of modernizing them. He even initiated a government-wide debt collection, particularly debt accrued by the private sector from trade tariffs. He was so frugal that, despite a senatorial decree to erect a mausoleum in honor of Pétion, Boyer never erected it. According to the Haitian historian Madiou, Boyer never constructed *anything*; during his tenure, "a parsimonious existence" was what he aspired to for the country.

His first political act was a proclamation invoking economic equality, protection from political interference, and protection of economic rights. It read:

The brave army of the Republic, lend me your strength to assure the peace and tranquility of our families; judges of the Republic, I am counting on you to respect and apply the laws. The Republic is founded on the holy right to property; the owner of one carreau (1.29 hectares) of land has the same rights as the owner of one hundred in the eyes of justice. That trade can operate freely.

This was a significant change in policy from Christophe and Dessalines, even from the French. Saint-Domingue's prosperity was grounded in the plantation system and economies of scale. Pétion and Boyer, on the other hand, believed in equality of private property. They believed that pride in working the land was intricately linked to owning it. It was this ideology that led to their consideration of compensation for the former French plantation owners. Boyer was decidedly more receptive to the proposition than Pétion and therefore received several royal missions as well as sent missions to France to explore the arrangement. This earned him recognition from the French as being a reasonable person, despite his blackness. Indeed, many Europeans writing during that time could be interpreted as sympathetic, even defensive of Boyer. Jean Baptiste Guislain Wallez (1783–1847), for example, in a biographical chapter that is widely cited, praised Boyer's military genius and leadership qualities, calling him the "founder of the public peace and national prosperity."[90] In 1826, Paul Émile Debraux described Boyer's presidency as a period of tranquility for Haiti, with Boyer having a soft yet firm hand as leader.[91]

Boyer was groomed to be a long-serving and effective president. He keenly observed Pétion's delicate mediation tactics between various parties. And he was a quick study. In 1835, de Laujon witnessed a scene that he described in great detail, leaving the reader with the impression that it revealed some traits of Boyer that were not readily discernible. De Laujon apparently experienced a "right place, right time" moment. Immediately after assuming the presidency, Boyer heard a case by a farmer, a mulatto, bringing an accusation of theft against another neighbor, who was black. Pétion had opened the National Palace for public hearings one day during the week, and Boyer upheld the tradition. He ordered the alleged thief to be brought to him. As expected, the latter denied having stolen the cow. Boyer then asked soldiers to accompany the man to church, where he would swear at the altar that he had not stolen the cow. Should he affirm the same, he would be left alone. With the racial divisions still palpable, better to let God decide, Boyer must have thought; it would be a decision no one would object to. However, with his strong spiritual beliefs dominating his logic, the man opted to face the wrath of Boyer rather than the wrath of God and confessed to the theft. De Laujon wrote that this incident highlighted Boyer's capacity for discernment. Perhaps, but it is also an example of how well Boyer understood the people he governed and how and when to leverage their vulnerabilities.

Considering that Boyer grew up in a slave colony and lived through the Haitian Revolution, his perspectives on whites and the potential for building a harmonious country of blacks, whites, and those of mixed ancestry are ambiguous. He has not been quoted by historians or contemporaries on the matter, but there were two incidents, described in detail by General Bonnet in his memoirs, that could give us some glimpse into Boyer's views.[92] During the colonial period, it was illegal for whites and mulattos to marry, and it was certainly illegal for either of the two castes to marry slaves. Boyer set up a commission to rewrite the country's civil code, and restrictions on social interactions between the castes became a prominent issue. After all, the initial motivation for the mulattos' rebellion was entrenched in the idea that they merited civil recognition by the French. In this new code, the article mandating the civil separation (and even the existence) of castes, was initially excluded—though not unanimously—as there were two (white) experts on the commission tasked with rewriting the legal code who wanted to preserve it.

However, coincidental to this legal debate, an old white farmer, wanting to legalize a relationship with his black servant—with whom he had had many children—applied for a marriage license. The issue was heated and riotous, with people even threatening to block the marriage at the church. Boyer, who had clearly underestimated the resentment that both sides still held, reversed the original decision, writing to the civil officer to revoke the marriage certificate. Thus, in Boyer's civil code, it was illegal for whites and blacks to marry. This incident exemplified the deep racial tension that even his military victory could not erase, as Boyer, the product of an interracial union himself, was clearly swayed by public opinion.

The second incident revealed Boyer's commitment to economic liberty, *despite race*. The government was still in the process of parceling out large plantations, transferring ownership from the French plantation owners primarily to the families of those who had fought in the revolution. However, there were still whites in the colony, and they also made requests to have their land returned. Most of these were met, but the request made by one particular officer, who had fought under Louverture, Dessalines, and Christophe, was denied by Bonnet. The officer sought a final decision from the president, and Boyer overturned Bonnet's decision. Boyer's arbitration in such cases was treated as precedent, and Bonnet duly restored lands to the descendants of white families who brought such complaints of dispossession despite having demonstrated an unwillingness to live under black rule.

Boyer's cabinet members have shared some insight

into Boyer and his meteoric ascension through military ranks to the country's most powerful seat. General Inginac, who served under both Pétion and Boyer for over thirty-five years in the presidential cabinet, wrote in his memoirs that Boyer considered other ambitious politicians as enemies and harbored a long-lasting resentment towards those who dared to oppose him.[93] Fellow general Bonnet, who led a column to successfully annex the eastern part of the island, wrote in his memoirs that Boyer was "gifted with a superior intelligence" and was an avid reader, but that "the simplest of orders regarding the most insignificant of subject matter had to come from him. Even the nomination of who would sweep the offices would need to be confirmed by him. He decided on all issues, administrative, even judicial, without losing time to consultations."[94]

However, Boyer was not entirely closed to receiving feedback, especially from his constituents. Or maybe he also saw the advantages of feeding the intelligence mill. Whichever was the reason, Boyer made himself very much accessible to citizens. Every Sunday was an "open house" during which public functionaries gathered, and ordinary civilians could ask for an audience with the president. Often, he was called to arbitrate a dispute. As early as 6:00 a.m., the doors of the National Palace were open. In the large hall hung the amateurly painted but ornately framed portraits of the young country's former revolutionary leaders: Louverture, Christophe, Biassou, and Jean François.[95]

Afterwards, everyone was invited to watch the military parade, giving an opportunity for the president to inspect the local units at Champs de Mars, a wide-open public space behind the palace. Scottish writer Michael Scott witnessed one of these military inspections under President Pétion when Boyer was the commander of Port-au-Prince. He described seeing a cavalry squadron of "splendid blue uniforms, with scarlet trousers richly-laced" that one might have mistaken for troops in Napoleon's army, if "it weren't for the black faces." Visiting just several weeks after Christophe's siege on the capital, Scott described the very chamber where Boyer received the public as being so bullet-riddled you could see the sky.[96]

Furthermore, Boyer's authoritative temperament, while having some merit, was, to some extent, imposed on him. In 1815 Pétion had been reelected to a third four-year term and decided in 1816 to amend the constitution to allow the Senate to elect a president for life. While not opposed to this, Boyer openly advocated for the office of a vice president, a proposal the Senate sent to Pétion several times, to no avail. After several such attempts, the Senate voted on the final version of the 1816 constitution, leaving out the article in dispute. Nevertheless, to some, Pétion began to resemble the tyrants that preceded him. This was a sentiment intimately felt by those from the Nord, who had defected from Christophe's kingdom for Pétion's republic. This issue, coupled with Pétion's neglectful administration and excessive tolerance of corrupt civil servants, created tension between the presidency and the Senate, and between Pétion and Boyer. Unlike his predecessors and Haitian presidents to come, Boyer never laid one finger on the 1816 constitution, which remained intact until 1843, after Boyer's fall.

Boyer was caustic, authoritative, and a micro-manager, yet reserved, family-oriented, and frugal. Boyer's own view of the world would have rounded out this personality profile. Unfortunately, while some of his intimate correspondence survived, fires, earthquakes, and explosions destroyed much of what was in the public domain regarding his official correspondence and documents. Thus, his profile is exact but incomplete.

There was another side to Boyer: He was playful and he had an appreciation for music and theatre. An adventure traveler, Vincent Fournier-Verneuil, wrote a memoir of his travels and experiences around the world, *Curiosité et Indiscrétion*, which included a short stay at a boarding house in Bordeaux, France, on the Rue Arnaud-Miqueu. It so happens that he occupied the room adjoining Boyer's. He wrote that Boyer had a "singular passion" for a French play, a three-act farce in Alexandrine verse, called *Les Plaideurs*, from which he was compelled to recite nightly scenes with Boyer. He also noted that Boyer incessantly played the clarinet, musing that he would have never thought that the art of governing could be mastered by playing a woodwind. Describing Boyer as "soft and gentle," Fournier-Verneuil reminisced that if Boyer remained the excellent young man that he knew, then his people must be quite happy.[97]

The final word is best left to his childhood friend, mentor, and commanding officer, Alexandre Pétion. On his deathbed, Pétion shared with General Inginac his fears regarding Boyer's eventual ascendancy, saying that Boyer was "too set in his ways to take the advice of those who could help him; he was bent on domination.[98]

15

"Niggers Speaking French": Boyer's Key Administrators

William Jennings Bryan, US Secretary of State. "Dear me, think of it! Niggers speaking french!", the Secretary reacted after having received a briefing about the country from John H. Allen, the manager of the Haitian National Bank in 1912.[99]

BOYER'S MAIN GOVERNING PRINCIPLE was absolute control of information. With everyone reporting to him, he was the central intelligence server, milling that information into appropriate packages for targeted recipients. "Interfering with everything" was the way British Consul Charles Mackenzie described it. Boyer mastered the "art of magnifying trivial matters into a preternatural importance" by making everything a presidential matter, he continued.[100]

But Boyer didn't accomplish this singlehandedly; for a quarter century, he was seconded by the most highly educated, sophisticated, worldly black men in the New World—a world in which most blacks were slaves and no doubt the reason Boyer's cabinet members were the talk of Europe and the United States. Admired for their competence and polish, this exceptionalism was diminished only by their blackness, as exemplified by William Jennings Bryan's reaction to a briefing on Haitian affairs. Fifty years after the American Civil War, it was still inconceivable that blacks could govern themselves; yet, Boyer's super-ministers had done so effectively fifty years prior to the American slave emancipation.

Unlike the modern Haitian government, early governments were lean and military led. In fact, for Haiti's first century of existence, all leaders were generals, whether they were elected or accessed power through violence. There were eight *arrondissements,* military jurisdictions with a general assigned to each: Port-au-Prince (which Boyer kept command of), Léogâne, Nippes, Aquin, Les Cayes, Jacmel, Mirebalais, Grand'Anse, and Tiburon. There were also seven functioning ports: Port-au-Prince, Miragoâne, Jérémie, Anse d'Hainault, Les Cayes, Aquin, and Jacmel.

Civil administration was assigned to military officers. Boyer's cabinet administered the entire island with a singular objective: to minimize public expenditures to the fullest extent possible. And one of the strategies of doing so was to assign civil service posts to military officers. [101] Despite his reputed bouts of jealousy when he'd sensed a fellowship germinating between Petion and his cabinet, Boyer retained the entire team; he also valued competence and experience.

Essentially, there were three super-ministers: Andre Dominique Sabourin (1771–1819), the high court judge, who supervised all areas for which notaries or lawyers were required including all births, deaths, marriages, arbitration, and land transactions; Jean-Chrysostôme Imbert (1779–1855), who managed the republic's finances, including foreign commerce and lending; and Joseph François Balthazar Inginac (1777–1847), the general secretary who handled both internal and external communications, represented the president at official events, and managed the rest of the public service.

Boyer lost Sabourin at the beginning of his presidency. The judge died shortly after Pétion, in January 1819. The historian Ardouin described him as being widely respected, "exquisitely" polite with the citizens he served. Sabourin was replaced by Jacques Ignace Fresnel, a member of the assembly drafting the constitution, former senator, civil court judge, and appeals court judge. A lifelong judge but aging, he was re-elected to the Senate in 1827, a less strenuous role, and was replaced by Brigadier General Jean

Auguste Voltaire, also a former senator. Voltaire was from the same generation of independence fighters as Boyer. He was squadron chief under Dessalines and is alleged to be one of those who conspired against him. He also was a member of the constituent assembly formed after Dessalines' death, which declared Haiti a republic and elected Pétion as president. Voltaire had personality; he even butted heads with Europeans who made outrageous demands. When Pétion realized, for example, that many of the traders anchored at ports in the Sud region rather than at Port-au-Prince due to their lax implementation of import tariffs regulations, he dispatched Voltaire, who did not hesitate to imprison white traders until they made payment. Later, he found himself in the Sud department as adjutant general at the very moment the Sud decided to formalize their separation from the Republic of Haiti. Since Voltaire had demonstrated fierce loyalty to Pétion, Rigaud, after the Sud's secession, guaranteed his safe passage to return to Port-au-Prince. Also appreciative of his long-running devotion, Boyer promoted Voltaire to brigadier general and placed him in command of the Azua department on the eastern side of the island. The historian Madiou fils described Voltaire as having a "soft and conciliatory nature" and being held in high esteem. He even kept his post as part of the transitional government formed after Boyer's departure, but died shortly after, on 22 July 1843.

Imbert, whom Madiou described as "a young man of rare probity," suffered from chronic asthma, had a less adventurous background, and was considered a gifted administrator. Just a few years younger than Boyer, Imbert was briefly a schoolteacher before becoming a clerk in the French navy in 1798. He was quickly promoted to administrative head of supplies in 1799 and posted in Jacmel as chief administrator. Imbert was still there when Louverture marched on the Sud region to retake it from Rigaud. He was assigned to Môle Saint-Nicolas, in the same position, and then reassigned to Cap-Haïtien in 1801. His sedulousness was compensated by a series of promotions that would see him become the secretary to the chief naval administrator in the Nord department, chief administrator of the Ouest department, and ultimately secretary of state finances of the Republic of Haiti, in 1808. The latter title would change, but Imbert held the post of what is essentially minister of finance for thirty-five years. Celigny Ardouin, a soldier who served in early administrations and elder brother to Beaubrun, the historian, described him as "inquisitive" and "devoted."[102] Imbert's fiscal discipline was so appreciated by the Senate that he was gifted a former sugar plantation, named Laval, near Anse-à-Veau, as a symbol of "national gratitude" for his "frugalness and fidelity to the welfare of the country."

Inginac was born just a year after Boyer and joined the army at the age of sixteen. He was near-sighted and never fought in war, having risen through military ranks via administrative roles. He was close friends with Judge Voltaire—so close that he stayed at Voltaire's house whenever he was in Les Cayes.

In 1798, Inginac was also working as a commercial agent in Port-au-Prince, when he was forced to emigrate to Jamaica after accusations of misappropriation of funds and a threat of several laches of the whip by Dessalines. He departed for Jamaica in 1799, where his father was also a commercial agent.[103]

He returned in 1802, after having heard the news that Napoleon's armada had landed at Saint Domingue with the intention to reinstate slavery in Saint Domingue. An intervention by Petion smoothed over his conflict with Dessalines, and the latter, in late 1803, thinking ahead as to what a post-independent Haiti would look like, asked him to undertake a count of shops in Port-au-Prince and to inventory their merchandise. The following month, Dessalines named Inginac Director of Land Affairs for the Ouest Department. Inginac's mission was to review all land titles—an enormous undertaking given that many owners had fled their plantations. Those who were not in possession of titles were dispossessed—even if their families had been in possession of the land for generations—except if their deeds had been lost to fires, natural disasters, or war. Haitian historian Saint-Remy described Inginac as "overzealous, rigorous to a point where he appeared unjust." Dessalines was pleased with Inginac's work and, from 1804 to 1806, also gave him the responsibility of auditing government transactions throughout the country.

In 1806, both Inginac and Boyer were battalion chiefs at the time of Dessalines' assassination, and both had signed the letter from military officers informing Christophe of his nomination as president and of Dessalines' death. But the two men must have met years before, as Inginac described their relationship as a 'long-running friendship".[104] In 1808, Inginac was appointed to the office of the state secretary, Division General Bonnet and quickly won Pétion's confidence—enough to replace Bonnet by 1810. The following year, he was assigned his own military unit and promoted to Pétion's aide-de-camp, eventually becoming his principal secretary. In 1815, he was a member of the commission to revise the constitution of 1816, then promoted to secretary general in 1817, and graduated to the rank of colonel in 1818. In 1820 he was promoted to brigadier general by President Boyer and delegated the special dossiers of public education and external relations.

Boyer trusted Inginac. He penned most of Boyer's international correspondence, including to the Catholic Church and to France, as well as the internal communications of public administration. The president sent Inginac to negotiate the resistance led by General Romain in 1821, and he was a member of the commission reviewing the French offer of recognition of Haitian sovereignty in 1825. Historian Beaubrun Ardouin described him as having a linguistic finesse—the talent of telling someone what they wanted to hear.

General Inginac also spun his own web of influence: His son, Duton, was the editor of *Le Phare*, a weekly periodical first appearing in August 1830. The newsletter was easily approved by the state printing house, which fell under the authority of the secretary general. *Le Phare* focused, in part, on economic policy, a pertinent subject given the various taxes imposed on the country to pay off the indemnity to France. Duton was also employed at the presidential secretariat, and the general even managed to marry him off to one of Boyer's nieces, Bonne's daughter Coquièrine. In all, Inginac knew Boyer very well. Aside from being related by marriage, he served as Grand Master of the country's Masonic order from 1834 to 1837.[105]

Lavaysse, the first of the French emissaries that came to Haiti to negotiate with Pétion in 1814, described Inginac as "polished and capable." De Cassagnac, a European traveler, described him as good-looking, despite his age, with a noble nature. He wrote that he spoke French well and could address complicated subjects. De Cassagnac was surprised - maybe even taken aback - at the refinement exhibited by someone "one generation removed from slavery".[106]

These three super-ministers masterfully managed Haitian public affairs, which was likely under a microscope by foreign powers.

There were two others who served Boyer loyally: Generals Jérôme-Maximilien Borgella (1773–1844) and Guy-Joseph Bonnet (1773–1843), born in the same year and dying only months apart. Together they established a military apparatus which dominated the island.

Borgella was born in Port-au-Prince. His father, Bernard Borgella, was a white plantation owner and lawyer, who served at one point as mayor of Port-au-Prince and was also a member and president of the Saint-Domingue Assembly before the start of the revolution. He was also an advisor to Louverture. However, Maximilien was ignored by his father, who could not legally recognize him at the time of his birth but also displayed no desire to do so when the right to French nationality had finally been accorded to mixed-race and free residents in the colony. He was raised by his mother until her death, then by her sister, and finally by his maternal grandmother and her companion, a white man named Ithier, who apparently had some wealth. A father figure, this man taught Borgella to read, ride horses, and shoot. Later, in 1792, when the law permitted, he took his father's name, just to spite him. At sixteen, he entered an apprenticeship to become a carpenter.[107]

Bonnet was born in Léogâne and also grew up without his father. After his primary schooling, he began working at a shop whose main commercial ties were in Bordeaux. The storekeeper, a Frenchman, was so impressed with Bonnet's diligence that he often left him in charge of the store while he took long sojourns in France.

When the French acknowledged the civil and political rights of mulattos in 1791, there was a wave of celebrations, and the mulattos of Léogâne had planned to travel to join those in Port-au-Prince. But the white colonists did not embrace the promotion in civil status of mulattos, leading to massacres throughout the colony. Unwittingly, Bonnet entered Port-au-Prince the very moment when Scarpin, the drummer boy, was being hanged. He was fortunately immediately imprisoned, which likely saved him from being massacred.

In his memoirs, Bonnet depicted a heinous scene upon his release from prison: Port-au-Prince burning, with bloody walls, and the bodies of men, women, and children in the streets. Boyer, also from Port-au-Prince, was spared this macabre experience, as he was studying in France. The eighteen-year-old Bonnet hopped on a wagon heading out of town. Serendipitously, it was headed to Croix-des-Bouquets, where the mulattos in the Legion of the Ouest had retreated. He enlisted. There, he met Pétion and others and was placed under General Beauvais' command. But when Andre Rigaud came north to consort with his fellow officers, Bonnet left to join the Legion of the Sud; shortly thereafter, he became Rigaud's aide-de-camp while the latter was valiantly fighting off the British invasion.

Upon Rigaud's last return from exile, Bonnet again deserted his post, along with a number of fellow mulatto soldiers, on the pretext that their lives were in danger in Port-au-Prince. Bonnet moved to the Sud department to take up arms with his old comrade. After Rigaud's death, Bonnet surrendered and was reintegrated into the National Army. Notwithstanding his Rigaudist attachments, both Pétion and Boyer had made good use of Bonnet, a trustworthy, operative, and skillful soldier. He aided Boyer in securing Christophe's Kingdom of Nord Haiti and, later, led one of the columns to take Santo Domingo.

For Borgella's part, it was while he was studying to become a carpenter that he learned of the persecution of mulatto families by plantation owners in retaliation for their advocacy to become French citizens, and also of the secret meeting of mulattos at Diegue, where the mulattos formed a militia to protect themselves against attacks by royalists and plantation owners. He dropped everything as well and went to enlist. The same age as Bonnet (fifteen), he was placed into an artillery battery. Borgella served briefly with Inginac, also under General Beauvais' command. In 1793, he was promoted to lieutenant; then to captain in 1794.

Born just three years before Boyer and despite being a gunner, Borgella apparently knew neither Pétion, who was an artillery master, nor Boyer as a child. Certainly, they did all meet at Diegue, when Boyer was still an adolescent, which is the earliest that they can be placed together. In 1798, while based in Léogâne under the command of General Beauvais, on one of many occasions that Borgella had been sent to detention for disobedience (the young Borgella was unruly), he met Inginac, who had been captured by the English. At this point in Haitian history, the English occupied most of the ports. The two men spent two and a half months in prison together and, upon being released, went directly to enlist in Rigaud's Legion du Sud, where Borgella was placed at the head of his own squadron.

When it was apparent that Rigaud had lost the war with Louverture, and the latter had offered amnesty to the rebellious soldiers and an opportunity to reintegrate into his army, a number of men decided to forgo amnesty and leave the country, including Rigaud, Pétion, and Boyer. Borgella, on the other hand, opted to stay. He had never been abroad, nor did he have the means to live in a foreign country. He escorted Rigaud to board the ship at Tiburon and then turned himself in. Borgella was brought to General Louverture directly, perhaps because the latter recognized the family name. The general asked if he was the son of his advisor, Bernard Borgella, to which he responded affirmatively. As is the case with the most bittersweet of life's ironies, Borgella was spared for having taken the name of the father that had forsaken him.

Bonnet fled to Curaçao with Pétion and with Rigaud's brother Augustin. Together, they mounted a plan to reassemble Rigaud's scattered troops and attack Louverture from the eastern part of the island. They arrived on 27 January 1801 at Santo Domingo, the same day that Louverture took possession of the city. Accepting his fate, Bonnet then traveled to Cuba, where he had relocated his wife during the hostilities. Upon arrival, however, he discovered that she had sold his belongings and fled to Jamaica with another man. Thus he remained in Cuba until Leclerc's expedition to retake Saint-Domingue from Louverture. In March 1802, Bonnet arrived in Saint-Domingue at Saint-Marc, among three hundred others who had self-exiled in Cuba, at the same time the French had won a decisive battle at Crête-à-Pierrot. In his memoirs, he claimed to have spent the night with Rigaud, who boarded a frigate the next morning, presumably to take him to Les Cayes, but which exiled him back to France. Hit hard by this deception, Bonnet decided not to reintegrate into the French army; he "moved in the shadows, avoiding superior officers." Eventually, he landed an administrative post with the head of the engineering unit; and, although it is impossible to know when they had crossed paths, Bonnet lodged with Boyer for some time in Port-au-Prince. Hearing about the continued resistance of African insurrectionists in the Nord-Est region, Bonnet traveled there to join them. They had refused to surrender to Rochambeau. In the end, Bonnet chose not to fight and negotiated passage on a ship to return to Cuba, where he remained for most of the war.

He returned after independence and worked closely with Pétion, who promoted him to brigadier general in 1807. He was soon after appointed to the position of secretary of state finances by the Senate but would be replaced by Imbert in 1810. He left once more to join Rigaud in Les Cayes, who had again, and for the last time, attempted a separatist movement. For his betrayal, he was exiled by Pétion. He lived in the United States for several years, first in Baltimore, then in Philadelphia, working as a cigar trader. When Pétion allowed him to return, he was assigned various projects, but he wasn't really re-called into active service until Boyer became president and made him the general chief of staff of the army. Boyer, it seems, also had a soft spot for Rigaud.

After his surrender to Louverture, Borgella was assigned to be the aide-de-camp to General Laplume. But they soon had a falling out, and Louverture was only too happy to side with Laplume, an African, over a mulatto whose African ancestry was "barely distinguishable." [108] Borgella was arrested again and sent to a ship whose passengers were intended to be drowned at sea. Fortunately, Borgella, also a Freemason, was able to leverage this affiliation to save his life. He had sent word to his fellow fraternity members, many of whom were white, who duly vouched for him, and so one of the coast guards hid him in his cabin. Perhaps feeling some remorse or perhaps the brotherhood had threatened him, Laplume ordered that Borgella be taken off the ship and instead placed in a cell. Eventually, in the most unexpected of outcomes, it was his father's intercession, a personal plea to Louverture to spare his child, that saw him released.

Borgella was well-liked and had an amicable nature, as described by British consul general Charles Mackenzie during his visit in 1826: "I found him a frank, open, manly soldier, without pretension, well versed in the history of his country, as well as in the character of his countrymen, and exceedingly friendly...Public opinion has long marked him as the future president of Haiti."[109]

These sentiments about Borgella were shared by many high-ranking officers and diplomats—so much so that, in 1827, the idea surfaced of replacing Boyer with Borgella. But he refused, explaining that "if we were to violate the constitution for such a rash undertaking, we would be authorizing everyone dissatisfied with government to do the same. And the country would never know stability. And as for Boyer, no one should doubt his patriotism."[110]

Borgella's popularity became apparent years earlier, when Rigaud, who had returned from exile in France, led yet another secession of the Sud department. Although he was initially against it, Borgella would also desert Pétion's army to join Bonnet and other mulattos. In 1810, when Rigaud was taken ill, the governing council saw it necessary to hold elections for a new general-in-chief of the Sud department, and Borgella was elected to the post by a majority. Leveraging his reputation and rank, General Borgella immediately issued a declaration that he considered the schism between the Sud and the Ouest to be an internal dispute and that their interests were indivisible.

Pétion welcomed the overture, and negotiations to reunite the country commenced in December 1811 in the commune of Grand-Goâve. Among Pétion's negotiators was Inginac. Pétion was offering one, indivisible country called the Republic of Haiti, governed by one president (Pétion) and a legislative assembly, whereas the Sud offered two sister republics who would collaborate on matters of defense but retain separate governing structures. Borgella and Pétion negotiated privately, while letting the other members debate, and finally it was arranged for the two "presidents" to enter Les Cayes, in a demonstration of solidarity. Borgella and the others eventually conceded. For suppressing any political ambitions and playing his part in the republic's reunification, Borgella was promoted to division general in 1812 and given command of the troops in the entire Sud department.

But there was no honeymoon for the parties to revel in the political victory because Christophe had begun his march south to take the Ouest department, presumably to enlarge his kingdom. The entire Sud army had to march north immediately.

On Monday, 6 April 1812, Christophe ordered cannons to fire on the capital of the Ouest, Port-au-Prince. It was 6 a.m. and Borgella, looking out into his telescope, was apparently himself being watched from a distance, as artillery fire hit the gabion behind which he was positioned. His officers, having described him as being "inflexible when it came to duty," were not surprised when Borgella exclaimed, "Since I wasn't hit with these bullets, I'll take this as a sign that I won't be hit by any bullet today." Bold and inspiring, he reportedly climbed up on the gabion wall to rally his troops against Christophe's attack.

For their valor, Pétion's commanders were rewarded with plantations of their choosing. Despite insisting that Borgella remain in the Ouest department, near him, Borgella chose to return to the Sud, a familiar place, with fertile land and friends from his secession days. He chose a plantation near Cavaillon named Custines, with 2,000 carreaux (2,580 hectares) of land, so that he could farm in peace.

Boyer's inner circle appears to have been exceptionally small, and Borgella was among them. The latter confided in him and complained freely to him, particularly regarding other cabinet members. Borgella was Boyer's wingman when it came to territorial conquest. He recalled Borgella into active duty in 1822 to lead the second military columns—Bonnet led the other—to take Santo Domingo, and Borgella remained commander of the eastern part of the island for ten years.

Generals Bonnet and Borgella were also lifelong collaborators with Boyer. Soon after reuniting the various regions under one government, Boyer unsurprisingly faced several rebellions, many of which the two generals personally extinguished. Bonnet had a reputation for impunity and was often sent to the Artibonite and Nord departments where sedition was endemic, and Borgella kept the historically rebellious Sud department in line.

On the foreign policy front, there was only one strategic objective: to get the world to recognize Haiti's right to exist as a sovereign nation. Both Imbert and Inginac played prominent roles in the démarche to obtain French recognition of Haiti's independence, which included a payment to indemnify the former plantation owners. During one round of talks, there were objections voiced regarding the wording of France's recognition of Haiti, and the emissary of King Charles X, the Baron de Mackau, intimated that another military intervention was a potential recourse. Inginac, indignant that the French could even entertain the possibility of such action after twenty years of Haitian independence, rose and removed from his cabinet several torches that he promised would be used to destroy all the property that they hoped to re-acquire. He would set the fires himself, he retorted. Historian Johnhenry Gonzalez observed:

> *These and other seemingly unlikely acts of defiance demonstrated both Haiti's early nineteenth-century military ascendancy as well as the skillful maneuvers of Haitian statesmen. Paradoxical as it may seem, Haitian governments enjoyed their apex of regional power and de-facto sovereignty precisely during the era in which Haiti was denied diplomatic recognition by foreign powers unwilling to accept its existence as an independent state.*[111]

Imbert, for his part, as the chief exchequer, mobilized the resources to pay the indemnity. He reorganized the tariff system to increase revenue and to palliate the burden of the indemnity, particularly on agricultural workers. For example, in 1827 he removed all taxes on goods destined for export, mostly raw materials, while raising tariffs on higher-value imports.

The support of Imbert and Inginac masked the fissures that began to appear in the relationships among Boyer's cabinet members. Borgella was vehemently against the indemnity and voiced his opinion to all who asked. And, despite more than three decades of collaboration, Boyer's relationships with Imbert, Voltaire, and Inginac did not end well. The former two were suspected to have colluded with the militants to unseat Boyer in 1843. Inginac, for his part, fled to Jamaica with Boyer in 1843 and was stripped of his Haitian citizenship. While there, he wrote his memoirs, including an acrimonious account of his time in Boyer's cabinet, painting him as intimidating and threatening, and asserting that the only reason that he had not resigned was because he was fearful of reprisal. The memoirs, written in a forcefully defensive tone, read more as Inginac's attempt to exonerate his role in what had become an unpopular administration. The effort bore fruit; He was regranted his citizenship in 1845, dying soon afterwards in 1847.

In his memoirs, Bonnet, who passed away two months before Boyer was toppled, succinctly summarized the latter's governing style and the impact that it had on administrators: "In wanting to manage everything, he destroyed hierarchy, undermining the authority of his administrators and inciting subordination." Bonnet explained that civil servants, upon seeing that initiative held no value for Boyer, decided to secure their own livelihoods, doing only the bare minimum for the government to function. "You have made a mistake in seconding discipline," Bonnet claimed that he told the president, concluding, "When the need for a functioning army arises, you will be disappointed."

These words would have been difficult for Boyer to hear. He was a strong and honorable president, who surrounded himself with a strong, honorable cabinet. Surely hearing the words "control," "management," and "authority" only triggered, in Boyer's mind, a verse from his favorite play, *Les Plaideurs*, in which the son of a terribly hard-working judge is trying to convince the latter to get some rest and let matters take their own course.

Si pour vous, sans juger, la vie est un supplice,
Si vous êtes pressé de rendre la justice,
Il ne faut point sortir pour cela de chez vous,
Exercez le talent, et jugez parmi nous.

Translation: "If, for you, not being able to judge is very painful [and] if you're in a hurry to render justice, there's no need to leave home to do so. Exercise this talent among us."[112]

16

"Damn these Haitians; they can't even fatten a pig."

WHY DID NAPOLEON SEND such a large army across an ocean to an island that was in a state of constant rebellion for over ten years? Why did the British maintain a presence on the island, even after being unable to hold the ports? How was Louverture able to strike a naval security deal with the Americans—what was he offering? The answers lie in the economic loss which Saint-Domingue represented for French investors. In 1789, largely considered the last "good" year in its history, Saint-Domingue possessed 792 sugar and 705 cotton mills; 3,099 indigo, 2,810 coffee, and 69 processing plants for indigo, coffee, and cotton; 173 guildives (operations that distilled rum from sugar cane), 3 tanneries, 313 large ovens, 28 potteries, and 33 brick-making workshops. With this economic infrastructure, the colony exported annually 47.5 million pounds of clayed sugar, 93.6 million pounds of muscovado sugar, 76.8 million pounds of coffee, 7 million pounds of cotton, and 758,000 pounds of indigo. By way of comparison, in the 1780s, Saint-Domingue's coffee production volume was fourteen times greater than that of all the British colonies combined. Napoleon could not stand the shame of losing the most prosperous colony that the world had ever seen at that point in time.

During the eighteenth and nineteenth centuries, the dominant economic system was known as mercantilism, an exclusive, centrally managed system organized around European metropoles, in which colonies were highly regulated for primary commodity production, based on slave labor. International commerce formed a geographic triangle: slaves purchased from Africa were sold to plantation owners in the colonies, where ships transported goods such as sugar, coffee, tobacco, and cotton back to the European metropole. In what British economist David Hume referred to as the "jealousy of trade," commercial interactions outside of the metropole were prohibited—the metropole, in this context, being the occupying European country. In such a system, rents were realized by both plantation owners, owing to the productivity of slave labor, and the metropole, owing to the monopsonistic commercial arrangement.

France operated this system with a slave corps of approximately 435,000, and the plantations were managed by 30,000 whites and others of mixed race. Commodities were not exported in an entirely raw form but were cleaned and processed on site; Saint-Domingue was populated with over 8,500 mills.

Saint-Domingue's collective productivity was impressive, owing in part to the brilliant planning of Jean Baptiste Ducasse, a French naval officer, who was named the first governor of Saint-Domingue in 1691. He is credited with setting up the French colonial administration and planning an agricultural system to produce at scale. He organized the first sugar plantations in 1698 with slaves that he had stolen from Jamaica, with as much as two million pounds that he had discovered when he looted the Spanish colony of Cartagena (now Colombia). They were so successful that Ducasse annulled royal concessions that were given as rangeland to cattle farmers, pushing them eastwards.

With this expansion came the gradual accumulation of slaves—gradual because, even though Africans were brought to the island as early as 1517, the corps of slave labor had to be renewed several times over. The Caribbean is particularly vulnerable to devastating hurricanes, which frequently destroyed crops and ravaged whole cohorts of slaves. There was also the matter of smallpox and malaria. Contrary to popular belief, the continuous importation of slaves was as much attributable to the extensive loss of human labor due to natural disaster and disease as it was to the desire for greater productivity. Between 1701 and 1790, the French had imported 1.3 million slaves to the Caribbean.

The colonial pearl that was Saint-Domingue had lost much of its luster by the start of the War of Independence in 1791. That year, Saint-Domingue's gross domestic product (GDP) was as high as 200 million French francs, using 1825—seven years into Boyer's presidency—as the year of comparative analysis. Its GDP did not attain this level again until the 1890s.[113] However, analysis over a longer time horizon revealed that GDP per capita began to decline as early as 1775 and appears to have plateaued from 1805 onwards. One of the reasons is the explosion of the population on the island. As is also the case in modern Haiti, the colonial administrators and early Haitian leaders did not implement the necessary incentives to curb population growth. Consequently, the moderate gains in tariff revenues had to cover the needs of a steadily growing number of inhabitants; GDP per capita vacillated between 100 and 150 francs for all of Boyer's presidency.[114]

Another reason for the decline in colonial revenue was the replication of the primary goods plantation system throughout Latin America and the Caribbean. Sugar became every colony's specialty. Barbados, Jamaica, and

Martinique also became successful, achieving scale in production, which, in turn, depressed world prices. While consumption tripled between 1700 and 1740, plantation owners experienced a 70 percent fall in prices. [115] This benefited European consumers; sugar became more affordable, and they began to explore innovative uses for it.

✳✳✳

The victory of the Indigenous Army over Napoleon was, as economic historian Victor Bulmer-Thomas put it, "greeted with a deafening silence by the rest of the world." [116] Completed ignored, Haiti needed reestablish trade relations with their former principal buyer, France, as well as with other European countries and emerging countries, such as the United States of America.

The leaders of the newly formed Republic of Haiti, some of whom were former slaves, inherited a colony organized for slavery, with no slaves. It was a challenge to maintain competitiveness while other countries in the region were extracting rents from slave labor. The other Latin American republics enjoyed this advantage for decades after Haiti's revolution. Slavery wasn't abolished until the last quarter of the nineteenth century in most countries in the region—in the United States, 1865; in Puerto Rico, 1873; in Cuba, 1886; and in Brazil, 1888, to name a few.

The break from France, the abrogation of slavery, and trade liberalization evaporated all profits. Instead of being metropole-directed, Haiti's fate rested in entrepreneurship and the identification of new markets. Since Haiti retained its plantation structure, power shifted from the metropole to the new landowners. Toussaint, Dessalines, and Christophe all practiced plantation agriculture by coercion. Soldiers were reassigned as plantation supervisors, to ensure that everyone not in a skilled trade worked on the farms.

Pétion, on the other hand, adopted a sharecropping model that largely favored remunerating with farming plots those who had served in the war. In December 1809, he carried out a massive land redistribution program. To each retired soldier, he gave 6.5 hectares in perpetuity; to each battalion chief, 19.4 hectares; and to each lieutenant, captain, and colonel, 32.3 hectares. Land sales were allowed but not subdivisions; and, military allocations excepted, no one could possess less than 12.9 hectares, as Pétion saw continued value in large-scale farming. Farm workers were to be contracted not coerced; however, the abandonment of a contract was severely punished. The revenue from commodity sales was capped at 25 percent for farm workers, the state took another quarter, and the balance went to plantation owners, whose responsibilities included housing and medical care for laborers. Finally, with a nod to ensuring that the health of workers was prioritized, women were not allowed to work after the third month of pregnancy.

The consequence of the various land management programs was that many of the former slave-soldiers were now landowners, and additional labor was needed to achieve the same level of productivity that had been realized during the colonial period. Furthermore, while productive capital was more widely distributed, its value was dependent on the extent to which Haitian goods reached foreign markets. This was the nature of the economy that Boyer had to manage.

This situation did not go unnoticed by French economists. Jean-Baptiste Say, a contemporary of Boyer, and famous for his argument that supply creates its own demand, observed that sugar, given the processing technology at the time, could only be as profitable as it was under slave production. It had become so much cheaper that at one point the Haitian authorities observed that, while they were making all efforts to sell their sugar abroad, sugar imported from the neighboring slave colonies had made its way into Haiti for local consumption. [117] Haiti's sugar was no longer competitive.

Slavery aside, Haiti's gross domestic product, from Dessalines to Boyer—that is, from 1804 to 1843—was relatively stagnant, at around 50 million francs. Annually, using 1825 as the base year, there was a slight, almost imperceptible uptick towards the end of Boyer's presidency. In other words, regardless of the model, Haiti remained a small economy in which productive assets had to be divided by an ever-increasing population, which had ballooned to a workforce of 935,000 by 1822.[118]

In a primary goods economy, the tariff structure demands special attention. Import tariffs were set high to incentivize and protect local production. Dessalines had introduced a tax on imports of 10 percent in 1806, maintained by Pétion and raised to 12 percent in 1819 by Boyer. Only Christophe had suppressed them, relying only on land taxes. By 1827, the whole island applied a 16 percent tax on imports except on goods from Great Britain and France. Trade privileges were granted to stimulate investment and secure formal acknowledgement of Haiti's sovereignty. To this end, Pétion lowered the tariff on British imports to 5 percent; however, Boyer raised them when the British crown did not hesitate to recognize the Bolivarian republics but still did not recognize Haiti. Nonetheless, as much as 33 percent of public revenue came from import tariffs.[119] Such was the attention accorded to tariff revenues by Boyer that, in 1836, he closed five ports— Aquin, Anse-à-Veau, Miragoâne, Saint-Marc, and Port-de-Paix—because the duties they brought in could not support their costs of operation.

While official recognition remained elusive, Haiti's

main trading partners remained France, the United States, and England. Half of Haiti's imports came from its closest neighbor, the United States of America, with 30 percent from the United Kingdom, and 20 percent from France. By 1832, US trade had dropped to 30 percent, as Haitians consumed more British goods, increasing that trade to 50 percent. By 1842, one year before Boyer's departure, Haiti's import share of French goods increased slightly, to 30 percent, while the United Kingdom's share dropped to 40 percent and the United States remained stable at 30 percent.

Haiti's exports and destination markets, on the other hand, remained relatively stable over the years, with the United States consuming 40 percent of total exports; and, as expected, exports to France increased slowly but steadily from 20 to nearly 40 percent by 1842. It appears that the American presidents from Andrew Jackson to John Tyler had adopted a color-blind policy regarding trade with the black republic.[120]

Haiti also had to adapt its agricultural model to the new social reality. Thus, it gradually moved away from labor-intensive sugar—as this demand was competitively satisfied by the surrounding slave colonies—and moved towards less labor-intensive commodities, such as coffee, cocoa, and tobacco. Of these, only coffee had been a prominent colonial export. Haiti also began exploiting other primary commodities found on the island, including precious woods such as mahogany. In 1826, the wood trade represented 18 percent of total exports and reached a high of 27 percent in 1837. By 1839, precious wood represented 43 percent of total exports, prompting Boyer to initiate regulations to limit extraction.

There was no going back to sugar anyway. Europeans, led by German initiatives, had begun to experiment with manufacturing sugar from beets.[121] Beet sugar technology gradually attracted more financing, after the first beet sugar factory opened in 1802. In France, the first factory dedicated to the extraction of sugar from beets was founded in Lille in 1810 by Louis Crespel-Dellisse (1789–1865). Where it related to cane sugar, there were also milling technology advancements adopted in Jamaica, Barbados, Trinidad and Tobago, Guadeloupe, and Martinique, rendering Haitian sugar even less competitive. By 1811, Bonaparte ordered the cultivation of beets in France. In the end, even the mechanization of cane sugar production could not compete. And, though it didn't happen immediately, all these colonies had to find other niches because the ramp-up of beet sugar production, a near-perfect substitute for cane sugar, lowered the international price of sugar below the cost of production. By the time of Boyer's death in 1850, almost half of the sugar consumed in Europe was from beet sugar. Cane sugar became commercially nonviable for most countries in the Americas by the late nineteenth century.

No longer holding preferential access to French

markets, Haiti was more exposed to fluctuations in world commodity prices. In addition to this vulnerability, it also had to contend with the scaling and rapid mechanization of colonies in the Americas, the emerging colonies in sub-Saharan Africa, and the exceptional productivity of the United States of America. The world was simply producing more, resulting in a depression of commodity prices. Between 1820 and 1843, cotton and coffee farmers experienced the largest reduction of prices, 95 percent and 98 percent respectively, from their average. Tobacco also experienced a fall in profitability, as the world price fell 87 percent from its average during the same period—though this could also be attributed to the rapidity at which the Americans achieved scale. Between 1820 and 1865, tobacco and cotton accounted for half of American exports. With its slave-based economy, the United States outperformed independent countries and colonies in North and South America, driving down commodity prices. By 1830, the United States had a 17.6 percent share of the world trade of tropical goods, while other independent countries in the hemisphere shared 42.5 percent among them.

Given all of the factors, coffee and cotton appeared to have the most potential for revenue generation in Haiti. Accordingly, the start of Boyer's presidency saw a dramatic increase in the export of coffee and cotton to France. Coffee sustained the Haitian economy.[122] Export volumes were 35.1 million pounds in 1822, increasing to 48.3 million pounds by 1835. Up to Boyer's departure, Haitian coffee exports averaged 40 million pounds annually. It was coffee that kept Haiti's trade balance positive, and this lasted for the entire first half of Boyer's presidency, until 1832. Afterwards, the country ran a slight trade deficit which averaged approximately USD $1 million per year.[123]

Haiti's modest export performance, in fact, mirrored that of the region. The United Kingdom abolished their slave trade in 1834 and emancipated those who were slaves in 1838. Like Haiti, those colonies experienced a 33.6 percent drop in exports; the French colonies—though they didn't abolish slavery until 1848—experienced a 27 percent decline in exports; and the Dutch colonies, among the last to abolish slavery in 1863, experienced a 28.2 percent decline. Few were the countries in the Americas that did better than the entire world when using exports as an indicator of economic performance. "The recovery of exports from the British and French colonies was hampered by the loss of the preferential treatment they enjoyed during slavery," wrote economists Frederico and Tena.[124] Exports per capita in independent American countries averaged $2.75–$3.32 in 1825, using exchange rates from 1913. While Haiti's exports in 1825 were slightly higher, at $4.92 per capita, assuming a population of 935,000 and exports valued at $4.6 million. As was the case in Haiti, the doubling of the population in the Americas from 3.7 percent of world population to 6.4 percent lowered the values of export indicators that are typically used to track country performance.

The new American republics became marginalized in relation to world trade flows. A look at global trade between 1800 to 1938 revealed that the fastest rate of growth was during the period 1816 and 1870; the world's economy grew, on average, 4.08 percent annually, realizing a cumulative growth of 804.3 percent. This expansion was still centered around Europe, where 60 percent of international commerce was destined and where the wealthiest consumers were located. Unfortunately for Latin America and the Caribbean, African and Asian countries also entered the primary goods market. And, as industrialization took shape, value addition processes occurred principally in Europe and the United States, where new technologies were able to increase output while using the same or even less inputs, effectively lowering industrial nations' demand for primary goods. Consequently, the share of primary goods of Latin American and Caribbean exports declined, on average, 11 percent annually. This shift was even observed within the United States; for example, cotton accounted for as much as 80 percent of exports in 1850 but declined to less than 30 percent by 1913 because it was replaced by manufactures. This was also the case for Italy, Germany, the Netherlands, and Sweden.[125]

One cannot also eliminate the racial and social divisions and its consequent political instability as contributions to Haiti's modest trade performance. However, this could be only a partial explanation, as both Christophe and Pétion, though they only governed parts of the country, had lengthy mandates, with enough time to reinforce institutions and restructure their respective economies. Equally tumultuous countries like Peru and Argentina experienced strong export-led growth; the former repositioned itself in the silver trade, the latter in cattle-raising.[126]

Cognizant of the regional trade dynamics, Boyer did what he could to stimulate domestic investment in local production. He banned imports of sugar products, wood, coffee, cotton, and wool. He also raised the customs duty to 12 percent on other imports. The idea was that if one million Haitians desired a certain product then they should produce it themselves.

Lastly, the main driver of imports that upset the region's trade balance was the need to reinforce defense structures, resulting in the acquisition of military hardware from abroad. The newly independent countries were obligated to militarize in order to preserve their sovereignty, spending substantial resources on defense. In Haiti, for example, between 1813 and 1815, revenues increased 88 percent, from 605,000 francs to 1.14 million, whereas expenditures during the same period increased 367 percent, from 357 thousand to 1.67 million francs. The difference is attributed to military spending. Realizing that this intensity of spending was untenable, the Senate passed a law in 1817 to increase export tariffs on coffee and cotton, expanding the resource envelope to support it. Cocoa, sugar, and wood saw similar increases.

To offer a wider perspective on the general sense of insecurity felt by newly independent countries in Latin America, between 1822 and 1860, military expenditures averaged between 50 and 77 percent of total government expenditures in the region. [127] France, Spain, and other former metropoles made several attempts to retake their former colonies. More pertinently in Haiti, by 1837, while public revenues amounted to 2.1 million gourdes, public expenditures reached 2.7 million gourdes, sixty percent of which were military in nature. In fact, during the whole of Boyer's presidency, military expenditures represented 50 percent, on average, of total public expenditures. [128] Investments included battleships like the *Philanthrope*, *Abolition de la Traite*, and *Wilberforce* acquired to constantly patrol the sea around Haiti. Other needs included the financing of army equipment like boots and uniforms, which by 1824, *Le Télégraphe*, Haiti's official gazette, estimated to be 60,000 men. [129] The opportunity cost of such expenditures (education, housing, agricultural, and other infrastructure investment) proved to be insurmountable and would alter the trajectory of Haiti's development.

$$***$$

Boyer, who was born early enough to remember the exceptional productivity of Saint-Domingue, made several attempts to kickstart the economy. Taking into consideration the challenges, Boyer and his cabinet published the *Code Rural*, six laws containing 202 articles of law passed by Parliament in May 1826. Among the headline articles, it organized the various labor classes, detailed the rights and responsibilities of both workers and employers, and established a rural police force to oversee farm operations and public works. Everyone who was not a farm owner nor a skilled worker was supposed to work on a plantation. All labor was to be contracted, the provisions for which —including work hours and salary— were outlined in the code.

The labor force was badly in need of direction. The census of 1827 revealed that Haitians numbered approximately 935,000, the Ouest department having the highest concentration, around 322,000, which was nearly one-third. Boyer was obliged to reduce the standing army to about 20,000 and place some proportion of soldiers on an annual rotation of military service for four months and eight months in private enterprise. Others were assigned to the supervision of plantations, while others were responsible for their own plantations.

Heavily regulated were any desired changes in residence, profession, choice of school, crops planted, livestock management, and land ownership. Agricultural priorities included grains, tubers, and fruit trees, and the rural police kept the accounting of harvests and administered its transport, which required a permit. Farmers were responsible for growing their own food and for their workers. Private commerce in rural areas was prohibited, except for sugar and cotton, which were designated to be sold within the country for milling before they could be exported. Tree felling required permission, accompanied by proposals to mitigate the environmental damage. The obligation to work was combined with Pétion's sharecropping model, in which plantations were subdivided into ten- to fifteen-acre plots, to allow for a larger, more diverse class of landowners. When the island was under French rule, the plantations were well over one thousand acres.

Idleness of land and labor were supposed to be severely punished, and there were legal provisions which addressed these transgressions. However, Boyer found resistance where it related to the application of the Code Rural. He was obliged to periodically issue circulars, such as this one released on 12 November 1829, urging farm managers to intensify their supervision of planters and to encourage them by explaining how essential farming was to the well-being of the nation.

Malgré l'adoption de différentes lois qui établissent une réduction de droits sur les principales denrées d'exportation, il était évident que cette mesure ne remplirait qu'imparfaitement le but proposé, si l'administration publique, abandonnant à eux-mêmes les cultivateurs, négligeait de les éclairer et de les diriger dans leur travaux.....l'ordre et la surveillance dans les campagnes étaient donc ce qu'il fallait organiser d'une manière plus régulière...Je n'ai cessé, soit par des circulaires spéciales, soit dans le cours de ma correspondance, d'appeler votre attention sur la nécessité de stimuler le zèle des agens qui vous ont subordonnés, et de veiller par vous-même, à la ponctuelle exécution des mesures prescrite...[130]

There were some avant-garde provisions in the Code Rural, which surpass even the modern labor laws of advanced economies like the United States of America. Haiti introduced, for the first time in its history - and probably the region as most of the surrounding countries were still slave colonies - the employment contract. For most workers, this could not be less than two years or exceed nine years. Employers were fined if workers were not contracted, and contracts had to be certified by a notary. Employers were responsible for registering with a health officer and seeking medical attention when necessary for workers. Pregnant women were not permitted to work after the fourth month and had an additional four months of leave postpartum. Everyone was entitled to a mid-morning break and a midday break, assuming a workday from sunrise to sunset. Laborers were free on Saturdays, Sundays, and holidays. And conflicts were arbitrated by rural police and justices of the peace.

Politically initiated in the Pétion school of governance, Boyer firmly believed that the forced labor model applied by Louverture, Dessalines, and Christophe was an encroachment on civil liberties. However, there was the supply-side problem of low labor productivity. Haitians had become reputed for no longer wanting to participate in rural economic activities; they wanted no part in agriculture or livestock management, nor anything else resembling their lives under French rule. "Damn these Haitians; they can't even fatten a pig," commented an exasperated Englishman to the British consul general Charles Mackenzie in 1826, recounting his experience of not being able to get Haitians to undertake manual labor. Mackenzie's own tour of the country yielded a similar, singular observation: Fertile land was largely idle and, where he did witness farming activity, it was small-scale.[131] This observation was seconded by Alcide d'Orbigny, a Frenchman and early environmentalist, who spent seven years traveling around Latin America and the Caribbean and arrived in Haiti from Cuba in 1826. He wrote that the farms appeared abandoned and unmaintained. [132] James Franklin, an American historian, believed that, given the recalcitrance of Haitian workers, Boyer was still too *laissez-faire*, despite the application of the Code Rural.

> *What is denominated as a coffee plantation, is neither more nor less than a large tract of land, throughout which grows spontaneously the coffee tree; not planted there by the people, but sprung from the seed which has fallen from those planted by the French, and which escaped destruction during the revolution. There are no divisions, no laying out of the lands, no order of planting in succession, nothing done towards improving and fertilizing the soil, in order to aid the growth of the tree, no lopping it of its excrescences, and pruning it to strengthen the parent stem; but everything is left to nature...It appears as if the work of civilization had not commenced, and that the people had not taken one voluntary step towards improving themselves in any one thing.[133]*

Most historians concurred that, despite its good intentions, the Code Rural was largely a failure. Foreign (and non-black) historians like Franklin and Baur attributed the comparative success of the earlier coercive models of Dessalines and Christophe to the nature of the black man. "It was evident to every man in Hayti, at all conversant with the negro character, that an attempt to keep up cultivation without force was impossible, and many of the proprietors, themselves negroes, knew that by force only could they obtain labourers amongst their people," wrote Franklin. Living in Port-au-Prince at the time of the announcement of the Code Rural, Franklin, though not a fan of Boyer, commented that Boyer "knew that indolence in the negro was innate, and that it was absolutely impracticable to carry on the work in the soil unless rigid laws were enacted to enforce it."

But the most logical explanation seems to have escaped everyone, even Boyer: These "lazy" Haitians were the same generation of slaves that catalyzed the legendary profitability of Saint-Domingue, propelling France into industrialization, and thus twenty-two years was simply not enough time to disassociate farming from the trauma of physical subjugation and the social and cultural demoralization of a people. As James Logan, a Scottish traveler observed from a trip to Haiti in the 1830s:

> *Unmercifully torn from his home and friends, treated like a dog, generally compelled to a labour he never before heard of, to adopt customs and views totally foreign to his nature, is it to be supposed that he works willingly, or that he has any desire to learn? It can only be time that will modify his mind and practice, and bend him to his situation, and, combined with other causes, may ultimately stimulate him to exertion for himself.*[134]

That agriculture would be the basis for wealth building was, nevertheless, a clear and logical cornerstone of Boyer's economic policy. His reasoning was based on Haiti's past economic performance and European consumption patterns. Boyer's Code Rural was an attempt to preserve the productivity of the plantation system; but, given the psychological trauma of slavery and the revolution, which endured thirteen years, it was inapplicable. Boyer tried to lead by example—he had his own plantation at Volant-le-Thort. On the road to Bizoton, it was originally Pétion's farm, which he had inherited by virtue of Pétion's partner, Joutte. His attempt to grow sugar on the approximately two-thousand-acre farm was largely unsuccessful.

While other former sugar-producing colonies reoriented their economies towards minerals, tobacco, bananas, and such, Haiti remained largely unmechanized and concentrated on the same colonial crops. At a time when much experimentation was taking place around the world on the refinement of primary commodities and value-addition, Boyer and his super-ministers surprisingly had few new ideas.

Recognizing that there was little enthusiasm for farming, Boyer's immigration policy was designed to stimulate the interest in black populations in the region to migrate to Haiti to fill the human resources gap. Relocation incentives were offered, particularly targeting black Americans seeking to flee an active slave system. Predating the Code Rural by several years, Boyer's December 1822 circular invited free blacks to come to Haiti. American Presbyterian minister Loring Daniel Dewey (1791–1867) answered the call. He was a member of the American Colonization Society, an organization promoting the resettlement of free blacks, primarily located in the Northern states so that they would not agitate the slaves in the Southern states. Dewey wrote to President Boyer on 4 March 1824 to inquire about what incentives and relocation assistance he was offering to the families. Boyer's reply, in English, was dated 30 April 1824: "My heart and my hands have been open to greet, in this land of true liberty, those men upon whom a fatal destiny rests in a manner so cruel." He offered aid with travel expenses; allocations of land and inputs to those who wished to cultivate; and to merchants and investors, a tax exemption of one year. He also assured Dewey that "as soon as they put their feet upon the soil of Hayti, they will enjoy happiness, security, tranquility, such as we ourselves possess."[135]

Boyer invested some resources in trying to make this a reality. The following year, in May 1824, he dispatched Pierre Joseph Marie (aka Jonathas) Granville (1785–1839), a proficient English speaker, to the US with a relocation plan. Granville was from the Nord department. His father was French and served as the tutor for Louverture's children. At age thirteen he was sent to France to further his education. The cohort with which he was sent included Isaac and Placide Louverture, the son of André Rigaud, and Séguy

Villevaleix, the stepson of Sonthonax, the French commissioner who abolished slavery in Saint-Domingue in 1793. Granville started medical school, but soon renounced it for the military, joining the French army as a cannon operator in 1806. A biography written by his son described him as being well-built and nimble; he excelled in dance, swimming, and equestrian sports. By several accounts found in Gallica, the French online archives, he fought valiantly for France and was granted his military pension at the rank of lieutenant from King Louis XVIII. Even though he was a Northerner, Granville decided to return in 1816 to Pétion's Haiti, as opposed to Christophe's kingdom. Pétion named him the land surveyor for the Ouest department and integrated him into the Haitian Army Corps of Engineers at the grade of second lieutenant. He held a series of appointments in the Haitian judicial system and in 1817 founded a school for boys. Also a Freemason, he was inducted into the Scottish chapter of Les Élèves de la Nature, Loge no. 10 in Les Cayes. Lastly, Granville was married to Joutte's cousin, which brought him into Boyer's intimate circle.

Boyer was prepared to receive six thousand Black American families to certain identified regions in Haiti. While he welcomed technicians and machinists, he encouraged Granville to recruit those willing to farm cotton, coffee, tobacco, and cocoa. However, when Granville arrived with the mandate to recruit and the resources to arrange for travel, he found the American whites hesitant. For reasons that are not clear, the American Colonization Society disengaged itself from the initiative. Minister Dewey presented the idea to what was essentially the bourgeois class of the state of New York. But even in the Northern states, slavery was still a legal practice, and in the 1820 census, there were still over ten thousand slaves there and was only slated to become illegal in 1827. Nevertheless, there were 29,000 free blacks who were living in degrading circumstances, and so several prominent American families (Jay, Wainwright, Griscom, Colgate, and Eddy, among others) formed another association called The Society for Promoting the Emigration of Free Persons of Colour to Hayti to facilitate Granville's task. Benjamin Lundy, a missionary sent to Haiti to learn of the conditions of immigrants, observed that eight thousand blacks of American provenance were there in 1827. He said that quite a number had prospered and appeared to have become influential members of society.[136]

However, Boyer was generally dissatisfied with these results and tried other, largely unsuccessful ways to stimulate the agricultural sector. The Customs Act of 1819 not only set import duties but also set preferential rates for local merchants. It also barred the import of commodities that could be locally produced, including sugar and sugar products, wood, coffee, and cotton. The hope was that this would incentivize innovation. In 1830 Boyer initiated a plan to purchase tobacco from farmers in the Sud department in hopes that the prospect of guaranteed income would boost productivity. Yet, that plan fell through, after the region suffered a drought followed by a hurricane in 1831. The effects of the hurricane were felt throughout the island, as many large plantations were destroyed.[137]

In fact, Haiti experienced many climate-related setbacks to its development strategy. On 26 September 1820 a hurricane formed in the region and hit the country two days later. Its field of devastation extended as far as South Carolina. Immense floods washed away herds of cattle and coffee plantations. There were equally devastating replicas in 1825 and 1827. During the latter, perhaps thinking they were safer on ships rather than on land, dozens of foreign crews - French, American, English - and their commercial vessels perished in the harbors around the island of Haiti. The losses for Haiti included the ships *L'Esperance, L'Irma,* and *Los dos Hermanos.*[138]

Boyer knew that economic rents could be found in mechanization and value addition, the identification of new markets in proximity to production, and the reinforcement of customs operations. But his frugality and obsession with stemming corruption worked against him. Bonnet recounted, for example, how disgusted Boyer was with the lavish lifestyle of a treasurer named Pigny, who also served under Pétion. Boyer had even ordered an audit of his office, finding nothing. "Parsimonious to the point of stinginess" is how Bonnet described Boyer.

Because there were very few "slips between the cup and the lip" under his management, corruption is not readily attributable to Boyer and his super-ministers, but neither was public investment. In fact, Boyer rejected nearly all proposals for investment in public works and education. With his economical disposition, he couldn't be convinced, no matter how compelling the idea, to disburse public funds, including those directed towards education and emerging agricultural technologies.

Though it is erroneous to conclude that Boyer was not at all interested in social and economic development. Education, for example, was a sector in which minimal investments were made. In a presidential decree of 1819, he established four primary national schools (for boys) and special schools for girls. Admission was based on parental military service. The rest were expected to attend private schools, the increasing number of which prompted him to create the *Commission d'Instruction Publique* to standardize and regulate teaching in schools. In July 1820, he passed a law creating local commissions in Les Cayes, Jérémie, and Jacmel and setting the minimum qualifications for instructors.

We also know that the Lancasterian model of education appealed to him. [139] Joseph Lancaster's educational methods, developed in England in the 1790s, were adopted in the public schools of most of the largest cities in the United States in the early decades of the nineteenth century. Lancaster's system used a single enormous classroom to instruct hundreds of poor children under a single master. Children were broken into small classes to recite their lessons under the tutelage of a more advanced student, or monitor. Boyer established ten such schools.[140]

After annexation of the eastern part of the island, he closed the University of Santo Domingo and used the location for a Lancaster school. School directors were Haitian, and instruction was in French. By 1839, there were a thousand students in total in primary schools and in the national high school, though the majority attended private schools. Nevertheless, if we postulate that one-fifth of the population was below the age of eighteen, which is conservative for developing countries, this means that there were over one hundred thousand school-aged children not receiving instruction.

Boyer also created the National Library in 1825. In June of that year, the government purchased property for the library from Louis Charles for 75 gourdes. The following month they disbursed 936.50 gourdes for 444 books. In 1826, the library was transferred to the house of a former senator named Daumec. The first chief librarian was Jean-François Acloque, who was also director of primary education in Port-au-Prince. Boyer also created a seminary for the development of local clergy in 1827.

In retrospect, significant public investment in education and vocational training would have probably placed the country on a slightly different trajectory. Instead, Boyer's education policy reinforced a class system, one in which the military constituted an elite caste and officers were rewarded for their continued loyalty. By 1830, about 10 percent of the population worked in the military or for the government, and 90 percent in agriculture - 40 percent worked on plantations and 50 percent worked on smallholdings.[141] Consequently, the Haitian economy was a two-class system, marked by the lack of agricultural diversification, the lack of industrialization, and the lack of investment in skills development.

Haiti exports under various regimes, in million pounds

	France			*Boyer*			
YEARS	*1789*	*1804*	*1818*	*1822*	*1832*	*1838*	*1840*
Sugar	141	48	2	0.7			
Coffee	77	31	20	35	49	50	46
Cotton	7	3	0.4	0.9	0.9	1.2	0.9
Indigo	0.8						
Cocoa		0.2	0.3	0.3	0.3	0.5	0.4
Logwood			6	2	21	13	43
Tobacco				0.3	0.8	2	2
Slaves	**455,000**						
Workforce				**935,000**			

Note: Author's compilation of various sources including Franklin (1825); St. John (1884)[142]; Madiou (1988); Ardouin (1958)

17

Black Diplomacy in a White World

JUST AS THE FRENCH, ENGLISH, AND SPANISH used Hispaniola as a base to conquer the surrounding territories like Cartagena (present-day Colombia), Curaçao, Jamaica, Grenada, and even Florida in the seventeenth century, the eighteenth-century independence leaders did the same.[143] In December 1815, the celebrated Latin American liberator Simón Bolívar landed in Les Cayes, Haiti, with his fleet of ten ships, after spending several months in Jamaica. He was fighting for the liberation of present-day Venezuela and Colombia from Spain. He came to Haiti to ask Pétion for reinforcements to continue their struggle for independence. Bolívar had no doubt heard about the government's zero-tolerance policy on the slavery issue, as well as the granting of Haitian nationality to all those fleeing persecution, but most of all the fervent call for peoples' freedom. As anticipated, Pétion generously offered Bolívar all that he could, conditional, of course, on the emancipation of all slaves in those regions. After four months in Haiti, Bolívar parted with, among other provisions, four thousand rifles, fifteen thousand pounds of gunpowder, and a printing press.

However, six months later, Bolívar was back in Haiti to plead for more munitions. On this second visit, he met General Francisco Javier Mina, who was fighting for Mexico's independence from Spain. "The Haitian capital was an interesting spectacle of men, of omnifarious origins, who sought refuge in its shade of liberty," wrote historian Beaubrun Ardouin of early nineteenth-century Haiti.

However, Bolívar and Mina were exceptions where it concerned Latin American respect and admiration for Haiti. Journalist and historian Carrie Gibson wrote that these countries feared the Haitian experience would incite black revolts, writing: "The idea of Haiti as a propagator of slave rebellions persisted throughout the century."[144] To hear them tell it, any and all disenchantment detected among people of color in the surrounding countries originated in Haiti, where its leaders were actively undermining their country's stability.

Rather than attribute the increasing social

insurrections to their intensification of slavery, the surrounding countries blamed Haiti for setting a bad example for their slaves. Haiti gave them hope, and even worse, aspiration. And yet these same islands benefited from Haiti's post-slavery lack of competitiveness. Its vast work force of nine hundred thousand were now paid laborers, making its commodities more expensive. Ironically, the surrounding islands were mostly Spanish colonies that in the eighteenth century had expressed a strong preference for livestock management rather than slavery-based agriculture but now had oddly developed a taste for it—or more appropriately an appetite for it, when they realized slavery's higher profit margins. In Cuba, for example, over 18,300 slaves disembarked in 1816, from 7,872 slaves just one year prior, a 233 percent increase. A direct beneficiary of the flight of experienced slave plantation owners from Haiti, Cuba's sugar production doubled from 89,090 metric tonnes in the period from 1792 to 1796 to 185,000 metric tonnes. By 1820, Cuba was producing 13 percent of the world's sugar, with a slave corps exceeding two hundred thousand. The Spanish colonies ostracized Haiti (and Boyer), refusing to recognize its independence. Even Bolívar did not keep his promise: While he liberated his own slaves—an estimated fifteen hundred—Venezuela, which declared its independence in 1821, did not abolish slavery until 1854.

World powers at the time may have permitted the

black republic to lead a subdued existence. However, Boyer took an active anti-slavery stance, intentionally seeking to interrupt the slave transport in the trade routes around Haiti by banning slave ships from entering Haiti's waters. He was aided in this noble endeavor by Casimir Panayoty, commander of the Haitian navy. Panayoty was born in Thessalonica, Macedonia, in 1762, became a naturalized Frenchman, joined the French navy, and was sent to Saint-Domingue during the American Civil War. He was promoted to lieutenant by Commissioner Sonthonax in 1796 and became the commander of the port of Léogâne in 1798, under Laplume. He chose the winning side in the Haitian Revolution and became well integrated into Haitian society. He was placed in command of the Haitian navy by Pétion, whose fleet included *L'Indépendence*, *La Constitution*, *La Guerrière*, *Le Flambeau*, and *Le Conquérant*. He was even elected to the Haitian senate and served as its president. Boyer named Panayoty *Contre-amiral* (rear admiral) after successfully retaking the Kingdom of Nord Haiti. He served Boyer loyally until his death in Port-au-Prince in October 1842, less than a year after having been promoted to the rank of general.

One notable example of Boyer's anti-slavery militancy occurred in June 1818. Boyer had sent *Le Philanthrope* to Jamaica to notify British officials of Pétion's passing the preceding March and his ascension to the presidency. On its way back, the ship crossed paths with a slave ship destined for Cuba. They attacked it, rescuing the 171 Africans aboard. Boyer had them all baptized, and those that were deemed capable were incorporated into the military.

On this point, the Kingdom of Northern Haiti (led by Christophe) and the Republic of Haiti had the same foreign policy stance. Because of its refusal to recognize Haiti's sovereignty, the United States of America, under the presidency of Thomas Jefferson, officially banned trade with both of them. Knowing that a ban of any kind on economic activity fuels informality and criminality—in this case, privateering and contraband—Haiti seized American ships that were in violation of their country's trade policy. The frequency of these seizures is evidenced by the numerous requests for intervention by the US Department of State to Congress. In 1817, for example, Septimus Tyler, an American agent, petitioned Congress to assist him in the collection of $132,000, the loss he incurred consequent to Christophe's seizure of his ship. Foreign merchants were continually trying to access Haitian markets without paying tariffs. There were so many cases, largely inactionable, that, in December 1841, Secretary of State Daniel Webster finally compiled a sizable dossier of complaints and supporting documents, which he forwarded to President John Tyler.

Periodically seizing ships or imprisoning foreigners was also a way of reminding other countries that Haiti, the black sovereign republic, was still around. Like a toddler misbehaving for attention, Boyer and his administration employed several tactics to remind the Old World that this young nation meant business. One target was John Dodge—born in Massachusetts but claimed to have lived in Cap-Haïtien for twenty years as a trading agent—who established an agency there to assist American traders gain access to Haitian markets. Boyer had imposed an annual fee of $1,600 for a trader's commercial license. Dodge claimed it was only imposed on American traders, while other nationalities traded freely. He refused to pay and, consequently, amassed a debt of $140,000. "The Haitians trample upon our rights but treat with great deference the claims of persons of all other nations," Dodge wrote in a letter to Secretary of State Edward Livingston in September 1831.[145]

More sensationally was a May 1837 case, in which two Haitians purchased a commercial vessel for $910 from an American named Ralph Plympton. They used the *Venus*, which they renamed *Deux Amis*, to export precious wood to the United States. On one such voyage to New York in late June, the previous owner spotted his ship being run by a crew of black sailors and seized it. The ship's captain not only filed suit in New York against Plympton but also brought suit in Haiti against the American commercial agent, Mr. George Swain, who had certified the sale. The latter was found guilty in Haiti and fined $7,776 to cover the cost of litigation, the loss of cargo, and repairs undertaken to the ship. He was unable to pay and thus imprisoned. Writing from a Haitian jail in November 1837, from the "hot and unhealthy" city of Port-au-Prince, where he "twice escaped death from fever and dysentery," Swain wrote to Secretary of State John Forsyth (serving under President Andrew Jackson), to intervene. He also wrote to General Inginac, Boyer's secretary general, pleading for his release. "The government of the United States has never corresponded with the Republic (of Haiti)," Inginac responded ten days later, "and so we do not recognize its commercial agents as public officials; rather, they are private citizens." He also urged Swain to file an appeal, but under no circumstances would President Boyer intervene in a private affair. Swain wrote to the State Department again in January 1838, pleading for action. The secretary of state must have sent an inquiry to Attorney General William M. Price, because there is a letter from the latter, dated 2 February 1838, acknowledging his awareness of the case and his commitment to follow up. There were also several exchanges between the attorney general and the New York state attorney, but to no avail. A few days later, the commander of USS *Ontario*, Samuel L. Breese, taken aback after learning that Swain was imprisoned, penned off letters to both Secretary General Inginac and Secretary of State Forsyth. Inginac's response remained the same. The American government also used the same logic in their response to petitioners! Regardless of merit, all petitions to the Department of State were answered in the same fashion: "Hayti has not been acknowledged by the United States, and we have no diplomatic intercourse with the persons in authority on that island." On 20 March 1838, Swain wrote to Forsyth, informing him that he had been released conditional on his agreement to pay the caution within six months. It is not obvious from the surviving documentation how the affair ended, but in July 1838, Swain again wrote to Forsyth that his six-month reprieve was about to expire, and he did not have the means to pay the indemnity.[146]

The lack of formal recognition didn't necessarily translate into a lack of trading partners. Boyer also actively practiced trade diplomacy, using a regime of preferential tariffs in return for political or diplomatic favors. As no country had recognized Haiti as a sovereign nation, *negotiants* or commercial agents were employed by their countries of origin to report back on the events occurring in Haiti. Officially, these agents were nominated, mostly by European countries, to organize the exchange of goods between the two countries and handle the finances, including the payment of tariffs. They were often sent with nomination letters and a petition seeking permission for their ships to come into port. The United States of America,

France, England, the Netherlands, and Spain all had trade agents assigned to and living in Haiti.

A proxy diplomatic corps, these agents did formally address Boyer after his installation as president. In a letter reprinted in the *Abeille Haytienne,* one of the first Haitian newspapers, on 16 April 1818, they expressed their sympathies for the death of Pétion and congratulated Boyer on his ascension. "We hope to have a long, prosperous future in closing the ties between the Republic and our governments. We anticipate being extremely satisfied given that your excellency is open-minded and energetic." They communicated their expectations of maintaining the same commercial arrangements as under Pétion and concluded by wishing Boyer success in his tenure.

This precedent was established by Pétion, who, in October of 1814, sent an emissary to London to ask Lord Liverpool to mediate between Haiti and France—in particular to broker recognition of Haiti's independence. England refused, but they were perhaps also aware of the imminent change of power in France. The Bourbons had been driven away a second time by Napoleon. In an attempt to sway them, Pétion reduced the import tariffs on British goods, but this didn't swing the pendulum in Haiti's favor. Neither did the return of Louis XVIII the following year. While diplomatic efforts with the United Kingdom stalled, commerce between the two countries continued. Pétion kept a general tariff of 10 percent on imports, with the exception of Great Britain, which he lowered to 5 percent. Haiti also freely traded, under its own banner, with other slave colonies like the English colony of Jamaica and the Dutch colony of Curaçao. "Commerce has always been and will always be the best way to achieve reconciliation," wrote historian Ardouin. Boyer retained this special dispensation for Great Britain: While general customs duty was set at 12 percent, the latter enjoyed a favorable rate of 7 percent. By 1826, Portuguese, Russian, and Spanish ships were pulling into the port of Port-au-Prince, and the Netherlands, Denmark, and Sweden also sent commercial agents to Haiti.

France, although embarrassed at having lost its beloved sugar bowl, was not embarrassed enough to neglect the economic opportunity which Haiti represented. In fact, one of the first commercial French shipments after independence was directed by a French agent named Dravermann. He captained a vessel hoisting the Prussian banner but carrying French goods like wine, dried fruits, and oils. He reportedly spoke frankly to President Pétion and was granted a concession and a local agent with whom to collaborate. This act by Pétion triggered a steady exchange with French merchants, which captured the attention of King Louis XVIII, who had been restored to the throne in 1815 after the defeat of Napoleon at Waterloo by an alliance of European armies. Or maybe it was the increase in trade revenue that caught his attention. In an attempt to capture the rents from this commerce, the king issued an order in March 1816, twelve years after Haitian independence, that, regardless of the banner they flew, all boats sailing from France with the intention of going to Saint-Domingue were required to register with the Ministry of the Marine and Overseas Possessions and that all commodities brought back were subject to the same import tariffs as those from other French colonies. Reference to its former colonial status was deliberate and careless. Louis XVIII didn't seem to have learned from his elder brother, Louis XVI, a mercantilist, who also insisted on heavily regulating private commerce. As expected, there would be no French ship ledger listing Haiti as a destination. "Merchant ships are the best negotiators," Pétion responded when informed of the practice.

Even before its declaration of independence, Haiti's foreign policy was characterized by trade diplomacy. Louverture's administration generally levied 20 percent on both imports and exports and created a corps of customs agents to ensure that the tariffs were indeed collected. Without officially recognizing the sovereignty of Saint-Domingue, many countries negotiated preferential tariffs with Louverture, informally recognizing his legitimacy. During the civil war between Louverture and Rigaud, preferential access to commodities and tariffs were granted contingent upon effective patrol of the seas around the Sud region in support of Louverture. Both the Americans and

British took up these offers. It was because of these established relationships that the ships carrying Rigaud, Pétion, and Boyer were captured by British and American frigates.

Louverture's success with these powers was, in part, attributable to timing. President John Adams was a Federalist, an early American political party which was firmly abolitionist and anti-French. The French still possessed the lands along the Mississippi River, west of the thirteen original members of the United States of America. However, American ally King Louis XVI was beheaded in 1793, and many Americans in France were imprisoned in the resulting social mayhem. The Federalists now considered France more of a threat than the possibility of a black republic. President John Adams had even sent the Indigenous Army of Saint-Domingue funds and foodstuffs in support of their liberation efforts. In 1801, the United States appointed Mr. Edward Stevens as consul general to Saint-Domingue, with the objective of renegotiating the tariffs, which he did successfully. Louverture lowered them to 10 percent.

However, relations with the United States would take a different turn with the election of Thomas Jefferson, a Democratic Republican who was very pro-French. The United States was small, fragile, and exposed on all borders. It needed to make alliances. When Napoleon asked them not to trade with Haiti, they acceded, partly because they had still not paid off their debt to France for its financial support during the American Revolution, and partly because they needed to navigate the Mississippi River. Haiti's defeat of Napoleon's army raised Americans' fear, especially among plantation slave owners. They made their views known through their representatives in Congress, who repeatedly blocked any attempt by the Northern states' representatives to establish formal relations with Haiti. Thus, Mr. Stevens' successor, Mr. Tobias Lear, was sent as a commercial agent, without a formal letter of nomination. Diplomatic relations with the Americans remained this way until 1863, when the Southern states had seceded and Lincoln, seizing the opportunity of their absence from the Senate, formally recognized Haiti's sovereignty.

In fact, Haiti's independence greatly contributed to American political discourse, not on human rights grounds but on the issue of political representation. With France heavily indebted and having lost its stronghold in the Caribbean, Napoleon did not see value in keeping the port of New Orleans or the lands along the Mississippi River. Known as the Louisiana Purchase, the sale of this territory, approximately 2.1 million square kilometers, substantially increased the landmass of the young American republic. Consequently, the practice of slavery migrated westward along with American frontiersmen. Southern states protested the tariffs imposed on their productivity, and Northern states—which were more industrial and liberal— protested the proliferation of slavery, provoking debates in Congress on the questions of representation and state autonomy. How would new states be admitted to the union, as slave states or as free states? The current practice was that every three out of five slaves were counted in terms of state population, which affected the number of representatives each state could have in Congress. Northern states, mostly slave-free states, argued that this placed them at a disadvantage when it came to federal appropriations. This issue remained unsettled until the American Civil War, but the immediate consequence was that the United States of America would not formally recognize Haiti and, in April 1819, Secretary of State John Quincy Adams, serving under President James Monroe, sent Jacob Lewis to Haiti as a commercial agent, again without diplomatic credentials.

In 1832, Boyer attempted to induce President Andrew Jackson to change the title of the commercial agents operating in Haiti to that of consul, thereby securing an implied recognition. In exchange, Boyer was willing to remove the additional 10 percent duty imposed on American imports. Again in 1838, after Boyer had negotiated a treaty with France, he wrote to the Americans for official recognition and was refused. In fact, during his twenty-five-year-long presidency, Boyer saw six American presidents come and go: James Monroe, John Quincy Adams, Andrew Jackson (for two terms), Martin Van Buren, William Henry Harrison, and John Tyler. He wrote to each asking for recognition, but to no avail.

The Americans had both economic and diplomatic concerns regarding the formal recognition of Haiti. Those who were opposed did not want to anger the French, as they still had a non-negligible military presence in North America and the Caribbean. Proponents of Haitian recognition made repeated arguments about Haiti's place in American trade revenue. This was particularly true during the Boyer years, trade with the US increased five fold, from 0.9 percent of total US exports in 1819 to 5.2 percent in 1820.[147] By 1823, US exports to Haiti were valued at approximately $2 million annually.[148] Yet the race factor outweighed the economic benefits: the last petition to recognize Haiti submitted for vote in the US House of Representatives before Boyer's departure was in January 1842, which was defeated 86 to 94.[149]

Nevertheless, these diplomatic "oversights" placed Haiti in a relatively good trading position. By 1822, imported goods from Haiti were valued at $2.26 million, and American exports to Haiti were $2.27 million, placing Haiti as the United States' sixth-largest trading partner at the time, behind England, France, Cuba, China, and the Netherlands. American exports mainly consisted of rice, meats, and flour. The Haitian government collected on average \$1.3 million annually in import duties from commerce with the United States of America. By 1839, Haiti sent more merchandise there than to any other country in the hemisphere, ranking it fourth behind Great Britain, France, and Russia.

President James Monroe, during his annual address to Congress in December 1823, outlined what would orient American foreign policy for decades to come. In what has come to be known as the Monroe Doctrine, the president expressed frustration with the trade and territorial disputes of Europeans. Their wars had become costly as well for the private sector, as American ships, and the cargo they transported, were regularly confiscated. Up until the 1820s, the only two independent countries in the region were the United States of America and Haiti; the others were mostly Spanish but also English, French and Dutch colonies. However, Napoleon's occupation of the Iberian peninsula and then Spain's popular revolt, which was not only against Napoleon but against autocracy in general, lessened Spain's stronghold in the American hemisphere. Just as the French revolution had inspired Saint-Domingue, the notion of self-rule inspired Spanish colonies as well. Given the spate of new republics throughout Central and South America, Monroe seized the opportunity to push Europe out of the hemisphere permanently. The Americas were "not to be considered as subjects for future colonization by any European powers." At the time of this speech, Chile, Mexico, and Gran Colombia (now Ecuador, Panama, Venezuela, and Colombia) had decisively fought off Spanish rule and declared their independence. Recognizing the end of the era of European metropoles, at least in the American hemisphere, Monroe went on to say that any attempt to retake a former colony that had already declared its independence would be seen as "dangerous to our peace and safety." Evidently, this shield from future European conquest did not extend to Haiti.

Refusal to recognize Haiti could probably be explained away with the many internal conflicts the country was experiencing. "We have concerns about political legitimacy" was a logical, and frequently used, excuse—and reasonably so, as the fractionalization of Haiti into three republics was disconcerting, and the world knew that all three leaders had fought together during the War of Independence. But, by 1822, Boyer had muted those excuses by uniting the island, including Santo Domingo.

Indeed, the annexation of the eastern part of the island may have fed the enmity which sprouted between the new Latin American republics and Haiti. This was a season of liberation. Brazil proclaimed its independence from Portugal in 1822, and, by 1824, Spanish rule ended in Peru, the last Spanish colony in the hemisphere. There was a need for these republics to confer on a number of issues, and so the Congress of Panama was organized in 1826. Haiti was not invited. This must have been the greatest indignity Boyer ever experienced, being forsaken despite having shown Bolívar perfect hospitality, allowing him to use the country as a base from which he would launch his offensives. Though some historians argue that it was Boyer's audacity in annexing Santo Domingo which angered Latin America, it should also be remembered that these republics remained slave-based economies. The independence they were celebrating only extended to whites.

Spurning Boyer and Haiti had more to do with the incompatibility of their economic systems and racism and less to do with the annexation of Santo Domingo. And yet, there were many things that these neonates had in common: The structure of their economies was plantation-based, and they were governed by military men. The early histories of these countries are not dissimilar to Haiti; they have had many coups and reversals of fortunes. Yet the generalized uneasiness felt by Latin America towards Haiti was articulated by Colombia's ambassador to the United States, José María Salazar. In a letter to Secretary of State Henry Clay inviting the Americans to attend the Panama Congress in November 1825, Salazar wrote:

On what basis the relations of Hayti, and of other parts

of our hemisphere that shall hereafter be in like circumstances, are to be placed, is a question simple at first view, but attended with serious difficulties when closely examined. These arise from the different manner of regarding Africans, and from their different rights in Hayti, the United States, and in other American States.

Mexico, however, stands out among the Latin American republics. On 30 November 1829, American Secretary of State Martin Van Buren sent a letter to Anthony Butler, charge d'affaires in Mexico, informing him that they had uncovered plans by Mexico to send a secret mission to Haiti. They were seeking assistance from Boyer to incite a slave revolt in Cuba. "It becomes the duty of this government to take all necessary precautions," Van Buren wrote, as he instructed Butler to investigate the situation and "keep a watchful eye overall on all the movements of the Mexican government regarding the project." Butler was to keep Washington informed so that the government could adopt the measures that they deemed "proper and necessary to avert the apprehended evils."[150]

The president of Mexico was Vicente Guerrero, who had taken power by way of a coup in 1829. Simon Bolívar, who had not freed the slaves in Gran Colombia, as he had promised Pétion, was not fond of Guerrero and referred to him pejoratively as *zambo*: someone of Indian and black descent.[151] He was of mixed heritage, unlike the other presidents in the Latin American region, who largely resembled their Spanish cousins. Also of the Masonic order, Guerrero had indeed reached out to Boyer soon after assuming power; to inform him that he had ended slavery in Mexico The intensification of slavery in Cuba disturbed everyone in proximity—the Americans had their eyes on the disproportionate number of slaves relative to the white population and the proximity of those slaves to Haiti. A successful coup in Cuba would make Boyer a very powerful man in the Caribbean. It was therefore untimely that an abolitionist took power in Mexico. Guerrero was reversed the following year, extinguishing whatever plans were in play.

As much as Boyer would have liked recognition from the Europeans and Americans, there was one principle he rigidly held: Haiti was a country of free men, and any black person who made their way to its shores was free. Boyer's commitment to this "free-soil" policy was tested several times, but he did not waver.

Harvesting from the salt ponds of the Turks islands, which were at the time part of the British colony of Bermuda, was hot work, involving standing in knee-high water and raking salt under the unforgivable Caribbean sun. Enslaved workers spent all day collecting and sifting the salt, and then spent all evening shoveling and measuring it. Unsurprisingly, many absconded and sailed to the nearby Republic of Haiti, the only safe place for them in the whole of the Americas. Sometimes the slaves stole the ships that came to purchase salt. Wood, Lightbourne, and Stubbs are among the salt traders who lost ships to audacious slaves. The Turks governor at the time, Daniel Bascombe, corresponded with President Boyer on the matter, via an envoy named Joseph Frith. The British even sent the frigate H.M.S. *Tamar* at one point in an unsuccessful attempt to recover the slaves from Haiti.[152] The H.M.S Tamar—as well as other ships sent to recover their slaves—may have left with merchandise but definitely left with a firm rejection of their requests.

While Latin America developed under the aegis of the Monroe Doctrine, Haiti was left unshielded and alone. This obviously created an atmosphere of anxiety felt by all Haitians. Boyer knocked on many doors, including that of one of its oldest collaborators, Great Britain.

However, Great Britain's presence in the Americas was not as prominent as it had been in the eighteenth century. At about the same time that Boyer became president, the British were also experiencing social change. King George III had passed away and was succeeded by his son, George IV, seen as decadent and wasteful. George IV was unpopular and unlucky, as his coronation date coincided with public debate on political reform, which had progressively intensified since the 1810s, culminating in the Peterloo Massacre in 1819. It had to be rescheduled.

Another reason for the diminished British presence was the fact that Great Britain had lost its taste for slavery as an economic system, which it would abolish in 1834. Their economy was rapidly industrializing, and they turned their attention to minerals and other resource extraction in the East, particularly in Africa and Asia. In 1825, England formally acknowledged Haiti as a sovereign country and named Charles Mackenzie as consul general. However, the expected recompense—a further lowering of tariffs—was not forthcoming. Furthermore, Boyer withdrew the customs abatement that Pétion had granted to the British. They had made the mistake of recognizing the sovereignty of Mexico and Colombia first, in 1823, and Boyer was offended.

In response to this action, on 1 January 1824, at the celebrations of the twentieth anniversary of Haitian independence, Boyer, bitter from several failed diplomatic attempts to negotiate recognition from not only Paris, but also Amsterdam, Brussels, and even St. Petersburg, nonetheless found some words of encouragement and *bienveillance* to his fellow citizens, warning them to hold fast against those who pretend to be friends of Haiti: "The triumph of our liberty was achieved with none other than our own energy and with honor we have managed to maintain our independence. The enemies of our freedom are blind with hate and prejudice. ... But you should always be proud of having defeated your oppressors."

It so happened that Boyer learned that the former Spanish colonies were, in fact, heavily indebted to England. Hence, England's recognition of their independence made sense in the context of facilitating repayment through international commerce. Boyer followed suit and sent an emissary to Bogotá, Colombia, seeking repayment for the support given to Bolívar during their independence struggle. He was not refused, and letters of credit were offered for reclamation at several British banks. The amount restituted was approximately 70,000 piastres, and Boyer used the money to purchase military reinforcements.

Formal recognition of the Republic of Haiti did come in 1821, from an unexpected corner, the Vatican. Abbe Henri Jean-Baptiste Grégoire (1750–1831) had written to Boyer in that year because of a schism that had arisen among Catholics in Haiti. Grégoire was a Catholic priest and an abolitionist. A member of the French General Assembly after the Revolution representing religious orders, he submitted a proposal to grant citizenship to the inhabitants of French colonies. When Napoleon proposed to reestablish slavery in the colonies, Grégoire, who had become senator, was the only one to vote against it. Many of the missionaries, who had accompanied plantation owners to Saint-Domingue, had ministered a doctrine of obedience and discipline to the slaves. Unwilling to accept this pro-slavery rhetoric, another faction of Catholic priests arose in support of the Haitian government's abolitionist stance. The conflict eventually became too much to manage, and Boyer expelled the leaders of both camps. It was in this context that Grégoire had penned a message to Boyer stating, "The Republic of Haiti, which had seen its way through a storm and elevated itself among the most civilized of nations in the world to become one of the phenomena of the nineteenth century," needed to be careful about the emissaries sent to its territory under the guise of religion. He advocated for a corps of national clergymen.

Boyer concurred. Efforts to nationalize the Catholic Church to ensure that its interests were in line with the principles of the Haitian constitution began with a series of laws to regulate church activity in Haiti; some voted as early as August 1818. They included guidance to ensure the effective administration of parishes, the lowering of taxes on church collections, the refusal to pay clergy salaries as had been done before Boyer, the assignment of clergy by the government to underserved communes, and the dictate that no sacrament could be refused to anyone who asked.

As Boyer saw it, his mandate was to fully execute the constitution of 1816, under which he was elected. Articles 48 and 49 treated the question of religion, stating that the

Haitian State was Roman Catholic, but all residents had the freedom to worship, regardless of their religion. In the spirit of religious freedom, the president welcomed several Baptist congregations to Haiti, who concentrated their efforts in education. However, Boyer and his contemporaries long suspected the Catholic Church to be a usurper, and that its priests were spies on behalf of the Catholic monarchs, sent to breed discontent and fulminate revolutions. Abbe Grégoire had attested to as much in his correspondence to Boyer. He thus established a seminary to train indigenous Catholic priests.

As intended, these measures caught the attention of the Holy See. Monsignor Pierre de Glory was sent to Haiti in 1821 as its apostolic vicar and even presided over the ordination of several apostolates during his visit. However, his presence proved to be divisive, and Boyer sent him away.

In 1822, after annexing Santo Domingo, Boyer moved to transfer the archbishop Monsignor Pedro Valera from there to Port-au-Prince; the latter refused while also protesting civil marriage and divorce, which Boyer had legalized. Valera was eventually expelled in 1830 and died of cholera in Cuba shortly after. Boyer went further in his efforts to weaken Catholic influence in Haiti by nationalizing all church land, consequently leading to the closure of the University of Santo Domingo. In January 1824, after what he thought was sufficient provocation,

Boyer wrote to Pope Leon XII to initiate the negotiation of a concordat, an agreement which would outline Catholic church management and administration in the country. How gratified Boyer must have been when he read the response dated July 1824, "His Excellency Mr. Boyer, President of the Republic of Haiti"—a small win.

18

The French Indemnity

GIVEN THAT THERE WAS virtually no global moral objection to slavery in the eighteenth century, the demand to indemnify France's former plantation owners could be construed as reasonable. Religious institutions, such as the Roman Catholic Church, displayed little appetite to expand their doctrine to include all of humanity. They were, on the other hand, more than willing to send missionaries to slave colonies, preaching submission and salvation from the simple sin of being born. An exceptional missionary sent to Hispaniola was Bartolomé de Las Casas, who became *the* abolitionist of the sixteenth century, advocating for the rights of the indigenous Taino people, who suffered abuses under Spanish rule. De Las Casas made several failed attempts to solicit the intervention of the Vatican in the slave trade.

Later on, in 1789, despite a large number of political assassinations on all sides of the political spectrum, the French National Assembly managed to find the moral superiority to publish the Declaration of the Rights of Man and of the Citizen, which on paper included all human beings, but in practice was only applicable to white male landowners. Neither did its predecessor, the American Revolution of 1776, manage to compel the United States to take the ideological leap of universalizing democratic principles. That didn't begin until 1865, with the passage of the Thirteenth Amendment to its constitution. Even then, all women in the United States, white and black, had to wait several decades longer for the right to vote. The oppressive nature of this precondition was borne by everyone who didn't have aristocratic origins – black and white. It wasn't until the Haitian Revolution in 1791—which germinated because of France's refusal to extend French citizenship to those born in the colonies—that there arose some resistance to the precondition of land ownership to enjoy certain rights, such as the right to vote or participate in politics. Yet this lonely black republic in the Caribbean was subjected to diplomatic containment so as not to contaminate the Latin American and Caribbean slave democracies which surrounded it.

The post-Haitian Revolution period was a turbulent time for Europe. Napoleon's defeat at Waterloo resulted in the Treaty of Paris of 1815, in which France was slapped with an indemnity of 700 million francs and set back to its 1790 borders. Even the Catholic Church confiscated French lands. As a show of good faith, the first installment of 100 million francs was paid in 1817, which initiated efforts by several parties to reset some national borders and, for other countries, to reestablish their monarchical positions. Hence the organization of the Aix-la-Chapelle Congress of 1818. The summit had, as its principal objective, to negotiate lost territory and indemnities, and was attended by countries such as Great Britain, Austria, Russia, Prussia, and France. However, with the American, French, and Haitian revolutions still ripe in everyone's minds, there emerged a movement, among some European leaders, to return to monarchical governance structures; some countries would adopt the hybrid version that we see today of reinstalling their royal families alongside representative political structures. The principal outcomes of the summit were that France would indemnify the "victims" of Napoleon's exploits, to the revised amount of 265 million francs, and remove their occupying forces. There were subsequent summits held in 1820, 1821, and 1822 to finalize border disputes and other claims.

The brooding French monarchy could only think of how easy it would have been to pay the indemnity by paying in kind, with commodities from its beloved Saint-Domingue. The last census taken of Saint-Domingue revealed a semi-mechanized economic system, designed to export exclusively to the French metropole commodities like sugar, cacao, coffee, cotton, leather, and indigo. There were 182 guildives and distilleries, 360 ovens, 29 potteries, and 36 briqueteries (brickworks). Over 8,500 rural properties were identified, along with 16,000 horses and 12,000 cattle, and 4,000 urban properties of various uses. This productive infrastructure was estimated to be valued, not including the slaves, at 1.45 billion francs.[153] Why not ask the Haitians for reimbursement as well?

On the Haitian side, the structure of the economy had not evolved; that is, Haiti was still set up to produce primary commodities for export. Since there was no longer an obligation to send everything to the French metropole, the challenge was to identify new markets. But this challenge was especially difficult for Haiti, as markets were inaccessible without official recognition. France, England, and the United States were open to trade, provided that it was undertaken through their agents, so as to limit contact between their blacks and the free blacks of Haiti. And, of course, there were no diplomatic communications between these governments, nor any government and Haiti. Pétion and Boyer judged this level of commerce as low intensity, given the volume of trade in the world at the time, and they decided that they needed to lead with diplomacy in order to secure new markets and greater volumes—hence Pétion's initial offer to indemnify plantation owners for their confiscated property.

Almost as soon as he returned to Versailles in April 1814, King Louis XVIII appointed a former Saint-Domingue plantation owner named Pierre-Victor Malouet to lead the Ministry of the Marine and Colonies. It is in his memoirs that we read the extent to which the loss of Haiti was an embarrassment for France.

> *Ainsi une calamité générale s'est étendue depuis trois ans en France, sur tous les états; ainsi ont disparu les sources de sa puissance et de sa prospérité; ainsi ont péri sa force militaire et sa considération politique; ainsi se évanouis les 80 millions dont Saint-Domingue avantageait annuellement la balance de son commerce, les ressources que ses ports en tiraient, les débouchés que ce superbe établissement donnait à ses denrées, à ses fabrications, l'aliment qu'il procurait à sa navigation; enfin, la fortune de plus de 20 mille familles, et l'occupation de plusieurs millions d'hommes.[154]*

Malouet assembled a mission of three envoys. The Haitians suspected that the envoys were sent under the guise of an indemnity proposal but were really there to surmise the state and military readiness of the former colony and render an opinion as to whether it could be retaken—a scheme that was confirmed when interministerial communication was found among the envoys' belongings. *La Restauration à Saint-Domingue* was a high-priority mission for the returning Bourbon royal family, and therefore they dispatched Dauxion-Lavaysse as head of this mission to Haiti that arrived in October 1814. In a June 17 letter to the envoys clarifying the mission, Minister of the Marine and Colonies Malouet wrote explicitly that they were expecting "an account of the state of the colony, its leaders and what disposition should be taken to put an end to the anarchy and minimize bloodshed in the establishment of the new royal government."[155] They proposed to Pétion that he accept the sovereignty of the French crown, and, in return, the king would be willing to discuss alternative governance models. Pétion convened his generals and, arriving at a consensus, made the offer to initiate negotiations for an indemnity, in exchange for recognition of the Republic of Haiti: « Les généraux et les magistrats de la République d'Haïti...ne peuvent compromettre leur sécurité et leur existence par aucun changement d'état...je proposerais à Votre Excellence...d'établir la base d'une indemnité convenue, et que nous nous engageons tous solennellement à payer. »[156]

Pétion and his advisors had been monitoring events in Europe. The return of the Bourbons was enough of a red alert that, several months earlier, he communicated with all generals that they should prepare for an eventual attack by the French. And so military preparations had already begun, including a ban on all food exports for the foreseeable future and plans for an additional planting season with the intention of storing tubers for a long war.

One of the three envoys, who went directly to the Kingdom of Northern Haiti, was arrested upon arrival and his belongings searched. King Christophe, for obvious reasons, was wary of both the Spanish and the French. The envoy, named Augustin Franco de Medina, was a Spaniard who had been living in Santo Domingo up until the start of the revolution. Among his personal effects were details of a plan to kill the recalcitrant blacks of Haiti in order to facilitate the repossession of the island and the importation of slaves. The cynical Christophe went through the mechanics of setting up a trial, only to execute him. King Louis XVIII was embarrassed and publicly disavowed the mission. The French laid low until 1816.

In October 1816, two warships, *La Flore* and *Le Railleur*, each bearing twenty cannons, appeared in the Port-au-Prince harbor. Among the soldiers disembarked the Secretary to the Minister of the Marine Charles François Hyacinthe Esmangart, who had participated in the Leclerc expedition. He was accompanied by de Laujon, a frequent visitor to Haiti. Between 1805 and 1814, de Laujon wrote several pamphlets advocating for France to retake Haiti. On this mission, he was to report on the general administration of the colony.

Their arrival made the country uneasy—it coincided with Bolívar's visit; General Mina of Mexico had just left a few days earlier, and there were Mexicans and Spanish Creoles circulating throughout the country. In a way, Haiti was the ideal place to hide out if one was staging a rebellion. Nevertheless, the French agents were received in a manner befitting their positions, though Pétion did not personally meet with them. The negotiations were undertaken via correspondence. This time the offer was constitutional sovereignty, which Pétion rejected. The only concession made by Pétion was to allow the return of French traders, under the French flag.[157]

By 1819, France was overwhelmed with debt. The *Niles' Weekly Register*[158] estimated that France's debt during the 1818/19 fiscal year was 307 million francs, with previous indemnity payments to its allies ranging from 108 million to 319 million between the years 1815 to 1818. So it came as no surprise that, in December 1819, the Haitian public received word from a Jamaican periodical that a French lieutenant colonel named Guillermin—a former plantation owner who had retreated to Santo Domingo after 1804 and was present when Dessalines attempted to annex the east—was willing to lead forces to retake the island and was actively advocating to launch the invasion from Santo Domingo. He claimed that certain French companies were willing to finance the effort under the promise that he could assemble twenty-five thousand soldiers. Propaganda or not, it made Haitians uneasy.

The Guillermin plan was real: He had formally petitioned the crown to sanction it. France's languishing economy was directly tied to the loss of its economic motor, Saint-Domingue, he argued:

« *l'inertie du commerce de la France, l'encombrement de ses manufactures, l'inaction de ses ouvriers, l'état languissant de sa marine, l'exubérance de sa population, exigent impérieusement le rétablissement de ses grandes colonies; il faut hâter de se rendre ses puissants véhicules de prospérité.* » [159]

By September 1821, the *Niles' Weekly Register* reported France's external debt at 263.9 million francs.[160] Haiti, for its part, was just getting by. For that fiscal year, it had registered 3.57 million gourdes in revenue and 3.46 million gourdes in expenditures. Cotton, sugar, and precious wood were the leading export commodities. In that year, an agent named Aubert Dupetit-Thouars arrived in Port-au-Prince with a more nuanced offer: In exchange for the recognition of an independent government, France would extend its military protection to Haiti as suzerain. Boyer, who was now president, counteroffered with an indemnity payment, conditioned by full recognition as a sovereign country. It was refused. For France, there was no amount for which it would relinquish the colony or repair its injured pride.

Just after Haiti annexed the eastern part of the island, in February 1822, the French vessel *Irma* appeared in Haitian waters. French plantation owners, who had retreated to Santo Domingo after France's defeat in Haiti, had written to an Admiral Jacob, stationed in Martinique, a French colony. They sought assistance in recuperating their slaves and transporting them to Martinique.[161] When reinforcements from Jacob arrived, they were met with resistance and left without even trying to berth. In retaliation, Boyer prohibited trade with the French for several months, but the president obviously realized that this wasn't the last mission that France would send and became preoccupied by France's increasing military overtures. He reorganized the national guard, ordered the regular inspection of all arsenals and maintenance on weapons, and mandated additional planting seasons to assure food supplies.

Shortly thereafter, in August 1822, Boyer's old friend, General Jacques Boyé, returned to Haiti. He had saved Boyer's life as a young officer, and the two remained in touch. The president asked Boyé to intervene on Haiti's behalf and negotiate with King Louis XVIII. Even though the last round of negotiations had failed, Secretary Esmangart and Boyer had exchanged several letters, with Esmangart recommending that Boyer send a delegation to France. Boyer thought that Boyé was the right choice—he knew and respected Haitians and he understood better the rapidly evolving political dynamics in France. Upon arriving in the Netherlands, General Boyé wrote to the King of France informing him that he had been named negotiator by President Boyer and that the latter would like to open another round of negotiations. Esmangart was sent again as the king's representative, and they conferred for several days but could not reach an agreement. During the negotiations, Boyé had walked back the offer of an indemnity and attached recognition to preferential trading rights—specifically, a reduction of import tariffs for French commercial vessels from 12 percent to 6 percent.[162] But the indemnity card had already been played, and now it was the French who insisted on it. President Boyer had shared with Boyé that he would even settle for tacit recognition of the country, via the assignment of a diplomatic corps. However, Esmangart countered that bilateral relations could be maintained by commercial representatives and now insisted on the indemnity. General Boyé made a final offer of reducing import tariffs to zero for a period of five years, which also was rejected. Mutually agreeing to close that round of talks, Esmangart wrote to the president proposing that the next time he should send a Haitian delegation.

Then in January 1824, Boyer committed a bargaining misstep: He offered the highest indemnity that he was willing to pay rather than the lowest. De Laujon returned to Haiti with a letter from Esmangart. Despite de Laujon's reputation of being a spy, Boyer received the envoy, who floated the figure of 75 million francs as indemnity; but Boyer, known for his ability to measure his words, uncharacteristically responded that he would give 100 million for recognition. He immediately realized his mistake and made the rest of de Laujon's stay so inhospitable that the latter decided to leave. But the benchmark was set.

Afterwards, Boyer sent new negotiators to France: Larose, a senator, and Rouanez, a notary public. They were instructed to negotiate a lower offer, but the French changed course at these negotiations. In a last effort to retain some form of influence over their former colony, the French offered recognition of "internal sovereignty" in exchange for the king's protection. Ironically, this was the offer that Louverture had made to Napoleon: that Saint-Domingue would be self-governing *and* remain as part of the French Empire. There was even talk of a military base, and a request that Haiti cede the eastern part of the island. The Haitian emissaries had no choice but to return to the offer of 100 million francs, and the king counter-offered with 150 million. There was no deal, and nine months went by without any correspondence between the countries.

The hesitancy with which France approached the indemnity issue was intimately tied to its diverse configuration of political interests. International commerce now had many actors, some of whom traded regularly with Haiti using foreign ships. The growth of private wealth, unassociated with the French monarchy, necessitated the creation of banks and investor groups looking for the next best opportunity. There remained also the old aristocracy of Saint-Domingue plantation owners, some of whom had been nearly ruined by the Haitian Revolution and others who had lost entire families in the war. This group pressed the crown for full restitution—the military solution was the only solution, not an indemnity.

A widely circulated monograph published in March of 1822, which the former plantation owners used to advocate for a military intervention, argued against any further negotiations for indemnity and the immediate repossession of Saint-Domingue. In addition to the natural wealth of the island, the expropriated Frenchmen argued that mulattos and blacks were not capable of self-governance: « C'est un proverbe dans toutes les Antilles, que les mulâtres ont tous les défauts, tous les vices des deux couleurs, sans avoir aucune de leurs qualités: ils le prouvent tous les jours. » [163] They also argued that, unlike what had transpired in Saint-Domingue, the right to property in the former British and Spanish colonies was respected: « En Amérique, on a voulu s'affranchir du joug de la métropole; mais les propriétaires n'y ont point été dépouillés, on y a respecté la propriété, l'humanité, la morale, la religion. » [164] Finally, they insisted that the mulattos were pressing negotiations because they found themselves in the same position as the plantation owners: outnumbered by those they intended to subjugate: « Mais sait-on pourquoi les mulatres veulent négocier, c'est parce qu'ils craignent d'être égorgés par les noirs, parce qu'ils espèrent que l'alliance de la France augmenterait leur force et ils auraient plus de facilité pour tyranniser les noirs. »[165]

But by 1824, the military solution was no longer an option. Among the concessions made in the Treaty of Paris (1814), which ended the Napoleonic Wars, was Article 8 which stipulated that France would be restored its possessions of 1792—a plan pushed back to 1790, after Napoleon escaped from prison and attempted to retake the empire—and this expressly included Santo Domingo (the eastern part of the island). Article 17 of the treaty, referring to native inhabitants of overseas possessions, stated that residents had six years to move to other lands falling under the jurisdiction of their respective empire should they find themselves in the situation where the colony in which they were living had changed ownership.

The native inhabitants and aliens, of whatever nation and condition they may be, in those countries which are to change Sovereigns, as well in virtue of the present Treaty as of the subsequent arrangements to which it may give rise, shall be allowed a period of six years, reckoning from the exchange of the Ratifications, for the purpose of disposing of their property, if they think fit, whether acquired before or during the present War, and retiring to whatever country they may choose.

Furthermore, in an annex to the Treaty of Paris, France and

the United Kingdom signed a separate agreement that the former would commit to reorganizing its operations so that, within a five-year period, any slave commerce happened only within its jurisdiction and not internationally.

> *His Most Christian Majesty, concurring without reserve in the sentiments of His Britannic Majesty, with respect to a description of traffic repugnant to the principles of natural justice and of the enlightened age in which we live, engages to unite all his efforts to those of His Britannic Majesty, at the approaching Congress, to induce all the Powers of Christendom to decree the abolition of the Slave Trade, so that the said Trade shall cease universally, as it shall cease definitely, under any circumstances, on the part of the French Government, in the course of 5 years; and that, during the said period, no slave merchant shall import or sell slaves, except in the colonies of the State of which he is a subject.*[166]

However these articles were interpreted, by 1824, the designated time frames for both articles had expired. Santo Domingo had been integrated into the Republic of Haiti in 1822, and the return to a slave-based plantation model was now out of the question.[167]

Then in July 1825, thirteen French warships carrying 528 cannons[168] appeared at the port of Port-au-Prince. King Louis XVIII had died in 1825 and was succeeded by his brother Charles X, who sent as head of the expedition, the

Baron de Mackau.[169] Mackau presented a decree by Charles X dated 17 April 1825: The ports of the French part of Saint-Domingue were open to all countries (putting an end to mercantilism twenty years after it had already ended). Tariffs would be equal for all countries, except for France, which would be lowered to half. And the inhabitants of the French part of Saint-Domingue should pay in five installments over the course of five years the sum of 150 million francs; the first payment being due on 31 December 1825. In return, the crown conceded the independence of the Haiti.

Again, as in the past, France's own indebtedness would orient its relations with Haiti. The French Bourbon royal family had participated in the Battle of Trocadero (1823), which reinstated their cousin, the King Ferdinand VII of Spain, who had been dethroned by Napoleon and kept in jail by other social factions wanting to convert to a constitutional republic. But this military campaign worsened France's debt position. Its debt-to-GDP ratio rose to 40 percent in 1825, and it was obliged to issue bonds to pay its own indemnities. The Haitians would not have made an indemnity offer without having some reserves. King Charles X took a chance.

Boyer convened his cabinet and the highest-ranking military officers to debate the king's proposal and offered to recuse himself from discussion so that everyone would feel free to express themselves. Secretary of State Finances Imbert presided over the discussions, which included Secretary of State Inginac, Chief Justice Fresnel, several senators, and military generals. It was 7 July 1825. The cabinet concluded consentiently that Boyer should accept the royal decree; the Senate concurred. Boyer addressed the public after the announcement of the Senate vote: "For 22 years, we renew the vow to live freely or die. Now we will add to this vow, another one dear to our hearts, that I hope will be favorably sanctioned by the heavens, that the agreement will bind us together forever, the French and the Haitians."[170]

But Boyer still had to convince the military hierarchy, many of whom had fought in the war against France. General Bonnet noted in his memoirs that they were divided into two factions. The opposing faction was led by the widely admired General Borgella, who was against the payment but deferred to Boyer's authority, saying, "What you decide to do is the best thing to do." With this simple concession, he unknowingly kept Boyer in power for another nineteen years.

While it is true to say Boyer formally had the full backing of his cabinet and the Senate to sign the agreement, it is not true to say that Haitian leaders were entirely happy with the arrangement. Haitian historian Thomas Madiou fils commented that the decree did have a different tone about it: « Les termes de l'ordonnance de 1825 blessèrent la dignité nationale, et l'on se manifesta contre l'indemnité dictée par une ordonnance au lieu d'être consentie par un traité. ». When Pétion made the offer of indemnity, it was conciliatory and, more importantly, consensual. This decree, however, touched the national dignity.

Inaction by the United States of America should not be interpreted as indifference. President John Quincy Adams had discussed the issue with his cabinet, and Haitian recognition had been introduced for congressional vote several times but was defeated by representatives from slave states. Adams spent as much time in politics as Boyer and was an early abolitionist. He served as Secretary of State (1817-1825), then president alongside Boyer (1825-1829), then Congressman from 1831 to 1848. He had defended the slaves from the Amistad – a slave ship upon which the Africans had mutinied and killed most of the crew. Paradoxically, Haiti accepting to pay France for its recognition signaled to the United States that it was no longer autonomous. Adams said, in a congressional speech in 1830:

According to that arrangement, if we possess correct information of its terms, the parent country acknowledges a nominal independence in the colony, and, as part of the price of this acknowledgement, Hayti agree to receive forever the produce of France at a rate of duty one half below that which is exacted, in the ports of

Hayti, from all other nations. This is a restriction upon the freedom of its action, to which no sovereign power, really independent, would ever subscribe.[171]

Adams articulated America's official stance on the Haiti issue. Yet, his diary entries signaled that it was more than a political matter; he may have found slavery distasteful but that didn't mean that blacks were capable of self-governance. In July 1827, Adams received a visit from the commercial agent assigned to Haiti, Andrew Armstrong.

He has been recalled in consequence of the refusal of President Boyer, and his Government to recognize him as the Agent, unless he should be formally accredited in that character— This has been declined on our part, as implying a recognition of the Independence of the Haytian Government. Armstrong has been there several years with an informal character in which they acquiesced until recently when the French and English Governments have appointed Consuls General to reside there. Since which President Boyer will hold no intercourse with an informal agent from the United States.[172]

A few months later, Armstrong was being considered for another post, and Adams wrote in his diary:

I left the determination to him, but acknowledged my

own propensity in favour of Andrew Armstrong,
heretofore commercial Agent at Port au Prince—recalled
thence because the tawny government of Hayti would no
longer recognize him inasmuch as we declined to
recognize them.[173]

One year onwards, the indemnity was still being hotly debated among Haitians. The Borgella faction had been meeting regularly at Ardouin's father's house, since the Ardouins and the Borgellas were intimate families. The idea was floated that they should assassinate Boyer and place Borgella as president. But the opposition remained superficial and didn't go beyond meetings and periodic publications arguing that Boyer had sold the country back to France. Under the leadership and loyalty of General Borgella, the army fell in line.

It is also probable that Boyer and his cabinet likely had no intention of paying the entirety of the 150 million francs—they simply needed to get those thirteen warships out of their harbor. And since they didn't know how many more ships were stationed at Guadeloupe and Martinique, there is evidence of this intention of reneging on the treaty in the last line of a letter the cabinet sent to Boyer to communicate their broad approval: "In any event, acceptance of this royal decree in its present form doesn't diminish or destroy the ability of the government and its means to resist all efforts to undermine it."[174] Boyer, in fact, had sent the French mission back with a formal request to the king to reduce the indemnity.

In November 1825, the government of Haiti contracted a loan for the first payment of 30 million francs from a consortium of French investors,[175] creating essentially two types of debt: the indemnity owed to the plantation owners and the interest owed to private creditors. Given the last inventory of the colony, Haiti did not struggle to find credit. From a creditor's perspective, this was a low-risk loan—the Haitians were surely wealthy and more so because they no longer had to pay off the extra layer of bureaucracy that comes with colonial administration. Haiti borrowed the 30 million, under the following terms: 6 percent interest over ten years, totaling 12 million francs, after which the interest rate would decrease to 3 percent annually. Less various administrative fees, the loan came to 24.3 million francs, and Boyer added 6 million francs that had been found in King Christophe's fortress.

The next indemnity payment wouldn't be made until 1849.

***

Haiti just could not raise the funds. It didn't make payments on the remaining balance of the indemnity, it didn't make payments on the principal borrowed, and it didn't even make the interest payments on the loan. In total, its debt amounted to 158.9 million francs, 8.9 million representing unpaid interest and fees. In fact, the Haitian government was never in a position to make the payments as prescribed in the royal decree—the country was just breaking even every year. For the first half of Boyer's presidency, Haiti ran a slight trade deficit of the equivalent of $1 million, and from 1830 onwards, the trade balance was positive but modestly so, also around $1 million.

Coffee exports kept Haiti afloat, despite great variation in international prices during the forty years post-Haitian independence. The beginning years of Boyer's presidency were excellent years to be a coffee exporter; the only time international prices had been higher was when Haiti was still a French colony. In 1826, coffee exports represented 77 percent of total exports. Eventually and unfortunately for Boyer, the price of coffee began to fall steadily, losing approximately 66 percent of its value during his first decade in office. The meager revenues were enough to cover the government's operations and not much else. However, towards the end of Boyer's presidency Haiti did benefit from a modest rebound of coffee prices, which coincided with some political distress with the lower chamber in Parliament, the Chamber of Communal Representatives, commonly referred to as the Chamber of Communes.

At the time the consortium of French investors granted

the loan, in 1825, many French economists argued that there was no indication that Haiti would be able to make the indemnity payments. But the French crown needed to save face and also wanted to replicate the British experience with the American colonies. Forty-nine years prior, Great Britain had recognized their independence and benefited greatly from its raw materials, which launched its Industrial Revolution. Whereas Great Britain was flourishing, French economists bemoaned the fall of an empire, likening France to ancient Rome. At a minimum, any payment on the indemnity would provide funds for investment capital and stimulate industry.[176]

Nevertheless, Boyer did intend to renegotiate the treaty to a more reasonable payment schedule—one that involved paying off the principal over a longer period of time, at lower interest rates. In fact, on two occasions, in 1829 and in 1830, the French reached out to offer more favorable terms. Boyer not only rejected those terms but, in 1831, restored original tariff rates for products of French provenance. The instability that characterized the previous forty years of French politics— including the replacement of royal families to the French throne— offered Boyer the opportunity to renounce the treaty, and he was not one to neglect opportunities. He would wait for a better offer.

King Charles X oppressed civil society, issuing, for example, a series of decrees that included dissolving the lower chamber in Parliament and restricting the liberties of the press. In the July Revolution of 1830, the French populace demanded his abdication for attempting to subvert what had evolved into a constitutional monarchy and revert to the absolutist rule that he had known in his youth. He was replaced by a cousin, Louis-Philippe d'Orléans, nick-named the "Citizen King."

Boyer hoped that the change in leadership would create more favorable conditions for Haiti. In fact, as soon as he received word of the new monarch's installation, Boyer tried again to renegotiate the terms. King Louis-Philippe, an age mate of Boyer's, was more receptive of Haiti's claims that its tariff revenue made it impossible to uphold its commitment to the plantation owners and its creditors. And finally, in February 1838, he offered more favorable terms, as did the financiers: The balance on the indemnity was halved to 60 million francs from 120 million, now payable over thirty years, without further interest payments on the balance other than what was contracted for the original loan of 30 million. The creditors agreed to accept payment of 1 million francs annually towards interest on the original loan.

Still no payments were made—but not for trying. Boyer was the most economical president the world has ever seen. Both his contemporaries and Haitian historians have written about his refusal to spend public resources other than on military salaries. Government expenditures were kept to a minimum, fluctuating between 2.6 and 2.9 million gourdes. Boyer even donated one year of his salary to the cause, as indicated in the following letter.

En faisant faire dernièrement à la Chambre une communication relative aux mesures à adopter pour la libération des engagements contractés au nom de la République, à l'occasion de la reconnaissance de l'Indépendance d'Hayti, j'annonçai l'intention que j'avais déjà conçue de contribuer personnellement à la liquidation de cette dette. Maintenant, je déclare que pour cet objet je fais don de la valeur d'une année de mes appointements (G. 40.000). Je dois ajouter ici que des sacrifices pécuniaires sont peu de choses pour le citoyen vraiment patriote et que tout bon haytien doit être toujours prêt à périr s'il le faut, en défendant la liberté et l'indépendance de sa patrie.
Port-au-Prince, le 5 avril 1826, an 23e de l'Indépendance

Then came the earthquake of 1842, which destroyed much of the North. The government of Haiti asked for a delay in payment. Again, in 1843 payments were interrupted by the coup d'etat against Boyer. Political instability continued to disrupt payments in the ensuing years, and a new agreement had to be negotiated. A final agreement on the indemnity, under Haiti's President Faustin Soulouque, was signed on 12 February 1848. According to that agreement, the 1843 payment would be made by the end 1848, and France would no longer pay tariffs on its trade with Haiti, giving some relief to the French merchants, but the government of Haiti would use half of its tariff revenue, presumably from other countries, to pay the indemnity. This time the agreement was based on real-time tariff revenues, those of 1845, which were valued at approximately 5.6 million francs. The five years of nonpayment amounted to 8.1 million francs annually and would be payable from 1868 onwards. Normal repayment would begin in 1849. Most importantly in this agreement, the debt-servicing fees—that is, what was owed to creditors—would not be paid until the indemnity itself was paid.[177]

Despite not making payments for three additional years—between 1867 and 1870, due to another civil war— Haiti finally made the last indemnity payment in 1883, fifty-eight years after the imperial ordinance of recognition.

How did life change for Haitians after the long-sought-after royal decree? French recognition signaled to other European countries that they could openly trade with Haiti, without incurring the risk of reprisal. The city-state of Bremen (now part of Germany) was among the first to emerge and send a consul in January 1826. Denmark, the Netherlands, Prussia, and Sweden sent consuls soon afterwards. Haiti had to wait until 1839 to receive the British ambassador; until 1841, for Belgium.

Even Spain, still hoping to retake the eastern part of the island but recognizing the fact that France was no longer in a position to give it to them, sent Brigadier General Don Felipe Fernández de Castro, the governor of the slave colony Cuba, to Haiti in February 1830. According to historical accounts, he was politely received, but he returned to Cuba empty-handed. Boyer did not mince words in a public proclamation dated 6 February 1830 in response to the Spanish demand.[178]

When the glorious resistance by Haitians forced the enemy to capitulate, wasn't it incontestable that this people would consider and declare, in the interest of self-conservation and preservation of its future, the whole territory as its property? ... That the vow to defend the entire country be in your hearts a sacred obligation and that the tree of liberty that I had the joy of planting among you grow forever with deep, indestructible roots.

The Haitian currency, the gourde, was now officially recognized. The gourde was actually a variation of the Spanish piastra—there were several different versions depending on the amount of gold in the coin—which was, at this point in international trade, a universally accepted currency. Letters of credit soon replaced the need to transfer large sums of gold species across the ocean. However, overspending could not be hidden. If a country's gold reserves diminished, that reduced its capacity to contract internationally. After paying the first installment of the indemnity, Haiti had nearly nothing left in its treasury. So Boyer issued a paper version of the gourde in September 1826, which was on par with the United States dollar. It was fairly well managed, considering it wasn't backed by any gold. It was probably one of the first currencies whose value was driven solely by expectations. Furthermore, with a view to replenishing the public treasury, Boyer ordered that foreign commerce agents were obliged to pay tariffs in species—one of the gold currencies—and the paper money was used for internal transactions. By 1842, one year before Boyer's fall, the gourde was worth one-third of the US dollar.[179]

To support the gourde, Boyer and his cabinet ensured that there was little wastage and no unnecessary expenditures. Public revenue per capita increased from ten francs to fourteen francs during Boyer's tenure,[180] and the debt-to-GDP ratio, which was 285 percent in 1825, had declined to 155 percent by 1840—three years before the coup against Boyer—and to 40 percent by 1860, despite the indemnity payments.[181]

***

Even before it had paid off the indemnity, Haiti began to borrow again—and irresponsibly so. In 1875, its external debt was about 16 million francs because of a loan taken out by President Michel Domingue, which raised its external debt to 44 million francs. Then, in 1895, President Simon Sam took out a loan of 39 million francs, presumably for public works. And in 1910, five years before the American occupation of Haiti, at the height of political instability, there was another loan of 65 million francs taken out, which wasn't paid off until 1961.[182] When the Americans invaded Haiti in 1915, its external debt amounted to 113.3 million francs ($22.6 million), higher than the indemnity.[183] Bizarrely, US-occupied Haiti took out more loans and in 1919 its external debt had reached the equivalent of $40 million.

In lieu of investment in productive capital, Haiti's principal expenditures were mainly to service debt and support the military, and trade tariffs were increased accordingly to meet these rising costs of doing so. The tax on imports, which had reached a high of 16 percent under Boyer in 1826, was increased to 26 percent in 1863, rising to 36 percent by the end of that decade.[184]

But Haiti wasn't alone in their debt management troubles. There was a financial crash in London in 1825, when the Bank of England raised interest rates to stem the flow of capital out of the country. The effects of the crash extended throughout Europe and Latin America, where several governments had floated bonds on the English market to finance infrastructure investment. International commerce slowed, and Argentina, Brazil, Colombia, Chile, Mexico, and Peru all subsequently defaulted on their external debts, unable to make payments as their tariff revenue from commodity exports fell.

Somewhat shielded by this depression in international commerce, partially due to its political isolation, Haiti's gross domestic product rose steadily during this repayment period.[185] Nevertheless, the austerity measures imposed on the Haitian people to meet the government's repayment obligations must have been difficult. Its adverse impacts and those of the subsequently contracted loans are better understood from the perspective of opportunity cost. What was odious about the French indemnity, and the opaque loans undertaken by Haitian leaders, is the social opportunity cost of debt servicing—that is, the foregone opportunities for infrastructure development and investments in human capital. This deliberate underdevelopment of Haiti is best examined in comparison to the younger Latin American republics, despite their early sovereign debt defaults in the 1820s.[186] As early as 1910, whereas the ratio of railroad miles per ten thousand people was between 8.0 and 8.6 in the Caribbean and South America, it was only 0.4 in Haiti, 106 years after independence. The 1910 ratios are similar for communication infrastructure: The ratio of telegraph miles per ten thousand people was 20.5 and 40.1 in Caribbean and South American countries against 0.7 in Haiti. Its population also began to explode, exerting pressure on social services. By 1910, Haiti had 152.8 people per square mile, while the Dominican Republic had 35.9, the greater Caribbean had 25.9, and South America had 8.2.[187] While Haiti was preoccupied with paying off the French indemnity, the slave-intensive colonies on either side, Cuba and Puerto Rico, were performing quite well. Their sugar output, which ranged from 55 percent to 80 percent of total exports, increased fourteen times as a result of infrastructure investments—particularly with the use of steam-powered mills and railroads to transport the sugar from farm to factory.[188]

In hindsight, the indemnity obviously contributed to Haiti's late technology adoption and suppressed growth. However unchecked population growth, a primary commodity-centered economy, and opaque loan contraction were and continue to be the drivers of underdevelopment in Haiti. Its underwhelming performance and small size are intimately tied to the nature of its consumption (import-intensive) and the fact that exports were increasing at a lower rate than that of the population.[189]

Royal decree of Independence of Haiti and Indemnity Payment, by Charles X of France, on April 17, 1825.[190]

2) Ordonnance du 17 avril 1825 :

« Charles, par la grâce de Dieu, Roi de France et de Navarre, à tous présents et à venir. Salut.

Vu les articles 14 et 73 de la Charte,

Voulant pourvoir à ce que réclament l'intérêt du commerce français, les malheurs des anciens colons de Saint-Domingue et l'état précaire des habitants actuels de cette île,

Nous avons ordonné et ordonnons ce qui suit :

Article 1. Les ports de la partie française de Saint-Domingue seront ouverts au commerce de toutes les nations. Les droits perçus dans ces ports, soit sur les navires, soit sur les marchandises, tant à l'entrée qu'à la sortie, seront égaux et uniformes pour tous les pavillons, excepté le pavillon français en faveur duquel ces droits seront réduits de moitié.

Article 2. Les habitants actuels de la partie française de Saint-Domingue verseront à la Caisse générale des dépôts et consignations de France, en cinq termes égaux, d'année en année, le premier échéant le 31 décembre 1825, la somme de cent cinquante millions de francs, destinée à dédommager les anciens colons qui réclameront une indemnité.

Article 3. Nous concédons, à ces conditions, par la présente ordonnance, aux habitants actuels de la partie française de Saint-Domingue, l'indépendance pleine et entière de leur gouvernement.

Et sera la présente ordonnance scellée du grand sceau.

Donné à Paris, au château des Tuileries, le 17 avril de l'an de grâce 1825, et de notre règne le premier.

Signé Charles

Par le Roi, le Pair de France, ministre secrétaire d'État de la Marine et des Colonies, Comte de Chabrol

Visa : Le Président du Conseil ministre et secrétaire d'État et des finances J. de Villèle	Vu aux sceaux, le ministre secrétaire d'État garde des Sceaux Comte de Peyronnet »

3) Mode d'évaluation du montant de l'indemnité fixée par l'ordonnance de 1825.

Les revenus annuels des propriétés des colons en 1789 étaient évalués, selon un tableau annexé à la loi du 30 avril 1826, à :

48.822.404 francs pour le sucre
70.299.731 francs pour le café
25.542.664 francs pour le coton, l'indigo et autres produits
Total :   144.664.799 francs
Plus :   5.000.000 francs pour les propriétés urbaines
Ensemble arrondi à : 150.000.000 francs

Outre-Mers, T. 90, N° 340-341 (2003)

Note: Author's charts based on data culled from a
variety of sources.

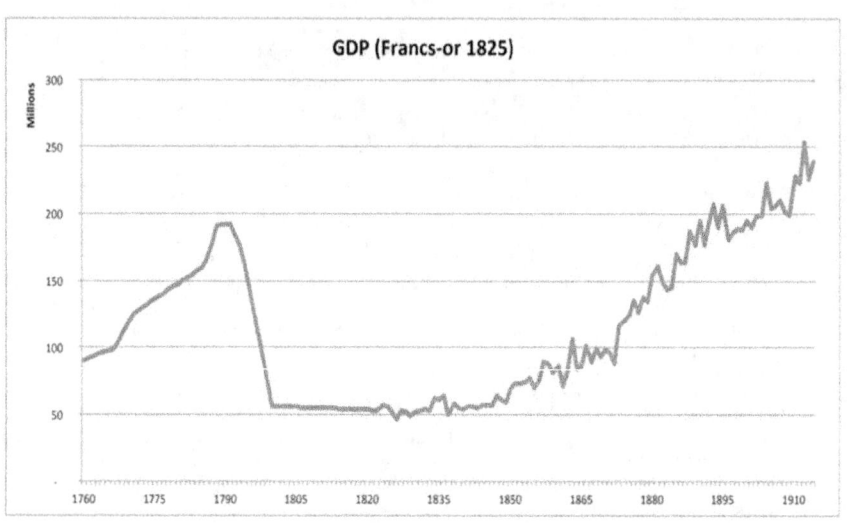

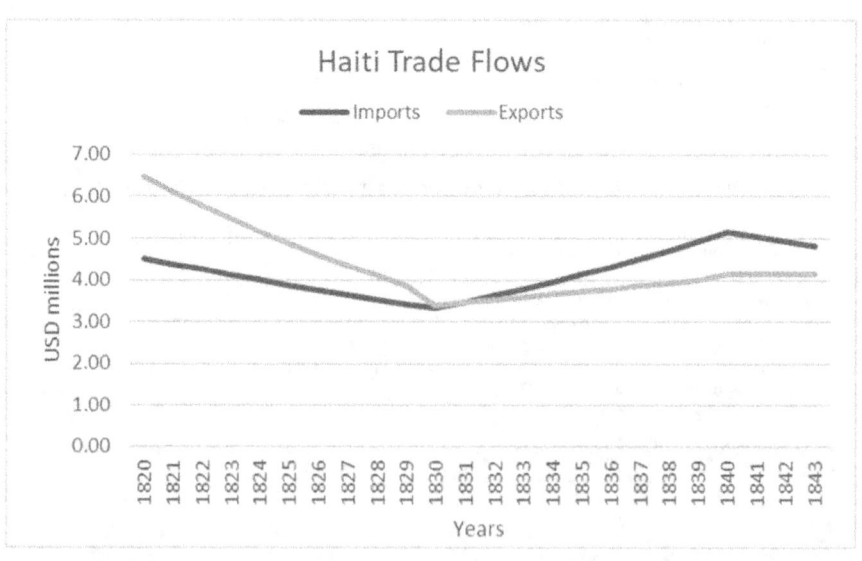

19

Unification of the Island

IT WOULD BE TOO EASY to conclude that Boyer was an autocrat who merely used good political reflexes to unite the island into one administrative entity. While this may be partially—even entirely—true, Boyer also had the constitutional mandate to do so. The project that was Haiti—the first blacks to free themselves from enslavement and charter their own futures—entailed the entire island and predated Boyer's presidency by seventeen years. As first referred to in its Declaration of Independence of 1804, the Indigenous Army gave the country the name Haiti after the Taino name for the island, Ayiti—the same appellation used in Haitian creole—and the declaration makes specific reference to the abolition of slavery on the entire island. That Dessalines did not negotiate with Rochambeau the transition of power in the Eastern department was an oversight on the former's part, perhaps as a result of inexperience. The subsequent constitutions of 1807 and 1816 both, in their geopolitical descriptions of the country, refer to the entire island of Haiti.

Shortly after the peace treaty with the French, Dessalines had attempted to take the eastern region militarily and failed. Pétion maintained good relations with the East, which had slipped back into Spanish hands by the time he became president, with the hope of reuniting the island. Not only was Pétion unable to recover the East, but the western part had been severed into three autonomously governed units during his presidency. In this sense, Boyer fulfilled the dream of the liberation leaders: a slave-free and republican island.

Pétion had managed to reincorporate the Sud department after Rigaud passed, but the Northern Kingdom of Haiti remained elusive. King Christophe was formidable—and a strategist. Upon hearing of Pétion's death, rather than communicate his condolences—as he considered the Sud and Ouest departments to be in rebellion—he issued a proclamation granting a royal pardon to all those that recognized him as the legitimate ruler. He also offered a guarantee that property owners would keep their farms, and all military appointments would be honored. In June 1818, he sent three emissaries to present the offer to Boyer, who never responded. Historians wrote that General Gedeon lifted Boyer in front of the emissaries, declaring, "This is the person that we have elected, the only person that we need. Go tell your king that we are determined to die to maintain him as president of the Republic."

Gedeon, whom Boyer once described as "heroic being his steady state," was a battalion chief who served under Dessalines but then, after speaking Pétion , joined the insurrection against him. He was black—and tall. He was promoted to colonel with six hundred grenadiers under his command—after divulging Dessalines' strategy to enter the capital and quash the rebellion. With these same men, in response to King Christophe's 1807 attack on the republic, he pushed back the latter's advance guard of four thousand infantry until he reached their cavalry. Later that year, he found himself in the middle of Colonel Yayou's own insurrection plans. Yayou was a friend, but President Pétion, suspicious of Yayou, had asked Gedeon to keep him informed of Yayou's movements. At a late hour on 22 July 1807, after Gedeon had just dined with Yayou, the revolt, which had already been planned, was launched. Gedeon rapidly assembled his men and went to protect Pétion in his quarters. It would seem that Pétion had momentarily lost faith in Gedeon's loyalty and thought that they had come to kill him, Petion later recounted. For his fealty, Gedeon was rewarded with the rank of general. And it was Gedeon that Pétion sent to the Sud region when Rigaud seceded in 1810. He was one of few generals willing to defend Port-au-

Prince, under Boyer's command, from second assault by Christophe in 1812. In that siege on the capital, Gedeon fought alongside Boyer and had also led the regiment that launched a counterattack to retake a fort that had been lost. Christophe burned alive the prisoners of that battle, so there was no love lost between them. For his service, Gedeon was promoted to division general and placed in command of Léogâne, a coveted port city. In 1815, he was elected to the Senate and was thus one of those who cast a vote for Boyer for the presidency. While the Senate entertained many candidates, including Bonnet and Borgella, Gedeon is rumored to have threatened the other representatives with violence if they didn't vote for Boyer. In fact, Gedeon lived across from Boyer on Rue du Centre in Port-au-Prince, and the two were no doubt friendly. Thus, his declaration to King Christophe's envoys merit attention: He reaffirmed the will of the Sud and Ouest departments to remain united and democratic, that Boyer had been duly elected as president, and that he had the support of the military.

Though the Sud's generals had capitulated, the insurrection led by Goman had not been resolved. Goman and his band of rebels occupied the forests of Grand'Anse and launched periodic attacks on nearby populations. On 8

January 1819, Boyer released a communiqué to reassure the Sud department that the ongoing insurrection there would come to an end because he had resolved to send the force he deemed necessary to realize that goal. It was essentially a final offer to Goman to surrender himself and the territory he occupied or to die. In this same declaration, President Boyer offered amnesty to any and everyone who thought that they might be in need of it and advised the public that the military would severely punish remaining rebels that were unfortunate enough to be captured.

The principal beneficiary of Pétion's military profundity, Boyer crafted a plan to recapture the areas occupied by Goman and chose none other than General Bazelais—the general chief of staff of the Haitian army since Dessalines, the commander of the very communes under attack (Tiburon and Jérémie), the father of Charles Bazelais (who would marry Azema, Boyer's daughter), and the very one who left him hanging during Christophe's siege on Port-au-Prince in 1812—to execute it. Three division generals—Borgella plus Generals Lys and Francisque, who had resigned from the military after the last encounter with Christophe—were reintegrated to second him. The president sent them written instructions, including maps of the areas they were expected to secure. Boyer had decided that the operation would start on 1 February 1819.

By all historical accounts Bazelais' men destroyed everything in their way, burning crops and houses in an attempt to dissuade any and all Goman sympathizers from assisting or sheltering the rebels. Finally, in June 1819, after four months of cat-and-mouse in the Grand'Anse forests, they descended upon Goman, whose scouts had not even the slightest inkling that Bazelais was so near. It is said that he fled with just the clothes that he was wearing. Afterwards, reconnaissance missions found correspondence between King Henry and Goman, who had been graced by the former with the title of Count of the commune of Jérémie. Neither Goman nor his two lieutenants, Malfait and Malfou, were seen or heard from again, nor were their remains ever discovered. Records do show, however, that Boyer, in a show of clemency, integrated Goman's son into the Republican army.

A song to celebrate Boyer's victory was printed in the 15 December 1819 edition of the *Abeille Haytienne*, a fortnightly periodical:

> *Ils sont de retour parmi nous,*
> *Les soutiens de l'Indépendance,*
> *Ils ont abattu sous leurs coups,*
> *Goman, tyran de la Grand'Anse ;*
> *Mais quel est l'illustre guerrier*
> *Qui sut diriger leur courage ?*
> *C'est le juste et prudent Boyer,*
> *Héros vaillant autant que sage.*

("They have returned among us, Those who support independence, They have defeated Goman, the tyrant of the Grand'Anse; But who is the illustrious warrior who led them? It is the just and prudent Boyer, a brave and wise hero.")

Peuple haïtien, people vainqueur,
Poursuit partout la tyrannie,
Et répètes toujours en chœur :
Gloire au héros (bis.) de la patrie (bis.)

("Haitian people, victorious people, pursuing tyranny everywhere, repeat as one" 'Glory to the Heroes of the fatherland.'")

Un suppôt d'un tyran jaloux ;
Depuis treize ans dans la Grand'Anse ;
Avait su braver le courroux
Des héros de l'Independence ;
Mais Boyer, semblable au Dieu Mars,
Lorsqu'en Thrace il vole à la guerre,
Parait, et ces brigands épars,
Tombent au bruit de son tonnerre.

("Partisan [Goman] to a jealous tyrant [Christophe]; for thirteen years in the Grand'Anse; he braved the wrath of the heroes of independence; But Boyer, like the god of Mars, who flies to war, the scattering brigands fall at the sound of his thunder.")

In April 1820, President Boyer hosted a dinner to celebrate the commanders of the Goman expedition. Among those seated at the high table were his old friend Colonel Segretier and Generals Bazelais. After formally inspecting the troops, he addressed the crowd that had gathered outside of the National Palace to get a glimpse of these intrepid generals. "Fifteen months have passed since I made the promise of bringing tranquility to the Grand'Anse region," Boyer began. In a word of caution to future insurgents, he continued, "I warn those who have private ambitions to separate them from the interests of the Haitian family, of which I am the father. I don't wish to use repressive tactics, and even Goman himself would receive a pardon if he gave himself up."

Up north, Christophe's despotism did not win him any fans. And his growing wealth caught everyone's attention. The port of Cap-Haïtien exported, during the year 1819, 15.5 million pounds of coffee, 2 million pounds of cotton, 1.5 million pounds of wood, and 1.2 million pounds of sugar, as well as smaller quantities of cacao and tobacco—approximately 75 percent of what the Republic of Haiti exported from five ports. There were also rumors of gold worth millions of francs stashed in Christophe's elegant palace, Sans Souci, which was built on the side of a mountain from which water flowed naturally and, in turn, irrigated impressive gardens. He was protected by a stone fortress, named Citadelle Laferrière, built at the top of the mountain, costing the lives of an estimated twenty thousand unpaid laborers.

Unfortunately, Christophe had suffered a stroke and was bedridden for some time. As soon as they got word of his incapacity, an insurrection germinated among the more rebellious of his officers in Saint-Marc and swiftly spread north to Cap-Haïtien. Like Dessalines, Christophe didn't see it coming. He had granted so much land and aristocratic titles with the hope that he would be assured of a long, prosperous reign. The rebellion resulted in a number of notable casualties, including his sons. Rather than be taken, King Christophe committed suicide on 8 October 1820. The leaders of the rebellion reached out to the neighboring country, the Republic of Haiti, asking for Boyer's support and recognition. They had planned to remain an independent state and had even selected General Romain as president.

However, Boyer saw that fortuitous communication as an opportunity to unite the country under one flag. With remarkable celerity, considering the preparations required to mobilize an army in those times, he marched his army north. He left Port-au-Prince and took Saint-Marc on the same day, 16 October 1820. Historian Beaubrun Ardouin didn't believe that the inhabitants there were even aware of Christophe's death; it was Boyer that brought them this news. Nevertheless, his peaceful conquest of Saint-Marc was all but guaranteed—he had already printed titles of land concessions for their military officers.

Upon realizing that he had profited from the element of surprise and had taken the plains of Artibonite, Boyer published an announcement on 17 October congratulating the Haitians in the Kingdom of Nord d'Haiti that served the cause of liberty and equality (by leading the rebellion). Officers who had not yet presented their submission, those mostly in Cap-Haïtien, and specifically those who had written to him, were welcomed to do so. "The Haitian state will show clemency." He sent advance warning that "soldiers that will be seen patrolling throughout the Nord" but they were "meant to facilitate conciliation and peace." As he wrote these words, his generals had already secured the inland communes of Verrettes and Hinche. On the eighteenth, he reorganized the army into four columns, all heading north, headed by General Magny (one of Christophe's men who had defected after the last siege on Port-au-Prince), and Generals Borgella, Bonnet, and Noel. On the nineteenth, while en route to Cap-Haïtien, Boyer received the submission of the commander at Gonaïves, the next commune in his path.

Two days later, he wrote to his partner, Joutte Lachenais, "It is impossible to describe what is happening here. Can you imagine living under the most horrible tyranny and suddenly overcome with joy and happiness? This is what I am witnessing here. … I am impatient; I can't wait to get to Cap Haïtien."

Upon hearing that Boyer had already taken Saint-Marc, the military commandment of the Nord sent four representatives from Cap-Haïtien to greet him and make explicit their intention to remain independent but that they welcomed an alliance with the Republic of Haiti. His reaction to their offer is illegible in the letter reprinted by historian Beaubrun Ardouin. The generals' first mistake was in addressing the letter to "Boyer, the President of Sud-Ouest d'Haiti." After that, Boyer was surely seeing red, as he identified himself as the President of Haiti in his response to them, assuring them that his only compass was the Constitution of the Republic of Haiti. He began with the carrot—"The men in the army advancing towards you are brothers and friends"—and ended with the stick: "Anyone opposed to their presence and tries to stop them will be met with the most unfortunate end."

Returning to Boyer's letter to his beloved Joutte, he was obviously undeterred in his ambition because, in the very next sentence to her, he wrote: "I don't want to waste any time; I am going to march on." He comforted her by encouraging her to remain calm: "There will be no unfortunate events". In the midst of a military expedition, he expressed his joy at having received letters from all his children and asked her to encourage them to write to him often, ending the letter with "I love you. ... All for you, Boyer."

J'étais hier, il est vrai, amplement dédommagé par les témoignages d'affection que le peuple me prodigua, mais je sens que mes forces m'abandonneraient déjà si l'amour de ma patrie n'enflammait de plus en plus mon zèle. Te peindre ce qui se passe ici est une chose impossible. La plus horrible tyrannie rendue tout à coup à la joie et au bonheur, tu auras encore une faible idée des scènes attendrissantes dont je suis témoin. Mon impatience est à son comble; déjà je voudrais être au Cap. J'ai reçu ce matin quatre députés du Cap (3) que je viens d'expédier avec quatre de mes aides de camp (4). L'intention des chefs de cette partie de (de l'île) est d'être alliés avec nous, mais d'avoir un gouvernement séparé. Je ne perds donc pas de temps, je brave tout et marche en avant. Sois tranquille, il n'y aura rien de fâcheux.

Saint-Marc, 18 octobre 1820, à 11 du soir

On 22 October, when all columns were near Plaisance, less than 50 kilometers south of Cap-Haïtien, Boyer wrote to the Northern generals that his actions were guided by "reconciliation and consolidation," as directed by the only guiding document that mattered, the Declaration of Independence of the Republic of Haiti, which was signed by Northerners as well as Southerners. The columns that were advancing would not fire a shot unless they were fired upon, and, in such a case, they were ordered "to unleash hell."

Less than a week later, on 26 October 1820 at 8 a.m., Boyer marched into Cap-Haïtien. "Children of the same family," he addressed the crowd, "I assure you that you will be protected by the shade of the sacred tree of freedom. Let us forget the past and ask the Lord to inspire us with ideas of peace and wisdom so that we can leave behind for our children, an assured existence, a free and independent country."

By 10 a.m., he was at his desk writing to his beloved Joutte. It is here we see the degree of mindfulness that he possessed of these historic events: "I am sensitive to all that I see in this memorable era. Fate, in choosing me to lead these extraordinary and happy events, seemed not to have given me the strength I need to match the courage that I have. While I have a burning passion to serve my country, my strength dwindles. All my glory is attributed to the pacification of the Nord, while not having shed one drop of blood."

Depuis environ deux heures, je suis en possession de cette ville, et mon premier moment de loisir est consacré à m'entretenir avec toi. Mon âme est émue à un tel point que les expressions me manquent pour te donner une idée de ce qui s'est passé à mon entrée ici. Les larmes veulent couler de mes yeux en t'écrivant ces lignes. J'ai trop de sensibilité pour tout ce que je vois dans cette mémorable époque. La Providence, en me réservant pour diriger des événements si extraordinaires et si heureux, semble n'avoir pas proportionné mes forces au courage dont elle m'a doué; car je brûle d'ardeur pour servir la patrie, tandis qu'elles semblent s'affaiblir. Toute ma gloire est d'avoir surmonté des difficultés infinies pour la pacification du Nord, sans avoir à déplorer qu'une goutte de sang ait été versé. Ah ! ma chère Joutte, je croirais avoir déjà assez vécu, si je n'avais ma famille que j'aime et qui a besoin de mes soins. Azéma, Fine, Antoinette, Célie, Coquièrine (1), trouveront ici l'expression de l'attachement que j'ai pour elles. J'ai reçu leurs lettres, dis-leur de continuer de m'écrire, elles me feront le plus grand plaisir. Quant à ma bien chère Hersilie qui est toujours présente à mon esprit, couvre-la de baisers pour moi, parle-lui de son cher papa et prends-en, le plus grand soin. Sois heureuse, ma chère et bien-aimée compagne, je t'aime et t'embrasse de toute mon âme.

Cap, 26 octobre 1820, à 10 heures du matin

He wouldn't see Joutte again until 17 December, two months after he had left.

It was an emotional reunion with the city of Cap-Haïtien; the last time he was there was in 1802 when he was nearly drowned by the French. Boyer toured the northern part of the country until December 1820, without incident.

After fourteen years in power, the aristocratic class that had emerged under Christophe's reign was not amenable to the republican values articulated by Boyer. Boyer's promise "to create an equal society" mortified them, as they envisioned their imminent dispossession of land. Unsurprisingly, as early as February 1821 there were armed insurrections against Boyer, and he handled them all the same way: decisively and summarily. All insurgents were executed.

***

Nevertheless, the instability in the Nord was such that Boyer was obliged to conduct a second tour of the region; this time with Father Jérémie, a Roman Catholic priest of the parish of Port-au-Prince. Saint-Marc, Gonaïves, Cap-Haïtien, Fort Liberté, Ouanaminthe, and Môle Saint-Nicolas were among the communes visited. It was on this voyage that he was approached by inhabitants on the Spanish side about unifying the island.

The French maintained possession of the eastern part, even after signing the peace agreement with Dessalines. An administrative error on the part of the Indigenous Army, there was no specific reference in the agreement to the island of Saint-Domingue, though Toussaint Louverture had already taken it from Napoleon. And it was in fact this annexation which provoked the massive dispatch of warships in 1802. Subsequent documents published, such as the constitutions of 1807[191] and 1816, clearly refer to the island of Haiti. Nevertheless, the French and other Europeans who had fled to the Spanish side promptly built fortifications to prevent a Dessalines-led incursion, re-established slavery, and didn't leave that region until July 1809 amid a war between France and Spain. The latter then attempted to retake their colony but were met with resistance by the inhabitants, some of whom were former slaves; others were European traders that had resettled during the Haitian revolution. In truth, Santo Domingo at this time was in a governance limbo. Some corners wanted to return to the Spanish kingdom; others want to be independent (they were led by Nunes de Cacérès); others wanted to join the Republic of Colombia, whose independence movement led by Bolívar was gaining traction in the region; and yet others wanted to join the Republic of Haiti.

There were multiple and opposing pressures building in Latin America and the Caribbean. The United Kingdom had abolished the practice of importing slaves, as well as the mercantilist system. Free trade was now gaining momentum. Spain was experiencing democratic pressures at home, King Ferdinand XII having been deposed twice. It was also under pressure to provide military support to its colonies, who were fighting off sequential slave revolts as well as colonial independence movements inspired by the American, French, and Haitian revolutions. And then there was the successful Bolivarian independence movement. Spain simply was not in a position to retake its former colony, and Boyer had taken note.

The president had other preoccupations as well. In November 1821, an American ship, carrying three representatives from the community of San Fernando de Monte Christi pulled into the Cap-Haïtien harbor. General Magny, whom Boyer had left in command of the Nord department, learned from them that several demonstrations had taken place and that the Haitian flag was already flying in northern Santo Domingo regions.

Dominican writer and revolutionary leader José Núñes de Cacérès (1772–1846) learned of the ship's arrival at Cap-Haïtien and decided to move first, within a month taking the capital of Santo Domingo and relieving the Spanish governor, Pascual Real, of his duties. They promptly hoisted the Colombian flag to replace the Spanish flag. At this point in Latin American history, the Republic of Gran Colombia, which occupied the north-west region of the South America. This symbolic gesture was meant to convey the desire for independence from Spain, which they promptly declared. Cacérès, a Creole and a contemporary of Boyer, had apparently caught the liberation fever that had spread throughout the region. But Cacérès had a difficult task: How was he going to unite a comparatively small population of approximately 70,000 on 50,000 square kilometers (twice the landmass of the western part of the island) around the idea of becoming a part of Gran Colombia, where slavery had not yet been abolished, when next door lay a formidable army who, based on very recent historical events, considered the entire island theirs, having won it militarily on the basis of slave emancipation?

Indeed Cacérès' actions mobilized his political opponents. Some of the Dominican communities like Monte Christe and Laxabon (now Dajabón), wrote again to Magny asking for munitions and protection. [192] Those letters were soon followed by similar requests from Azua, Saint-Yague, Neybe, Saint Jean, and Porte Plate, who, in addition to expressing a desire to be part of the Republic of Haiti and "submitting to its laws," affirmed their intention not to return to slavery. The commander of Porte Plate, Antonio Lopez Villanueva, also wrote separately that they were against Cacérès' declaration of independence in favor of Colombia and "were eager to collaborate as friends, as brothers." The *Niles' Weekly Register* had already heard about the political realignments happening in Santo Domingo. On 29 December 1821, it was reported: "It is stated that the city of St. Domingo in the island of St. Domingo or Hispaniola, alias Hayti, has surrendered to 'the patriots.'"[193]

Haitian sociologist Jean Price Mars cautioned against

interpreting these testimonies of loyalty as popular sentiments. The vast majority of settlers in the eastern part were largely indifferent to who was governing them. The Haitian army, estimated to be 20,000 would not have seen much resistance. The War of Independence and subsequent civil conflicts had not disturbed their traditional livelihoods of cattle raising and wood trade. The leaders who wrote to Boyer were worried about their political futures and thought the best way to secure them would be to align themselves with the nearest, powerful army.

"Dear Senators," Boyer wrote on Christmas Day in 1821, "article 40 of our Constitution sets the administrative limits of our Republic to include the entire island and even the adjacent smaller islands. It was necessary therefore to reach out to our brothers in the East to orient them towards a uniform administration." He went on to describe that there were other forces that were oppositional to the "natural direction" of the political future of the island—he was referring to the declaration of independence of Santo Domingo that Cacérès had published on the first of the month—and insisted that he had to undertake a "moral revolution" to bring them back on course *and* to preserve Haitian independence. "If the responsibility of the public tranquility and the maintenance of the integrity of the state falls on me, it falls on you Senators. I submit to you that, in order to preserve its independence, there needs to be a unified and indivisible population under one government."

This was true—Haiti's sovereignty was better ensured by a unified island—but it was not the only truth.

Another truth was that the two populations were very different. General Bonnet outlined as much in a letter to Boyer, the elements of which were coincidentally repeated by Cacérès during his speech of concession of power and authority over the city of Santo Domingo upon Boyer's arrival. Language is the most obvious difference, even though the two royal families in France and Spain were related. Second, the Spanish part was more Catholic—with an archbishop, Pedro Valera, assigned by the Pope, as well as the first cathedral in the Caribbean—and thus marriage was the foundation of families; whereas, in Haiti, the vast majority were not Catholic, though it was the favored religion of the elite. Haitians founded their families without any formality, an arrangement known as *placage*. Additionally, the structure of their economies was different, though compatible; the West had a plantation/sharecropping system, whereas the East practiced primarily cattle farming.

By mid-January 1821 Boyer had received from Santo Domingo a sufficient number of submissions to his governance to declare that he was "accepting" them and that he would deploy the army to their territory to facilitate incorporation. He went on to write that any pillaging or violations of private property would be met with the death penalty. The pro-unification voices became stronger, and a week later Cacérès wrote to Boyer a letter submitting the capital, Santo Domingo, to his authority. "The municipality of Santo Domingo, accompanied by its military chiefs, unanimously submits to the Republic of Haiti, with no reservations that the President, a brother, friend and father, will embrace us in peace..."

Excellentissime Seigneur, Hier à midi, je reçus le Messaqe officiel de Voire Excellence du 11 courant, et je m'empressai de réunir la Municipalité et les chefs militaires afin de leur en donner lecture. Ils convinrent tous unanimement de se ranger sous les Lois de la République d'Haïti et d'en arborer le pavillon en cette ville, ne doutant point de trouver dans leur digne Président le frère, l'ami et le père qui offre de les embrasser tous en paix et de les rendre heureux. Que Dieu accorde de longues années à Votre Excellence.

Santo-Domingo, le 19 janvier 1822

This is how it came to be that Boyer, a man who relished taking his chances, marched twelve thousand men to Santo Domingo. The incursion was done in two columns: A northern column, led by General Bonnet, entered from Ouanaminthe, and a southern column, led by Boyer himself, entered from Lascahobas. It was 9 February 1822. The reunification of the island complete, Jean Pierre Boyer became the first and only president of the island known as the Republic of Haiti.

Of course, he wrote to Joutte the very next day. He assured her that he was in good health and not tired, despite the hurriedness with which they marched to Santo Domingo. He described the city as beautiful, with superb structures. He also recounted having met the local Catholic clergymen. Boyer spent one month in Santo Domingo, setting up administrative structures. He placed General Borgella as the commander of Ozama, what would become the sixth administrative department of the Republic of Haiti for the next twenty years.

20

Insurgency, the National Pastime

AT ITS ESSENCE, Haitian history is a seemingly unending series of resistance movements—a perpetual cycle of strong men designing different ways to repress a people who refuse to be repressed, followed by retaliation. Boyer's presidency was no exception. Rebel leaders used the narrative that Boyer had "sold" the country back to the French, using the indemnity payments as pretext to mobilize locals—who, by their rebellious nature, were already predisposed to believing *n'importe quoi*. This inflammatory rhetoric caught on and remained, up to 1838, the principal propaganda upon which several conspiracies were elaborated. After 1838, it became evident that a new generation had come of age, one that had not taken part in the war against France. They had been born in a free country, and having taken for granted the liberties that were won by the Haitians before them, they exercised their rights to education, to choose their profession, to mobility, to marry, and, unfortunately for Boyer, to mobilize. And their chief complaint of Boyer and his super-ministers was one that the young always have against the old: their resistance to change.

There were two factors working against Boyer from the beginning of his presidency, and both had roots in Pétion's constitution of 1816. Unlike his predecessors and many of his successors, Boyer did not amend the constitution under which he was elected. The last modification before assuming the presidency was in 1816 by Pétion; the next would be in 1843, after Boyer was deposed.

The first factor was the creation of the Chamber of Communal Representatives, a second parliamentary house. Municipalities, *communes* in Haiti, now had representatives with a five-year mandate and who were remunerated directly by the communes themselves. This added a different dimension to the political economy of Haiti, distributing power and influence to local businessmen, planters, craftsman—presumably successful—with now the opportunity and voice to influence the affairs of Port-au-Prince and advocate for the economic interests of the commune. Up until this point, the Senate was the only law-making body, and it was typically filled by military heroes; and despite being from all over the country, they were based in Port-au-Prince. This system of compensation from local municipalities also created a built-in incentive to pay taxes, because it was from these revenues that representatives would be remunerated.

The second factor working against Boyer was the clause giving the president a life-long term *and* the right to nominate his successor. This clause was troublesome by itself, but it also juxtaposed the two legislative chambers because the president was elected by the Senate, the upper house, which only had twenty-four members, who were entitled to a nine-year term. The article concerning presidential life tenure was disconcerting because Haiti was just a stone's throw away from a country that had decided to hold elections every four years, and because this generation had fought against three autocrats: Napoleon, Emperor Dessalines, and King Christophe. However, in its treatment by Haitian historians, that article doesn't appear to have been widely contested; they typically mention it as part of a list of amendments that were made to the previous constitution of 1806.

Pétion had mastered the dynamics of the Senate, and Boyer had acutely observed. Senators were traditionally military officers who had demonstrated loyalty and valor, specifically during the War of Independence and against

King Christophe's incursions. There wasn't much negotiation needed between the Senate and the executive; they were all old war buddies. However, as they began to age and some died, Pétion did not nominate replacements nor organize elections. In fact, Pétion was reelected in 1816 with only five senators remaining. In February 1817, the first elections were held for the Chamber of Communes, under the new constitution. While the executive branch could directly influence the Senate by nominating people who were sympathetic to their ideology and way of doing things, the lower house evolved into a different beast. Their representatives were local leaders, businessmen, and they seized this political opening to dilute power from Port-au-Prince to trickle out to the departments. This infidelity to older, traditional political structures was inherent in the Chamber's design, as the communal representatives were paid by the communes and thus were beholden to local economic interests.

The twenty-five representatives passed some interesting legislation during their inaugural session, more so because of their enthusiasm over their newly gained power than from any subversive intentions. By the end of the first legislative session, the Chamber of Communes had demonstrated that they had taken their mandate to legislate seriously: They passed no fewer than sixteen laws, including the budget framework and laws establishing public health centers, pharmacies, and health officers throughout the country. These laws required the government to pay for food and lodging for public health officers, patient medications, and accountants to oversee the administrative management of each center. They also passed laws to regulate the functioning of mayoral offices and the process of undertaking public infrastructure projects. They also created an appeals court, established other regulations to modernize the judicial system, and fixed the salaries of all public servants.

Another legislative act coming out of this first cohort of communal representatives was the redistricting of communes, and thus representatives, based on their distance to the capital. Consequently, Miragoâne was now a Sud commune. The Ouest department was now divided into ten communes; the Sud, sixteen. Each would be assigned a justice of the peace, a military commander, a civil officer, and a council of notables, which replaced the municipal structure. The members, who were nominated by the president, had no military rank, and were responsible for the maintenance of local infrastructure and the functioning of schools.

Indeed, the movement to unseat Boyer began in the House of Representatives and with this first cohort—"The seeds of opposition, the seeds of contestation between government branches of power, within this first legislative session, critical of the administration and defensive of the rights of the military," echoed historian Thomas Madiou.[194] This opposition was mitigated, even muted, by Boyer's allies for a number of years, until it grew in number and scale and could no longer be silenced.

Boyer had acted too quickly for there to be a vacuum of power in the Kingdom of Northern Haiti, and in the eastern departments of Ozama and Cibao. However, there were still clusters of resistance throughout the island. One of the most prominent was an insurrection that lasted over a year and was led by General Prince Paul Romain, who had been second in command to Christophe in the Nord department. General Romain was one of the original senators who had elected Christophe as president of the new Republic of Haiti and was in Port-au-Prince when Christophe attacked the city. Whereas other senator-generals were taken aback by Christophe's aggression, Romain and other generals decided to join him. For this reason, he was removed from the Senate, but Christophe would duly recompense him by naming him the Duke of Limbe, a northern commune. He even slept in an apartment next to the king at the palace.

Even though Romain was at the head of several thousand infantry, most of Christophe's officers had capitulated to Boyer, incentivized by the latter's distribution of land titles to ensure loyalty. This was standard practice among Haiti's strongmen. Dessalines was killed as much for his land management policies as for his cruelty. While the clause in his 1805 constitution confiscating all property belonging to French colonialists was celebrated—understandably so in the euphoria of independence—his immediate acts revealed other intentions. At several turns he launched a verification process of land titles. [195] This wasn't because he was paranoid—the mulatto children of former French plantation owners had indeed seized the opportunity that the exodus of whites presented to make claims on those properties. Dessalines was against the practice of illegitimate mulattos inheriting land that he believed belonged to the new nation. He was killed just after commissioning a verification mission in September 1806 and thus unable to realize the redistribution that he had yearned to see.

Pétion, on the other hand, did not try to undo what had taken place: a redistribution of land to mulattos, transforming them into a large land caste. Most were army officers anyway, and he needed their loyalty. He used the plantations that remained in the public domain to keep the peace when required, giving out small concessions of 5 to 10 carreaux, ultimately creating a second caste of smallholders.[196] In the same vein, Boyer continued Pétion's land management policies in Christophe's kingdom, rewarding officers for their allegiance and permitting subdivisions among them.

Despite assurances that he would maintain his wealth, General Romain balked at the concessions offered. He maintained that he was next in line for the throne, since the people had killed Christophe's sons. He tried to mount a resistance and motivate the surrounding populations of Saint-Marc and Gonaïves, moving from camp to camp deep in the forests of the Nord department, but was soon arrested.

Throughout the month of March 1821, whereas nearly all Romain's battalion chiefs were executed, President Boyer offered the general clemency if he swore allegiance to the Republic of Haiti. He refused, and Boyer had no choice but to place him under house arrest in Léogâne, where his most trusted General Gedeon was commander. That his life was spared lends credence to the observation that Boyer was deliberative in temperament. After all, General Romain was among the oldest and most admired generals who had fought Napoleon's army. He had first emerged in the Louverture-Rigaud conflict, as a colonel under Christophe's command in 1799, and then was promoted to the rank of general by Dessalines.[197] That he ended up on the losing team does not negate the fact that he was a symbol of freedom for an entire generation and a human repository of early Haitian military history.

He remained under house arrest for over a year. General Gedeon allowed him to communicate freely— which he exploited by sending letters almost daily—and also gave him the liberty of a daily walk around the city. After some time, correspondence outlining a coup d'etat was intercepted. Included in the scheme was a plan to implicate Gedeon, who had fought alongside Boyer in Christophe's 1812 siege of Port-au-Prince, a battle where many generals had abandoned the president-to-be. When Boyer summoned Gedeon to the capital to brief him of the plot, the latter insisted that he needed to return immediately to Léogâne, even though Boyer assured the general that he did not believe in his involvement as insinuated in the letter. In August of 1822, General Romain was shot dead during one of his daily promenades, and the circumstances around his death remain ambiguous to this day.

Scarcely a year went by without some conspiracy to overthrow Boyer being exposed. Most only receive a passing mention by Haitian historians. One notable scheme was led by Brigadier General Quayer Larrivière, which included members of the infantry all the way to the elite presidential guard. Accompanied by several members of Boyer's presidential guard, Lariviere went as far as to march an entire infantry column through Lascahobas and Hinche, which was, at the time, the eastern part of the Ouest department. His objective: to replace Boyer with the legendary Borgella, the commander-in-chief of the eastern departments of Cibao and Ozama. In order for this change of power to succeed, securing the stretch of land between the eastern department and Port-au-Prince was strategic. If he wanted to, Borgella could march right into the capital, meeting with little resistance. Borgella had, in fact, declined to participate in that conspiracy and many others that followed, but the officers felt that he would assume responsibility for the nation if only the deed was done. During the inquisition on the case, presided over by super-minister General Inginac, the officers involved did not deny the plot to unseat Boyer. They cited his agreement with King Charles X of France to indemnify the former plantation owners in exchange for formal recognition of the Republic of Haiti as their motivation to conspire against him. When pressed further about their motives, they defended their scheme by arguing that the president had "compromised the honor, dignity and interests of the nation." All were executed in July 1827. Historian Beaubrun Ardouin, who was present, noted the courage and calmness with which they met their deaths. Boyer, faithful to his psychological profile, also remained calm; a minor shakeup of military assignments was all he ordered.

His moderation was admired and attracted many high-ranking functionaries to the presidential palace that Sunday. Ardouin wrote that Boyer was the most eloquent that he had ever been and would be that day. After laying out the facts of the conspiracy to those assembled, Boyer directed his comments to an old family friend he noticed in the crowd, an officer named Colonel Adam: "You who knew my African mother and how honored I am to be her son and how much I love and respect her...". His voice began to rise. "Don't you know that I was nearly drowned by the French?" Now Boyer was talking to everyone; the ebullition betrayed his normally stoic demeanor. "How can they accuse me of sacrificing my country to France; my citizens, my brothers to the French?" he roared to the assembly. Ardouin wrote that even the question mark at the end of his address echoed, shattering the habitual elegance of the Sunday assembly.[198]

A bit later into Boyer's presidency, another plot to undermine him was uncovered in the Nord department. The eldest son of a prominent Cap-Haïtien family, the Isidor family, had marriage difficulties, which quickly became a legal affair. The family won a judgment against the woman, who, knowing well how the president was prone to micro-management, traveled to Port-au-Prince to solicit Boyer's final judgment. Boyer indeed decided in her favor, and, in doing so, ignited a conspiracy that nearly toppled him. Battalion Chief Belonie Narcisse learned about the conspiracy but was slow to react, and Gabriel Isidor, commander of a mounted company and one of the conspirators, discovered that Narcisse was aware of at least some part of the conspiracy and decided to send a letter to

Boyer denouncing Narcisse with the same accusations. Again, Boyer, who was not one to use a machete to swat flies, asked a certain General Leo to convene a military hearing to investigate the accusations. Narcisse maintained his accusations of Isidor; but without any proof, he was seen as an ambitious slanderer and demoted.

But the Isidor conspiracy was real and long-running—the Nord department still had a vision of being a sovereign republic. A month later, in December 1836, Division General Guerrier sent an envoy to Port-au-Prince to inform Boyer that the conspiracy was real and that he had been approached by another conspirator. On 28 January 1837, at nine o'clock in the evening, Isidor—apparently feeling that time was not on his side, as he was unable to persuade the highest-ranking officers in the region to join him—decided to act and called his company to mount. Like Lariviere, he was betting that there would be no opposition to the insurrection once it took shape. However, General Leo, informed of the call, ordered the arsenal closed to all military personnel and gave the guards permission to defend any forced entry. Though only followed by half of his company, Isidor managed to take control of the arsenal but was eventually outmatched. He then fled with his troops to another arsenal at Milot. There, he successfully distributed arms to civilians, inciting them to join the rebellion on the pretext that Boyer had sold the country back to the French. The indemnity itself was insufficient to ignite a revolution, but Boyer's arrogance and condescending attitude created a vortex of offended people. Fortunately for Boyer, Isidor was unable to convince the rest of the Northern troops to join him, Isidor was abandoned by the other half of his squadron and hid in the vast forests of the north. Boyer ordered the hunt, and Isidor was ultimately found and shot, along with his son. Boyer duly reinstated Narcisse and promoted the officers who had not taken part in the insurrection.

There is a verse in Boyer's favorite play, *Les Plaideurs*, in which an aristocrat, a countess, expresses how much pleasure she derives after receiving the winning judgement in a case.

> *Monsieur, tous mes procès allaient être finis.*
> *Il ne m'en restait plus que quatre ou cinq petits.*
> *L'un contre mon mari, l'autre contre mon père,*
> *Et contre mes enfants. Ah, Monsieur, la misère !*
> *Je ne sais quel biais ils ont imaginé,*
> *Ni tout ce qu'ils ont fait*
> *Mais on leur a donné*
> *Un arrêt, par lequel moi vêtue et nourrie,*
> *On me défend, Monsieur, de plaider de ma vie.*
> *[Further along she adds]: Je n'en vivrais, Monsieur, que*
> *trop honnêtement.*
> *Mais vivre sans plaider, est-ce contentement ?*[199]

Banned from pleading any future cases, the countess expresses a certain gratification that she derives from mounting a defense. While it might seem that Boyer was unsettled by these multiple schemes to overthrow him, he perhaps derived some pleasure in both exposing them and administering justice.

21

Next-Generation Rebels

THROUGH ALL OF THESE FAILED PLOTS to remove him from power, Boyer remained consistently passionate and enthusiastic about protecting the foundational values of the republic and, according to historian Beaubrun Ardouin, "His heart was more inclined to indulgence rather than punishment." Nevertheless, Boyer's fate began to take form soon after the Isidor conspiracy. The new legislative session opened in April 1837, and per protocol, Boyer addressed Parliament. He mentioned the Isidor incident, painting the antagonist as insatiable, asserting that the vast majority of Haitians "simply wanted to enjoy the rights that they had fought for."

The immediate consequence of the Isidor rebellion was that Boyer, amidst a widely held belief that Nordists were characteristically militant, appeared strengthened by the support that he received from the generals in the Nord department. But his speech didn't have the intended impact. Boyer had not realized that the revolution had ended, after all, thirty-five years prior, and these parliamentarians knew nothing about war. In his address, Boyer used words like "conspiracy," "order," "maneuvers," "machinations," and "maturity," and these references dated him. Furthermore, by this time, Boyer had lost several generals who were devoted to his idea of a republic and loyal to him: at least six of his generals had died by 1840, including Gedeon.

This new generation of young men, who had only *heard* of the War of Independence from their fathers and uncles, had their own champions, like Rivière Hérard Dumesle. President Boyer's first contact with Dumesle was when the latter read a eulogy in honor of Pétion. Ceremonies of remembrance had been held throughout the country, and in Les Cayes in the Sud department, where he was from, Dumesle made a speech that was eventually published in a circular on 3 April 1818. Several days later, on the eighth of April, Dumesle sent to Boyer a letter of congratulations. Boyer replied on the thirteenth, expressing that he was appreciative of the gesture, and, in reaffirming his intentions to respect the constitution and to preserve the independence of Haiti, he was "counting on help of the true friends of the country" and would always be "open to the opinions of those who were motivated by love of country." Dumesle was a simple citizen when he wrote to the president, but his tribute to Pétion had gained him some attention, and he was elected to the Chamber of Communal Representatives four years later, in 1822, representing the commune of Les Cayes (Sud department).[200]

One year prior, in August 1821, the lower chamber had shifted slightly in Boyer's favor. After annexation, Boyer invited the Nord and Artibonite departments to hold elections, and the Chamber of Communes ballooned to fifty-six representatives, with twenty-seven from the newly annexed territory.[201] This addition helped Boyer rebuff a serious attempt to amend the constitution that year. On 9 November 1821, the upper chamber, the Senate, addressed a private letter to Boyer expressing their intention to revise the constitution of 1816. This notice, combined with the Chamber's previous attempt, proved the issue could no longer be ignored. "Circles of commerce" had sprouted throughout the country; they were composed of entrepreneurs and traders who resented the preferential tariffs accorded to foreign agents and even their presence on Haitian soil. They argued that the trading system wasn't entirely liberalized because it retained the monopsonistic colonial model in which foreigners came to Haiti and dictated prices. They advocated for the expulsion of these agents and asked President Boyer to mandate that countries wishing to trade with Haiti do so via local agents. Boyer refused, and this initial grievance morphed into a more threatening criticism relating to the life term of the president, which he also refused to respond to. "Wisdom and duty demanded that the leaders of the country remain faithful to its social contract," he responded to the Senate. He concluded that any amendments to the constitution should be undertaken at the appropriate time, which practically meant at his death, when the Senate would have to convene to choose the next president. [202] This communication and others that followed would fuel what historian Thomas Madiou called a "mutual distrust" between Parliament and the executive branch.

Following the integration of Santo Domingo into the republic, 1822 saw the addition of sixteen representatives from the eastern departments of Cibao and Ozama to the Chamber of Communes, raising the total to seventy-two. Boyer apparently thought that the twenty-seven from the Nord and Artibonite departments and the sixteen from Cibao and Ozama gave him leverage in Parliament because he articulated as much in his address to the Chamber: "We are beginning a new era—nowhere on our soil is there a foreign power. Finally, we get to prove to the world how civilized Haiti is." He asked members to guard against the "machiavellism" of Haiti's enemies, those who would undermine Haitians' liberty and independence. He urged the representatives to avoid these passions and to seize the lessons learned to "fortify our fraternity and the consolidation of the common welfare."[203]

In the same year, just after the suppression of General Romain's coup, an African named Félix Darfour, who had come to Haiti several years earlier, made official allegations in the Chamber of Communes against the president, accusing him of sedition and of selling the country back to the French. Darfour appeared to have been supported by a number of representatives, who gave him a voice in the Chamber. The two earliest versions of this story, as told by Madiou fils and Ardouin, differ materially. According to Madiou fils, who published the first volume of his anthology in 1847 and who credited Beaubrun Ardouin for his assistance, angry citizens arrested the conspiring representatives, whereas Boyer convened a military tribunal for Darfour. He was found guilty and sentenced to death. The six representatives were held in captivity in different areas of the country and released after several months. No reference is made in Madiou about a trial for them; however, they were officially removed from the Chamber by their fellow representatives and denounced in public communications by both branches of government.[204] Historian Ardouin, who was physically present and who was frequently in Boyer's company—but who didn't publish his anthology until 1856—wrote that Madiou's version the 'official' version, and it was adopted by both houses of Parliament as attested to by their public communications regarding the incident. "Boyer didn't possess powers of seduction; he preferred intimidation," Ardouin wrote.[205] In the end, the historians converged on the consequences of the Darfour affair: The ensuing legislatures were only superficially oppositional, as the punishment dispensed had effectively tamed ambitious spirits. Boyer would enjoy relative tranquility, until the 1832 legislative session.

Although the 1832 elections occurred a decade before Boyer was forced into exile, it could be argued that the revolution against Boyer germinated during this time. The fourth legislative session saw the Chamber of Communes stacked with young, ambitious, learned men. Not one of them had taken part in the War of Independence. Les Cayes had elected Hérard Dumesle; Acquin, an adjacent commune, elected David Saint-Preux; and Cap-Haïtien chose Jules Solime Milscent as their representative. There was no coincidence that these three communes, cradles of rebellious spirits, sent three rebels to Port-au-Prince.

Satiated with power and evidently bored with long-standing protocol, Boyer improvised his speech at the opening ceremony of the 1832 legislative session. Milscent, on the other hand, had been elected president of the Chamber and prepared his speech in advance. Milscent had started the biweekly newspaper *L'Abeille Haytienne* and was often critical of the president in his editorials. His editorials were unpleasant but tolerable, since Milscent was part of the committee that drafted the country's civil codes—legislation for which the legislative and executive branches of government collaborated over several years. However, he did become increasingly critical as time passed. Milscent began his parliamentary address by recognizing the president's achievements, including the unification of the island, one of the few issues that Haitians were largely in accord with. "You have done a lot, Mr. President, but you have a lot left to do," he concluded.

But that was just the official speech. After the opening ceremony, the Chamber sent a delegation to the National Palace with a letter of policy recommendations, which historian Ardouin suspected was written by Dumesle. One of the demands was for the formalization of electoral procedures. On this point, the president conceded and asked the Chamber to form a special commission whose objective was to draft a proposition of law, a task taken up by Dumesle as well. The president then convened a review committee, which was chaired by super-minister Inginac. The commission's members, which included the usual suspects Milscent, Dumesle, and Saint-Preux, all trained lawyers, found themselves at odds regarding certain aspects of the electoral code. Eventually, Milscent found himself in opposition to his Southern colleagues, Saint-Preux and Dumesle.

But in 1833, it was Dumesle who found himself in

opposition. On 12 July 1833, he made a motion for a closed session to debate how the president nominates and dismisses his ministers. There are two backstories: Boyer had replaced the high court judge without consultation or explanation, which constitutionally was a presidential discretion. But it was also true that the high court judge released a circular that forbade civil servants to assume elected positions in Parliament. If they chose to run for elected office, they were expected to resign their posts. Generally, this was a clever maneuver to better distribute the meager resources of a government, giving Boyer more positions to distribute as political favors. But Dumesle placed himself in opposition to this policy.

The president of the Chamber put the motion to a vote, which ended unanimously against the idea of establishing the practice of having closed sessions. Curiously, the following week, on 17 July 1833, the representative from the commune of Saint-Yague (in the east), Raphael Servando Rodriguez, addressed his colleagues that "under the guise of the public good" there had evolved a "violent opposition" within the Chamber. He must have smelled something brewing.

Dumesle would go on to make the same motion several times, the last one being a convocation of the high court judge to answer questions. None were successful. Dumesle had become unpopular in the Chamber, and there was a geographical division forming between the representatives from Les Cayes and the rest of the Chamber. In fact, one month later, on 13 August 1833, the House called an emergency meeting to discuss the two festering sores, and they barred Dumesle and Saint-Preux from the rest of the legislative season, referring to them as "turbulent, provocative and generally obstructional to the Chamber doing its work." The representatives debated a motion to expel the two from the Chamber entirely, which succeeded.

From 1833 to 1836, Dumesle was essentially a political outcast. He left the capital to return to the Sud region to re-work his telic approach. And this wasn't the last of him. In November of 1836 Boyer received a personal communication from Dumesle, delivered to him by an intimate friend, Louis Mesmin Séguy-Villevaleix. Bedridden with fever, Boyer asked a visiting Ardouin to read the letter to him. In the letter, Dumesle tried to persuade Boyer of his good intentions, including his loyalty to the constitution and to the public interest. He asked the president if he could return to Port-au-Prince so the two could meet. According to Ardouin, who felt comfortable enough with the president to speak frankly, he suggested to the latter that Dumesle was popular in his commune, that he would likely be reelected to the Chamber, and that it would not be a bad idea to let him come and at least think that he had won some favor with Boyer. The president dismissed the proposal, stating that "he should just comport himself as an honest man and citizen."

The year 1837 was difficult for the Chamber of Communes. Elections were held for a new legislature, and Dumesle and Saint-Preux were sent back to Port-au-Prince. Disappointed to see them back, President Boyer, in his inaugural parliamentary address, made reference to the nation demonstrably "having an aversion to ambitious coup-plotters," as evidenced by how quickly the nation rallied against "a smaller number of miscreants." For Boyer, this was a "demonstration of good sense by the people, their commitment to order, and their preference for constitutional government." While calling on the new parliamentarians to be "mature and prudent," he didn't officially respond to any of the correspondence coming from this legislative session. In fact, during that session he did not send a single proposition of law for the Chamber's consideration. Feeling the frigidity from the National Palace, the cabinet, and even the Senate, the Chamber wrote to Boyer on his birthday that year: "The Chamber, which represents the people, also represents its affections, and is deeply persuaded that you are loved by them and sends you the warmest wishes."[206]

But Dumesle didn't stay in conciliation mode very long. On the last day of the 1837 parliamentary session, he dropped key words and expressions which outlined the moral argument underpinning the eventual call to arms in 1843: "By voting us to the Chamber, you have given birth to the future [by placing emphasis on the new ideas] of social rejuvenation...[It will be] necessary to develop [new theories] and renounce old theories [that that demonstrated themselves to be incongruent with innovation]...[We must continue with the].regeneration of the government's institutions...[Even though we accomplished little during this parliamentary session, we certainly did not] compromise futures or alienate hopes....[207]

The figurative declaration of war came in the last sentence of his address: "These hopes have not been thwarted, and in attesting to the glorious past of our country, these memories inspire sublime devotion; considering the protectiveness of the President, we are promised a coming political and moral rebirth."

Those words launched a revolution. For the 1838 session, the Chamber of Communes elected Dumesle as its president. With his steering, the assembly send an open letter to the President, dated 20 April 1838. They had observed stagnancy in Haitian society and shared some new ideas of "regeneration". They asked him to reconsider the responsiveness and efficacy of the country's institutions. Specifically, they asked for new legislation regarding policing, coastal security, a reorganization of the courts system, improved trade and customs administration, and better management of public servants. They also appealed for new laws to regulate lending, agricultural activities, the arts, and public works, as well as better administration and control of public resources. This detailed correspondence summarized the vision of a reorganization of Haitian society and outlined the desired agenda of this newly elected core of legislators.

For the politicians of Boyer's youth, the issues had been slightly different, but equally divisive. The amalgam of diverse political movements included debates about race but also about the distribution of resources. As was the case during the colonial period, not having slaves meant lower levels of production. Not having French nationality meant there would be no access to French schools and vocational training, or even the right to mobility. Not having political representation at the National Assembly meant not having input into tariff rates and other commercial measures.

This open letter to the president made its way throughout the country. When the commune of Jérémie (Sud department) read it, they decided to honor the Chamber's president, Dumesle, with a medal and sent out an invitation for contributions. A banquet was held in his honor. Eventually the public servants that had organized and participated in the ceremony, in both Jérémie and Les Cayes, were fired.

The letter was persuasive, and some took it on themselves to remove the president. The first of May is Labor and Agriculture Day in Haiti. In 1838, as was the custom of the time, it was celebrated with a Catholic Mass. The president was accompanied by both the presidents of the Senate and the Chamber of Communes as he walked to the church. They were followed by four men, Desfontaines, Raymong, Gabriel, and Manga, three of whom were active and/or former soldiers, one of whom later recounted that he thought himself close enough to shoot at Boyer with his pistol—but owing to his placement decided against it for fear of the projectile hitting Dumesle. Strategizing on their next best opportunity to assassinate Boyer, they concluded that they would kill super-minister General Inginac, which would prompt a very public funeral, during which they would easily be able to get to Boyer. One of them was tasked with knocking on the general's door at 2 a.m. with the pretext of having an urgent correspondence. When Inginac opened the door and took the letter, he was shot in the back of the head. However, the scheme (which included quite a few military officers) began to fall apart when it was learned that Inginac did not die. The conspirators were duly tried and executed.

The truth came out at trial: Inginac was simply collateral damage; it was Boyer they wanted. The Sunday after the trial unsurprisingly drew a larger than normal crowd to the National Palace. It was 20 May 1838, and Boyer waited until a large number of people had amassed in the visitation hall before declaring, "The Chamber was pleased to agitate people by its public address, which had a long list of reforms but not one proposition of law." The president announced that if this behavior continued, he would put aside the constitution to arrest and punish everyone who sought to disturb the public tranquility. This was taken as a declaration of war.

Boyer assumed a martial stance, but, according to Madiou fils, the incident shook him. He proposed resigning to both Joutte and his friend, Séguy-Villevaleix; both of whom persuaded him to remain in office. He had not yet identified a suitable successor, as per the constitution. Séguy-Villevaleix had participated in the indemnity negotiations of 1838 and would be elected to the Senate in 1842. He probably believed that Boyer still had a considerable political base.

It is also true that Boyer thought that he could outmaneuver this growing opposition. Super-minister Inginac owned a hotel where most of the parliamentarians from the outer communes stayed while parliament was in session. Together, they devised a strategy to form a majority bloc in the Chamber of Communes. After a great deal of politicking, they were able to assemble a majority of thirty-one representatives; they released a statement on 05 October 1839. "Several members of the Chamber are trying to impose their opinions and what they believe to be fact on the rest of the Chamber...We declare our determination to no longer participate in the sessions until there is a demonstration of the desire to achieve harmony." They urged the president to publish the statement, as Saint-Preux and Dumesle had been doing with the publication of their correspondence to Boyer in the newspapers in an effort to sway public opinion. But Boyer had other plans: On Sunday, 06 October, after the customary military inspection and parade, during the gathering of dignitaries and military officers at the palace, Boyer announced the retrenchment of numerous civil servants, all associated with the rebellious representatives. He also declared to the assembly that the army had been placed on alert due to threats to the national tranquility. On Monday, 07 October, he banned public protests, and the newspaper that had previously printed all of the letters from Dumesle and the like, *L'Union*, suspended its operations. By Tuesday, 08 October, six additional representatives broke from the opposition to join the majority, increasing the number of representatives on Boyer's side to thirty-seven. That was all they needed; they met that day to expel Dumesle, Saint-Preux, and others and elected a new president and secretary.

Rumors of militarization surfaced and even reached the United States of America. *Niles' Weekly Register* reported that there was a rebel army fifteen thousand strong. By November 1839, several American newspapers that were largely favorable to commercial and diplomatic relations with Haiti, were describing Boyer as "tyrannical."[208]

By 1841, the president's resistance to change

radicalized the peoples' champions, and Milscent wrote a song about Boyer, which, at that point, was met with more popularity than the President.

J'entends en maintes occasions Prêcher contre l'ambition : Mon âme en est ravie (bis). Mais ceux qui nous parlent si bien, Regorgent d'honneurs et de biens ; Cela me contrarie (bis). Faire droit sans exception À toutes les réclamations, Mon âme en est ravie (bis)i Mais refuser à l'équité Ce qu'obtient le rang, la beauté ; Cela me contrarie (bis) Respectez le Chef de l'État, De ses faits, publiez l'éclat Mon âme en est ravie (bis).

(Translation: "I often hear preaching against having any ambition, and my spirit is pleased. But those that preach to us are stuffed with honor and land, and this disturbs me. Make laws without exceptions to entitlements; my spirit is pleased. But refusing to equitably acknowledge merit and beauty; this disturbs me. Respect the Chief of State and his deeds; publish the explosion; my spirit is pleased.")

This was exactly what the sociologist Jean Price Mars had inferred about the Dominican annexation, which could at the same time be characterized as both an invasion and a response to a call for help. There was nothing untrue in the song, but it wasn't the whole truth.[209]

Alternatingly eloquent and autocratic, Boyer would

either win people over with rhetoric or force. Those were his only two political tools. When the previously expelled representatives were reelected in 1842, Boyer chose force and reacted by banishing a total of twenty-eight representatives of the seventy-two elected. This time, he included the representatives from Santo Domingo. « Je ne veux point être un juge en peinture, » Judge Dandin said to his son, in *Les Plaideurs.*[210] The thought "I no longer want to have the *appearance* of a president" began to play on a permanent loop at the back of Boyer's mind.

That year, he didn't address Parliament. Instead, he sent super-ministers Inginac and Voltaire with his message to them. It was 12 March 1842. Upon leaving, the super-ministers, already in their seventies, were unable to mount their carriages and needed the help of their aides-de-camp. The young Parliament was repulsed. Well into his sixties when the 1842 Chamber of Communes session opened, Boyer also appeared to be irrelevant, a political dinosaur.

Thinking that he could leverage the Senate to keep the Chamber in check, Boyer wrote to the upper house on 15 March 1842.

It appears that the same members, known for their subversive projects who were expelled in 1839 to restore the harmony between the three branches of government, have been reelected. Is there any other way to interpret their reelection than as an act of hostility? No one more than me respects the independence of elected assemblies. But can we allow the vote of a small number of electors to destroy the sacred vote of the majority? Could the Senate allow these representatives to be certified after expelling them several years prior? Citizen Senators, in always wanting to surround myself with your light and patriotism, I would like your opinion on these serious issues.

Boyer had flagrantly violated the constitution and provided the political justification for his unseating. No longer operating within the confines of the law, the banished parliamentarians began to organize the change that they had been hoping to realize, and that Boyer had actively impeded. Historian Ardouin concluded similarly that Boyer had created the opposition because he didn't respect their opinions and because they were a consequence of his "excess of principles." [211] Post-expulsion, they formed the Society of the Rights of Man and Citizen, based in Les Cayes. The outcome of their meeting was a document entitled The Praslin Manifesto (Praslin was a farm outside Les Cayes), which detailed their grievances with Boyer. This manifesto quickly made its way around the island.

Finally, to add to the political conflict, there were two disasters which pivoted popular opinion in the rebels' favor. Another marker of big events in Haitian history was a severe earthquake in the Cap-Haïtien region in May 1842.

Nearly all communes in the Nord department were impacted, and Cap-Haïtien was flattened. The country regularly experienced extreme weather or earthquakes; this time, however, peasants and military soldiers plundered the city, while six thousand of their countrymen, half of the population of Cap-Haïtien, were buried in the ruins. On the heels of the earthquake was a fire in Port-au-Prince, where a large portion of the city was burnt down. They were considered bad omens: "Is this a sign of the fate of ruin of our institutions?" wrote François-Élie Dubois, a lawyer based in Jeremie and among the public servants fired after Boyer learned of the medal of honor conferred to Dumesle.[212]

22

Money Matters

ON 7 MAY 1842, A VERTICAL DISPLACEMENT of the Septentrional Fault under Île de la Tortue, an island just off Cap-Haïtien, jolted everyone along Haiti's northern peninsula from their supper tables. It was half past 5:00 on a Saturday afternoon.[213] The sound of the earthquake—a muffled roar deep underground but rapidly approaching—was heard first; no one seemed to recognize it. Then came the violent tremors, which left nothing nor anyone standing. Finally, an enormous dust cloud thickened the air and added to the terror. Seismologists' records estimated that the earthquake lasted less than a minute. There was no time to react; buildings collapsed instantly, and nearly everyone who was indoors at that time perished.

The earthquake itself was a terrifying experience, but

within minutes it became gruesome. Cries were heard from all corners, "Run to the mountains!" The sea had regressed, some say as far as 60 meters, but it was now on its way back. A wall of sea water 5 meters high descended upon the towns along the northern peninsula of Haiti. Six times these waves struck the Haitian towns; the last wave went as far as the island of Saint John, 816 kilometers away. Although the epicenter was at Cap-Haïtien, reports of damage from the earthquake and the tsunami were received from Cuba, Jamaica, and Puerto Rico.

Only at sunrise the next morning could the damage be assessed. Between five and six thousand people, half of the population of Cap-Haïtien, did not live to see 8 May. Some had fallen into the large crevices that opened up across the city. Others were buried under the rubble of their homes or drowned by the tsunami. Fires throughout the night destroyed whatever structures had resisted the water. When the earth finally settled, the largest cities in the Nord department were flattened: Cap-Haïtien, Port-de-Paix, Môle-Saint-Nicolas, Fort Liberté, and Saint-Yague. Aftershocks were felt several times per day for three months. The earthquake was felt as far as Anse-à-Veau, and, in Gonaïves, the ground opened up in several places to release heat, igniting uncontainable fires throughout the city.

One of the ways in which Boyer chose to deal with low productivity and commercial exclusion in the international arena was by creating a new monetary instrument. Money first became problematic under the mercantilist system, because the habitual payment in metals proved cumbersome and more costly to move as the volume of trade grew and commerce expanded over an increasing number of markets. There was little mining activity in the New World at first and most of it was undertaken by Spain, for which gold was the metal of choice. There were two main internationally recognized currencies: the livre and the piastre or peso. Both were in coin form, having different values depending on the quantity of precious metal—gold, silver, or copper—used in their minting.[214]

The merchants in Saint-Domingue accepted all metal coins, even those from England and Portugal. The currency with the largest circulation in Latin America and the Caribbean was the Spanish piastre, a consequence of the pillage of Mexican and Peruvian gold reserves. The piastre was in such short supply that merchants offered price reductions if traders brought the species rather than promissory notes. The piastre went through several additions due to counterfeiting. The fifth edition of this coin was minted from 1731 to 1771 and was called the *peso gordo*.[215] It became the principal means of commerce in Saint-Domingue and is the origin of the gourde, the Haitian currency.

After Haiti's independence, monetary policy was the responsibility of the executive branch. There was no institution resembling a central bank. Cash management and reporting was the responsibility of super-minister Imbert, who reported annually to Parliament on government revenues and expenditures.

At first, Haiti used the coins that were already in circulation. However, metal currency was hard to police, and authorities in Haiti, as in other countries, were challenged by counterfeit pieces in wide circulation. Hence there was a need and expense of periodically changing the minting. Furthermore, to save money, traders now came to buy Haitian commodities with promissory notes from financial institutions; consequently, there was not enough money in circulation in the country, as the gold remained in Europe. Faced with the acute shortage, President Pétion had the remaining coins in the country pierced in the middle, naming it the new Haitian gourde. With the middle bits, he minted new coins. This palliated the shortage, but he needed a more sustainable solution. In 1813, he introduced paper money, which locals used to pay customs duties and other taxes. Bills valued approximately 300,000 gourdes—the gourde was trading at parity with the United States dollar—were printed. But faced again with the inability to effectively curb counterfeits, the government recalled these bills in 1817.[216]

In April 1826, President Boyer proposed to Parliament the creation of the Bank of Haiti. He thought that these money matters would be better left to a dedicated institution whose main role was to preserve the value and adequate circulation of the national currency. But unable to gather sufficient seed capital to launch the initiative, Boyer decided to again introduce paper money in September 1826. This time, however, he retained a dual currency system: import tariffs were paid in metallic species (gold or silver), and the paper money was used for domestic transactions. The value of bills issued amounted to 3.5 million gourdes— still at parity with the dollar—whilst there were only 1.3 million gold piastres in the treasury. Perhaps the world was still under the illusion that Haiti possessed the same wealth as Saint-Domingue and/or they were exploiting the gold known to be located in the northern region of the island. The world also believed, as well as many Haitians, that Christophe had left a tremendous repository of millions of gold coins. How else could he have financed the construction of the fortress and castle? And why else would both Pétion and Boyer offer to indemnify the French for the loss of their plantations? Though both Pétion and Boyer were aware of the gold reserves in the Nord department, they did not have the technology nor the means to exploit them. The paper gourde was nothing more than paper. As economist John Maynard Keynes wrote: "When the object of desire (money) is something that cannot be produced and the demand for which cannot be readily choked off ... there is no remedy but to persuade the public that green cheese is practically the same thing and to have a green cheese factory under public control."[217]

The paper gourde was not without precedent. The Second Bank of the United States had issued paper money. In fact, it was created in part to stabilize the value of the dollar, as there were, by this time, hundreds of private banks in the United States, that were issuing letters of credit. The distrust of the currency and the operations of the bank incited then-president Andrew Jackson to withdraw the government's deposits and place them in state banks in 1833. This move was in line with his personal ideology that government should be near to the people and of service to them. Indeed the move increased circulation of the bills across the states. However, the United States would run into the same problem as Haiti- the supply of gold and silver in the country had dwindled as it remained in Europe, largely at the Bank of England, with promissory notes used to facilitate trade, thus raising concerns about the value of the paper dollar.

The paper gourde effectively raised the supply of money in circulation, increasing the government's cash flow. French economist Robert Lacombe estimated that the government took in $701,166 annually, in US dollar equivalent, which increased to $900,000 by 1837. The Haitian treasury was able to build a surplus to approximately $1.5 million.[218]

With the economy growing steadily though modestly, the currency stable, and having just obtained a lowering of the French indemnity in 1838, Boyer sensed that the public's confidence in his monetary management had improved. He was certain he could raise the capital to launch the national bank. He submitted the proposition to Parliament, but the Chamber of Communes, stacked with the young opposition, rejected it.

Returning to the May 1842 earthquake, despite the macabre scene, the disaster was followed by pillaging that began even before the aftershocks had ceased. Peasants from the countryside descended upon the towns—not to help, but to plunder. Violent clashes ensued between the marauders and the survivors. Despite suffering considerable losses, the Northern generals organized themselves to suppress the criminality. However, the insalubrious environment caused a fever, from which several hundred others died.

In Port-au-Prince, the opposition grew more bold. The same printing press that had nourished revolutionary movements in Venezuela and Mexico was used to highlight the Boyer government's shortcomings. They were critical of what appeared to be a tortoise-like response.

Vous disiez, il y a quelques jours, que le Gouvernement était fort; c'était ici le moment de prouver cette force en faisant respecter la loi.... Si vous ne forcez pas les bandes qui se sont gorgées de pillage à baisser la tête devant la toute puissance de la loi, la loi ne sera plus qu'une lettre morte. »[219]

Le Patriote, a newspaper created by a group of youths, taunted Boyer. Boyer, who mentioned frequently how strong the country was against potential foreign invasions, could not quell the looting and killing. They insisted that if he couldn't impose the law, then the law was no more than its letters—like his paper money.

On 18 May, some believed too late, Boyer released a statement in the state newspaper, *Le Télégraphe*. "A horrible event has propelled thousands of families into mourning," he began. He described how each of the cities had been affected. He expressed indignation at the "depraved, inhumane individuals" who were pillaging and refusing to aid those trapped under the rubble. However, he reassured the afflicted families that, though their problems appeared insurmountable, they should not let themselves be defeated. And even though its means were limited, the government "would not abandon them."

Life recommenced as survivors established themselves in other cities. Commerce shifted to the port at Gonaïves. President Boyer dispatched a team to Cap-Haïtien with food provisions, medications, and medical personnel.

Parliament passed a law which exempted Northern residents from the payment of property taxes and business permits. And donations were made by thousands of citizens. But by December 1842, Cap-Haïtien was still ashes and dust, and the opposition began to criticize the government's lethargy.

The eventual reconstruction projects in response to the earthquake attracted unsavory characters and thus counterfeiting and scams. The government observed an unexplainable devaluation in the gourde, when it should have been in high demand given the scope of investment required to rebuild. But the gourde had fallen to a third of the value of its gold coin equivalent. Boyer and his cabinet decided to recall the gourde note that was widest in circulation, which was the 10-gourde bill. Doing so revealed that there were 17,900 counterfeit bills in circulation.[220] Unable to distinguish between them, Boyer's government had to reimburse all holders of the bills, an additional unforeseen cost.

The counterfeit was an indication that there was not enough money in circulation to satisfy everyone's needs. But is there ever enough money in an economy to satisfy everyone? Some degree of scarcity preserves the intrinsic value of the currency. Despite the counterfeiting episode, Boyer had established a successful monetary system, a paper-based currency that had only slightly depreciated over a twenty-year period and was not backed by any precious metal reserves, and which modestly accomplished the objectives of attracting commerce and increasing the liquidity of government. The Haitian monetary system was prescient in that it functioned on expectations, as is now the case for many modern currencies.

Despite the monetary fraud, 1842 was a very good year for Haiti. Government receipts were 3.3 million gourdes, up 23 percent from 1840. That year, Haiti exported 41 million pounds of coffee and 19 million pounds of wood. And despite the calamitous earthquake, expenses were 2.5 million gourdes, down 8 percent from 1840. But this wasn't enough to mute the growing opposition.

23

The 1843 Revolution Against the Boyer Gerontocracy

TOWARDS THE START OF HIS PRESIDENCY, Boyer had a scare. The day after having celebrated Haiti's fifteenth anniversary of independence, he decided to venture out in his carriage. Normally reclusive, he didn't have a sense of the public's mood after the death of Petion. Had they accepted him? Would they cheer if they saw him?

One of the lug nuts fell off a carriage wheel, and it became visibly loose. The chauffeur had not initially felt the instability; rather, several onlookers signaled to him that something was wrong. He had a difficult time stopping the galloping horses, and it turned into a spectacle. Nevertheless, Boyer safely descended the carriage and walked back to the National Palace. There was no cheering, but there were also no jeers. Just respect. After the carriage was repaired, he restarted his journey. But the newspaper *l'Abeille Haytienne* quoted him as having said, "Once again I avoid danger." By 1843, what Boyer had perceived to be luck must have now seemed like providence.

A premonitory one-man rebellion occurred in 1839. A sugar plantation owner named Honoré Féry decided that he would no longer pay taxes to protest Boyer's tax policies. Bazelais, Boyer's son-in-law, and Madiou fils, who was Bazelais' secretary at the time, were sent to Jérémie to negotiate with Féry. "Féry's protest was a moral one", wrote Madiou fils, and [as a reputable farmer and citizen] "his defiant stance carried much weight with others living in the [southern peninsula] region". [221] Eventually Féry capitulated and agreed to pay the various taxes imposed on farmers. "An oracle", Boyer called him, after the delegation had recounted the details back at the national palace.

Every calendar year in Haiti begins with celebrations to mark the anniversary of its independence on the first of January. On this day in 1843, it was raining and the mood was grey, like the sky. Boyer had decided not to participate in the festivities, and there were few high-ranking public officials in attendance. On the ninth of January, there was a further deterioration in the national psyche: Division General Bonnet, who had been unwell but had participated in the festivities to celebrate the country's independence, succumbed to his illness on the ninth of January. Though Bonnet and Petion had locked horns over several issues, Boyer had relied on Bonnet's patriotism and his eagerness to serve: He had extinguished many insurgencies and played a key role in the annexation of the East. Boyer lost his first ally.

The ideological movement that had developed in opposition to Boyer's republic of aging generals transformed so rapidly into a revolution that it was nearly spontaneous. The first meeting of the newly formed secret society, called the Society of the Rights of Man and of the Citizen— comprised of lower chamber representatives and others chafing under the old guard—had taken place on Christmas Eve in 1842 in Jérémie, a commune in the Sud.[222] At that meeting, they reached a consensus that they should organize themselves militarily. Their decision was expedited to the society's Les Cayes chapter, another Sud commune. The Les Cayes meeting was held in the first days of January 1843. At that meeting, they agreed to take inventory of the armaments in the region and identify officers who were inclined to support them, and a man named Charles Rivière Hérard, the head of the Les Cayes chapter and Dumesle's cousin, was placed in command. The intensity of communication between the two chapters and the conviction of their beliefs was such that by 15 January 1843, barely two weeks later, the attack date was set for the week of 20 February.

These two groups probably could not have led a successful revolution by themselves. The southern peninsula of Haiti is a vast territory of forests and plantations that was sparsely populated. However, just a week later, on 22 January, the news of the arrests of several members of the group circulated among the residents of Jérémie. True or not, it became a call to arms—the residents even started to make their own munitions. That day was a Sunday, and it was national custom to organize a modest parade of soldiers in the communes. Overtures were made to the soldiers posted at local forts. On that same day Rivière Hérard sent another message asking for them to march "to save our country, our mother, from despotic attacks. ... The signal is given, and any hesitation will compromise our movement."[223] Rivière Hérard asked the Jérémie forces to come to Les Cayes on 27 January.

Rivière Hérard secured the commitments of two generals, Lazarre and Riché, and by 1 February, the communes of Anse d'Hainault, Dame-Marie, Petite Rivière, and Tiburon had mobilized and joined the resistance. It was now a generalized revolt of the southern peninsula. Upon witnessing the movement, Boyer's closest ally in the Sud, General Borgella, sent a correspondence to General Segretier—a long-time friend of Boyer, who had served with him under Pétion's command during the Revolution against the French—warning him that an armed insurrection was en route and that he should block the principal road from the southern peninsula into Port-au-Prince.

After Borgella had spent ten years as the top military commander on the eastern part of the island, a hurricane in 1831 motivated him to ask Boyer for leave from his post in Santo Domingo to return to his plantation in Les Cayes. This hurricane was truly devastating, having destroyed several public buildings and prominent houses, including Rigaud's former home, and flooding caused considerable damage to crops. Historian Madiou wrote that, during this deadly storm, people formed circles and held hands to keep from being sucked up by the wind. Boyer granted the transfer, and that is how Borgella found himself in the geographical middle of a coup.

His letter was intercepted by the insurgents. But Segretier had also written to Borgella, asking him not to resist. Segretier had also conceded to Hérard on the promise of a promotion from brigadier general to division general in the transitional government that would follow Boyer. However, by the end of that year, Segretier would resign his post, alluding to regret that he'd participated in such a movement.

The first victory of the rebel militia was at Pestel on 21 February 1843; the second was at Jérémie on 25 February.

On 26 February, Colonel Bazelais, Senators Ardouin and Villevaleix, and General Inginac went to the national palace. They had not been summoned, and Boyer wasn't expecting them. Bazelais brought the news of the defeat at Jérémie and the defection of four regiments at Anse à Veau. The four discussed their opinions about the way forward. Ardouin and Inginac published different accounts of this meeting. According to Ardouin, Bazelais intimated that Boyer should stand down. Boyer was inclined, but he needed time to organize his affairs, as did the other members of his political class. To gain such time, he decided to continue a minimal military campaign, which included sending Inginac and Villevaleix to Léogâne. A defeat at Léogâne would constitute a signal for immediate departure. In his memoirs, Inginac, on the other hand, claimed that, though he was aware of Bazelais' news, he wasn't at the meeting in which it was decided to march the troops forward to Léogâne and, that when he received the orders, he had to leave immediately, without having had the chance to voice his objection. His reticence was understandable: Léogâne was where Inginac had planted roots and where he had important commercial investments. Nevertheless, he went to Léogâne but soon retreated to Gressier when the news arrived that the commune of Jacmel had joined the rebellion and contributed several hundred troops to the cause, who were already heading to Léogâne.[224]

The rebel militia advanced until 12 March, when they overtook Léogâne, a commune just thirty kilometers from Port-au-Prince. Their troops were reportedly eight thousand men strong,[225] though the size of the militia varies depending on the source.[226] In any event, their numbers did not match Boyer's standing army, and the latter had no appetite to kill their fellow citizens. By most historical accounts, they yielded.

There had been attempts to undermine the insurgency by disseminating misinformation regarding the well-being of its leaders. For example, in late March, *La Presse* (Paris) reported that there were rumors that Rivière Hérard had killed himself, and the forces that he was leading had fled into the forests. However, the newspaper called into question this version of events, citing the large number of insurgents they had confirmed on 27 February.[227] In all, the misinformation campaign proved ineffective.

Around this time, the Great March Comet could be seen for several weeks. Its bright dust tail intermittently illuminated the skies above Haiti. On 28 February, it was reportedly visible throughout the day. The people saw it as a good omen and threw their support behind the rebel militia. "The revolution was won in the battle for public opinion", wrote Ardouin, as he described how civil servants had ceased reporting for duty several days prior, which is why he went to the palace almost daily to assist Boyer.[228]

One year prior to these events, super-minister Imbert was suspected of having passed on information to the rebellion's parliamentary representatives. It was the nature of his position to have frequent contact with the head of the Chamber of Communes' finance committee, who was David Saint-Preux, the other delegate that had been expelled with Dumesle. Boyer, who had not seen Imbert in six months, was growing suspicious of him, and decided to replace him with a subordinate named Pilie. He prepared the official announcement of Pilie's nomination to the post in February 1842, citing Imbert's poor health. He arranged for Imbert to be informed the night before the notice. However, fate prescribed a different future for Boyer. That evening, Imbert suffered a stroke and thus could not be informed before the publication. In this way Boyer inadvertently catalyzed the coup d'etat against him. Already suspected of being associated with the political opposition, Imbert publicly began to voice his criticisms about Boyer's governance style and aligned himself with the recently formed Society of the Rights of Man and of the Citizen, who now had as members all of the prominent political leaders of the Sud region, including Imbert and his three sons. No documentation of his participation in the coup could be found, but validation of his complicity with the opposition movement would come later, after Boyer's departure, when he would be the only one of the super-ministers not inculpated; in fact, he was recalled to his post.

A chronicle of the events of 1843 written by François-Élie Dubois of Jérémie, who served in the Peoples' Army, as the insurgency named itself, as captain under the command of General Lazarre and, after their victory, served as the general administrator for the commune, described Boyer as "enlightened" but "infatuated with the ideas of the men of his time," giving credence to the hypothesis that the revolution was at its base a generational one. "Too nostalgic" and overly committed to the country's independence leaders and post-colonial traditions, Boyer was closed to alternative ideas and spurned all proposals to embrace industrialization and modernity. Using the French indemnity as an example, Boyer, obsessed with paying it, rejected all petitions for public works, even capital investments in education and health. For Dubois, the revolution was indispensable; after all, the population, without any power, had repeatedly made proclamations to a "deaf government."[229]

Accused from all corners of the country of leading a government that was "rusty, retrograde and indolent," Boyer had no choice but to resign.[230] Beaubrun Ardouin, who was now a sitting senator but who assumed the role of Boyer's secretary during his last weeks, was tasked with organizing the Boyer family's departure. He arranged for the British warship HMS *Scylla*, which lay anchor in the Port-au-Prince harbor, to accommodate the entire family; they would leave at sunset on 13 March. Once these arrangements had been finalized Ardouin returned to the National Palace to transcribe Boyer's letter of resignation to the Senate. Boyer had positioned himself on a couch, partially laying down, suffering from an inopportune cold and fever.

> *Vers 7 heures du soir, je retournai au palais pour lui (Boyer) rendre compte de ma mission auprès de M. Ussher [the British consul]. Nous étions convenus qu'un canot et une chaloupe de la Scylla se rendraient au coucher du soleil le 13...Le Président m'ayant demandé si j'avais rédigé l'acte d'abdication, je lui répondis que je l'avais commencé chez moi, et que je l'achèverais s'il me donnait une plume et de l'encre. Sa femme, Mme Joutte Lachenais, me fournit ces objets. Je m'assis près d'un guéridon qui était dans un petit salon au nord du palais, tandis que Boyer était à moitié couché sur un canapé ; il était atteint d'un gros rhume et avait un peu de fièvre.*

Ardouin, born in 1796, did not fight in the War of Independence, but his father, a soldier, was a contemporary of Pétion and managed a *magasin de l'état* (a state-run store) in Port-au-Prince until his death. In order to limit arbitrage, these stores sold items acquired directly from local producers. Beaubrun was twenty-two years old when Boyer assumed the presidency. He studied law and was named commissaire in Port-au-Prince, a coveted post, close to power. He would later be named judge to the Appeals

Court, and eventually be elected senator and, for some time, president of the Senate. Among the first locally printed school manuals in Haiti was his *Geographie de l'Isle d'Haiti*, published in 1832.

The first paragraph of Boyer's resignation letter was a succinct summary of his twenty-five years at the National Palace. He reminded the population that he was elected to the presidency after the untimely death of Pétion, when the Republic of Haiti was just the Ouest department; since then, it had expanded to the entire island and gained recognition from world powers. The second paragraph discussed the frugality with which the country was administered, and that Boyer was leaving 1 million piastres in the treasury. "In wanting to avoid any possibility of civil war, of malevolence, I am leaving voluntarily," Boyer said, concluding that he had only one wish: "that Haiti finds the happiness that my heart has always desired."

> *Citoyens Sénateurs, Vingt-cinq années se sont écoulées depuis que j'ai été appelé à remplacer l'illustre fondateur de la République que la mort venait d'enlever à la Patrie. Durant cette période de temps, des événements mémorables se sont accomplis. Dans toutes les circonstances, je me suis toujours efforcé de remplir les vues de l'immortel Pétion, que mieux que personne, j'étais en position de connaître. Ainsi j'ai été heureux de voir successivement disparaître du sol, et la guerre civile et les divisions de territoire qui faisaient du peuple haïtien une*

nation sans force, sans unité, j'ai pu ensuite voir reconnaître solennellement sa souveraineté nationale, garantie par des traités dont la foi publique prescrivait l'exécution. Les efforts de mon administration ont constamment tendu vers un système de sage économie des deniers publics. En ce moment, la situation du trésor national offre la preuve de ma constante sollicitude, environ un million de piastres y est placé en réserve, d'autres fonds sont en outre déposés à la caisse des dépôts et consignations, à Paris, pour compte de la République. De récents événements, que je ne dois pas qualifier ici, ayant amené pour moi des déceptions auxquelles je ne devais pas m'attendre, je crois qu'il est de ma dignité, comme de mon devoir envers la Patrie, de donner, dans cette circonstance, une preuve de mon entière abnégation personnelle, en abdiquant solennellement le pouvoir dont j'ai été revêtu. En me condamnant en outre à un ostracisme volontaire, je veux ôter toute chance à la guerre civile, tout prétexte à la malveillance. Je ne forme plus qu'un vœu : qu'Haïti soit aussi heureuse que mon cœur l'a toujours désiré. 231

On what was likely a breezy evening due to Carême winds, the HMS *Scylla* set sail with the Boyer family on Monday, 13 March 1843, at sunset. Boyer, costumed simply in black, decided to leave ahead of everyone and meander through the empty streets of the capital before heading to the harbor. He was on horseback, and following him, at a respectable distance, was the presidential guard. The hot, arid air did nothing to soothe his malady of the preceding evening. Accompanying him on the voyage was, according to Ardouin, his partner, Joutte Lachenais; his daughter and her husband, Azema and Charles Bazelais; his sisters Mariette and Bonne; Pétion's daughter Hersilie and her husband, Jean Pierre Edmond Coquière; Coquerine Coquière, the widow of General Inginac's son; Inginac himself and his wife, Zelmire Morisseau; Pierre Faubert—Boyer's aide-de-camp—and his wife Josephine; and Thomas Madiou (the historian's father) and his wife, Antoinette Moulut. A modest crowd had assembled on the quay. Many wore white head scarves; some carried torches. Everyone was silent.

Ardouin had gone to the harbor to see the president off and described him, in the last moments, as having a last surge of defiance. Indeed, Boyer was reluctant to cede power to singular ambitions. After all, hadn't Haiti received the long sought-after recognition of its sovereignty? Hadn't he negotiated a lower indemnity? Hadn't Haiti carved out an, albeit small, space in international commerce? Ardouin attempted to mollify him by responding to the questions affirmatively and reminded him that he [Boyer] had also lived the civil war between Louverture and Rigaud and, later on, that between Christophe and Pétion. Boyer acquiesced; he decided that he didn't want that legacy for himself and boarded without further hesitation.

They arrived safely in Jamaica. Before disembarking, Boyer penned a note of thanks to British Admiral Charles Adam, who was responsible for his transport. He expressed gratitude for the respectful treatment that he and his family received while onboard.

Les événements politiques qui ont eu lieu récemment en Haïti m'ont déterminé à abdiquer le pouvoir dont j'étais revêtu comme Président de la République afin de la préserver des horreurs de la guerre civile. Mon intention était de me rendre en Europe, mais la faiblesse de ma santé m'a décidé à faire d'abord une station à la Jamaïque où je désire vivre dans la plus profonde retraite avant de réaliser ce projet. Appréciant La grandeur de votre caractère, j'éprouve le besoin de vous exprimer ici les sentiments de ma haute considération. Permettez que j'exprime aussi ma gratitude pour les procédés obligeants dont j'ai été l'objet de la part du Commandant de la Corvette de S. M. B. la Scylla.

Boyer also wrote to the governor-general of Jamaica, still a British colony, named Kincardine, requesting permission to disembark, which was granted. And though he was invited to meet with the governor, Boyer lay bedridden for over a month and the two didn't meet until 17 May.

On 4 April 1843, Charles Rivière Hérard entered Port-au-Prince as provisional president, and Dumesle was named minister of foreign affairs. Rivière Hérard's government declared that Boyer was guilty of high treason, and all his property should be forfeited to the republic. Borgella, Inginac, Ardouin, and Séguy-Villevaleix, among others, were named as accomplices. They would face trial by national jury, some in absentia.[232]

The young revolutionaries went to work, drafting the constitution of 1843. Setting up a political administration to incentivize civil participation was an ideological break from the previous forty years of governance. Historian Louis-Joseph Janvier called it the best work to come out of the revolution of 1843.[233] Overall public administration was conferred to civil agents, who were supported by local councils. Civil agents were nominated, but elections would be held for seats on local councils and for mayors, who governed the communes. In fact, in an attempt to put an end to the military's omnipresence, this constitution specifically restricted public administration to civilians.[234]

But it appears that not everyone who sided with the youth shared their vision of a participatory democracy. Rivière Hérard didn't last five months before being replaced by the seasoned General Philippe Guerrier, who was eighty-six years old. He had fought with Dessalines and had taken the side of Christophe in the first civil war. He banished Rivière Hérard and Dumesle from Haiti. However, he died in office a year later, and between 1844 and 1847, there were three additional presidents: Jean-Louis

Pierrot (1845–46), Jean-Baptiste Riché (1846–47), and Faustin Soulouque (1847–49); the latter named himself emperor in 1849 and reined until 1867. Furthermore, in the cruelest of ironies, Boyer received news from his contacts in Haiti: The only political consensus that the Peoples' Army leaders could reach was that they would revert to the 1816 constitution.

The international press coverage of the bloodless coup against Boyer was varied and largely inaccurate. Articles coming out of the United States reported that he first landed in Jamaica, with $3 million, while others reported that he left with just the clothes on his back. "The revolution in Haiti is now complete," the *Boston Liberator* reported. In a movement that only started twenty days prior, the fifteen-thousand-strong Peoples' Army were "making advances in republican reform." Haiti was free of Boyer's tyranny but half a million dollars poorer. [235] He had even fled with Christophe's crown, according to the *New Orleans Bee.*[236] *Le Journal de Toulouse* reported that Dumesle was the principal agitator, and that he had been forced out of the Senate by Boyer's bayonet but that his constituency repeatedly voted him back. Such was his popularity that he was able to assemble six thousand men within a few days. [237] *Le Journal des Débats Politiques et Littéraire* published similar reports but added that Boyer had fled with the equivalent of 4.3 million francs.[238]

"What has changed in Haiti since the fall of Boyer?" wrote a French traveler in 1844, answering, "The public servants, that's all. Before it was Pierre that consumed the public's resources; now it is Jean. ... The Republic [of Haiti] has no agricultural or commercial policy. The few capable men that it possesses only want positions; everyone wants to lead."[239] Haiti would remain a military state for the next hundred years.

24

Boyer's Final Years

JOUTTE LACHENAIS DIED on 22 July 1843 in Jamaica.[240] Her death was sudden, but she was buried the very next day. She might have been helped along by the physical environment. A violent earthquake in early June had caused so much devastation that Boyer felt obliged to send a note of condolences to the governor's office. Additionally, an intense fog had settled around the island, rendering navigation quite dangerous and negatively affecting the air quality.

Joutte's impact on Boyer's life cannot be overestimated. In General Bonnet's memoirs, he intimated that Boyer received his assignment as head of the president's guard while he was only a colonel because of Joutte's influence. She intervened again when promotions were being given for brigadier general. [241] Certainly, without Joutte, Boyer would not have been well-positioned to succeed Pétion at his death, with more senior and more experienced officers around. The Senators were unlikely to vote against a man who simultaneously held the posts head of the presidential guard, commander of Port-au-Prince, and commander of his own regiment of grenadiers, holding the rank of general. Partner to two presidents over thirty-seven years, Joutte likely mastered the art of politicking. Nevertheless, from the few personal communications that survived, Boyer's love for Joutte was sincere, and their blended family showed no signs of conflict. In her funeral announcement, she was referred to as Madame Boyer.[242]

Exactly one month later, Boyer and his family left Jamaica for England, where he remained briefly and then sailed for France. He and his family touched land in Rouen on 25 September 1843 and proceeded by road to Paris. Among his first interviews was with the *Journal de Toulouse*.[243] The observant journalist at the port described Boyer as looking about sixty-five to sixty-eight years of age and "having the gestures of an intelligent, distinguished man." Boyer was accompanied by his mother, who was in her nineties, and the family's luggage appeared modest, given the rumors about his pillaging of the state treasury. Despite the trauma of the previous six months, the journalist commented that he had a noble air about him and spoke with resignation. Upon arrival he stayed at the Hotel

Victoria on Rue Chauveau-La-Garde in Paris.

He was formally received by King Louis Philippe d'Orléans.[244] The visit, which took place sometime around May 1844, was described as a "long conference" and amical, with several historians recounting the following anecdotal exchange between the heads of state, with little variation:

LOUIS PHILIPPE. Is your majesty enjoying his stay in France?

BOYER. Certainly, but, if your Majesty permits, I would like to remind him that I am not royalty, but a simple president of a country.

LOUIS PHILIPPE. When you have governed over a people for twenty-five years, you are royalty.

Votre Majesté est-elle satisfaite de son séjour en France », lui avait demandé le roi? « Enchanté, Sire, mais Votre Majesté me permettra de lui rappeler que je ne suis qu'un simple président de République », répliquait modestement Jean Pierre Boyer « Monsieur le Président, reprenait son royal interlocuteur, quand un homme a gouverné pendant vingt-cinq ans un peuple, il est toujours une Majesté.[245]

Boyer was offered the Château de Pau as a permanent residence but declined. Pierre-Eugène de Lespinasse wrote that it was because Boyer wanted to be free from all surveillance and have the liberty to return to either Jamaica or Haiti, depending on emerging events.[246] But it could also have been his frugal and reserved nature, mentioned repeatedly by contemporary chroniclers. By their accounts, he always lived simply at the National Palace in Port-au-Prince; his principal indulgence was being surrounded by his family.

After hearing that the Senate had confiscated his property and stripped him of his nationality, Boyer applied for and received approval for a travel document from French authorities. In April 1844, the French press reported[247] that Boyer traveled to Le Havre to book passage to Southampton and then on to Jamaica. He felt that he needed to be closer to his homeland to appeal the decision.

But there was another reason. Hérard was having trouble keeping the country unified. The mutinous Sud department was living up to its reputation, and the Nord department wanted a president from the region pushing their interests. *L'Echo Francais* published a letter from Division General Lazare [248] from Jérémie, one of the communes that had joined with Hérard, that provided the public vindication that Boyer was hoping for. General Lazare complained of the mulattos in Port-au-Prince wanting to occupy all the seats in Parliament and the influential positions in public administration and being unwilling to accept a rank below colonel. "It is as if the revolution was achieved by them, for them. Even the despotic Boyer shared the power." He went on to complain that even though blacks had joined the "regeneration" movement to chase the tyrant Boyer, the mulattos were treating them as if they could not manage anything. Finally, General Lazare confirmed in the letter that Boyer had indeed left one million gourdes in the national treasury, which had been pillaged by the mulattos. As confirmation, a few months later, the same newspaper published an announcement that the Minister of Foreign Affairs had approved a pension for Boyer.[249]

Boyer had written several letters of protest, asking for a revision of the decision taken in 1844 to strip him of his nationality and property.[250] "I feel that I am obliged to not let the world believe that because of my silence, I am resigned to being dispossessed and the violation of my rights. ... As a consequence, I protest ... against the execrable abuse of power, the violation of my inalienable rights, and the redistribution of my properties." [251] Eventually, it was Beaubrun Ardouin, who had been exonerated and was still a Senator, who proved instrumental in lifting the seizure of Boyer's property for his descendants in 1846.

Boyer learned that his successor, Rivière Hérard, along with Dumesle, had already been exiled and were also in Jamaica. It happened that his resignation had not sufficiently appeased the various factions—they chose power and militarization in lieu of modernity and industrialization. In the midst of the battle to occupy the National Palace, yet another rebellion emerged in the Sud department led by Jean-Jacques Acaau. The eastern departments of Cibao and Ozama also saw an opportunity and did not hesitate. They were finally able to unite under a single vision and declared their independence from Haiti on 28 February 1844. These were tenebrous years for the country, yet none of these events put an end to Haiti's predilections for strong, autocratic men.

International media were also paying attention. *The New York Herald* reported eyewitness accounts of mass executions of opponents to the new regime. [252] Their reporting was based on letters sent by American and other foreign merchants, which described the crippling economy. In general, there was widespread insecurity, shops were closed, and large stocks of provisions could not be sold. "I don't think Hayti will be longer habitable for civilized man," wrote one reporter. They described targeted massacres of mulattos amid calls to revoke all licenses held by trading agents—the same demands that were made to Boyer by the young revolutionaries.

Upon hearing that Boyer had returned to Jamaica to recover his families' holdings, the hubristic Dumesle—the young turbulent communal representative whose re-election campaigns to the lower house were based on promoting a "fresh and modern" democratic governance—begged the former president, in vain, to return to the country. He made several requests for a meeting with Boyer, all of which were ignored. Dumesle went to the ex-president's residence anyway, where both proverbially and quite literally on his knees he begged Boyer to return to the country and set it right. Having recited the play *Les Plaideurs* hundreds of times, Boyer instantly recalled Dandin, the judge: « Ouf ! Je me sens déjà pris de compassion. Ce que c'est qu'à propos toucher la passion ! Je suis bien empêché. La vérité me presse. Le crime est avéré, lui-même il le confesse. »[253] Inspired by the verse, Boyer responded, "One shouldn't kneel in front of a man. I have already pardoned you for all wrongs done to me, but I can't pardon you for the wrongs that you have committed against your country."[254]

In March 1845, Boyer would lose another beloved on Jamaican soil, Hersilie, Pétion's daughter who had married his nephew.[255] She was twenty-six years old. Nevertheless, the family stayed in Jamaica this time, and, in April 1846, Boyer sent her husband, Colonel Coquière, to Haiti to negotiate the reinstatement of the family's properties. Despite being deeply troubled and only wanting to live the rest of his years in the country of his birth, we see in his correspondence to Coquière a man committed to certain life principles. He reminded Coquière in a letter to him soon after his arrival, "Always be honest, measured, and prudent."[256] Coquière failed in his mission, and so Boyer submitted another public statement dated 6 November 1846. In it, he makes his case that the accusations of treason against him and the government's decree to seize his property are illegal and barbaric, considering that he had not committed any crime and had resigned at his own initiative to avoid internal conflict. The public note ends with his characteristic eloquence: "No matter how long this persecution endures, my soul, with the help of God, will rise above this perversity, my comportment will be dignified, and my wishes as well as my attachment to my country will only end with my death." This last communique provoked an extraordinary session of the Senate on 13 November 1846 to debate the confiscation of Boyer's properties. The country had already experienced many political reversals—Dessalines, Christophe, Hérard— none of which resulted in the confiscation of properties. Furthermore, Boyer was not accused of having obtained these properties from any illegal activity. The resolution to restore properties that had not yet been sold was adopted. For those that had been, the state would indemnify his designated heirs.[257]

His properties were restituted by decree by President Riché in 1847, who had served as a young soldier under King Christophe, and who had some degree of respect and admiration for the man that had unified the island—and spared his life. Riché, after all, had massacred hundreds of mulattos in Christophe's kingdom and had persecuted the Spanish-speaking inhabitants of the eastern departments. He was never prosecuted. Furthermore, in an effort to dissuade further defections from the army during the coup against him, Boyer had, at one point, sent Ardouin to Les Cayes with orders for Borgella to announce promotions, among which included the promotion of Riché to division general.

However, Boyer never returned to Haiti. Rather, he decided to settle down in Paris, where he lived quietly and modestly at 11 Rue de Castiglione. When one newspaper, *Le Courrier Francais*, intimated that Boyer was house-hunting, Boyer asked them to make a correction in the following issue—such was the importance of the perception of modesty.[258]

Boyer spent a lot of time reading and apparently never lost his passion for prose. He gifted *L'Académie de Jeux Floreaux de Toulouse* three thousand francs to establish an annual prize for authors of fables in rhyme.[259] Among his last actions was to establish three scholarships at the College of Paris for people of color.[260]

Jean Pierre Boyer died on 9 July 1850, at the age of seventy-four. With him were Charles Bazelais and Edmond Coquière, his sons-in-law, who evidently loved him a great deal—both named their first sons after him, Boyer Bazelais and Boyer Coquière. There is no record of Boyer having had a son. However, Bazelais recounted that after the death announcement had been released, a young man in a French infantry uniform appeared at the house asking to salute the former president. With much hesitation, they directed him to where Boyer lay. The young officer laid down on his belly and said a prayer. When asked for his name, he declined. Bazelais wrote that the young man resembled Boyer.[261] Boyer had been in France during his short exile, along with Rigaud and Pétion, in 1801. Any child of his would have been born between 1801 and 1802 (because Boyer was part of Leclerc's convoy), making this child forty-nine or fifty years of age at the time of his death. This "young soldier" had either inherited Boyer's youthful looks or was more likely a grandchild.

"Before closing his eyes for the last time, he made his final wish of happiness for the country," wrote *Le Moniteur Haitien*, the country's official newspaper. The paper informed Haitians that Boyer died with all his physical and mental faculties intact; that his doctors had diagnosed him with a gastroenteritis, resistant to all treatments; that he was attended to in his last moments by his nephew Edmond Coquière and his grandson Boyer Bazelais; and that his body was embalmed.[262]

Many notables died that year, including Rivière Herard, who died in exile in Jamaica; John C. Calhoun, former vice president of the United States who had served under Presidents John Quincy Adams and Andrew Jackson;

sitting American president General Zachary Taylor; the Daoguang Emperor of China after a thirty-year reign; and the poet William Wordsworth. Even the King of France, Louis Philippe, passed one month after Boyer. Boyer nevertheless was not forgotten in the international press. His death was announced by all the major media houses of the day. Coverage had even begun before his death as word had circulated regarding his poor health. "Boyer, ex-president of the Republic of Hayti, is ill in Paris and not expected to recover," wrote *The New Hampshire Gazette.*[263]

His funeral was intimate, attended by family and close friends. The service was held at L'Église de la Madeleine, on 11 July 1850, at 10 a.m. He was buried at the Père Lachaise Cemetery in the 20th arrondissement in Paris, and his eulogy was delivered by his old friend Séguy-Villevaleix.

His will, unsigned and undated, commenced with a declaration, giving some insight into his state of mind.

Je meurs dans la religion catholique dans laquelle je suis né.
J'ai toujours été dévoué à ma patrie que j'ai servie avec zèle et fidélité.
Par suite d'une ambition effrénée, quelques hommes étaient parvenus à égarer et entraîner une partie du peuple à bouleverser l'état, sous l'astucieux prétexte de parvenir à des améliorations.

Le monde entier sait, que pour préserver mon pays des horreurs de la guerre civile j'ai, par abnégation, abdiqué le pouvoir. Je ne parlerai pas des iniquités dont j'ai été la victime; ma conscience est en paix, je suis tranquille sur le jugement de la postérité.

(Translation: "I die as a Catholic, just as I was born into Catholicism. I have always been devoted to my country, whom I served energetically and faithfully. The government was toppled by people who had been misled by an ambitious group using the pretext of bringing improvements. The whole world knows that, to spare my country the horrors of a civil war, I relinquished power. I'll not speak of the injustices of which I was a victim; my conscience is in peace, and I am tranquil regarding the judgment of posterity.")

Boyer left half of his possessions to Azema, his daughter, and the other half to Hersilie's children. An inventory of his belongings found several artifacts from his long presidency, and four notebooks handwritten by Boyer, which were his account of the War of Independence.

What became of Boyer's stalwart super-ministers?

Division General Bonnet did not live to see the fall of

Boyer's government; he passed away at the age of seventy in January 1843. Despite the lack of resistance against the rebels, Division General Borgella was charged with treason and imprisoned for a short time, but this was a strategic act – rather than a patriotic one - to ensure that his popularity would not catapult him directly to the National Palace in place of Rivière Hérard. Borgella never denounced Boyer; he was liberated and died peacefully soon after in March 1844 at age seventy-one.[264]

General Inginac, Boyer's Secretary of State, had the most difficult time of all. He had also fled to Jamaica, but not with Boyer. According to his memoirs and contrary to Ardouin's account, he was at home when he had learned of Boyer's departure that same night. Inginac had been with the president several hours earlier, and nothing about his resignation and departure had been mentioned to him. After several hours under the protection of the French consul general, he boarded a vessel to Jamaica.[265] While there, he lost his wife. The provisional government tried him in absentia for treason and stripped him of his nationality. He returned to Haiti in November 1844, blind and frail. The government allowed Inginac to stay, and he died in 1847 at seventy years old.

Imbert and Chief Judge Voltaire served as members in the provisional government established in the wake of Boyer's departure, but the latter died before elections were held in July 1843 at eighty-two years old.[266] After Riviere Herard was elected to the presidency, Imbert, whom Boyer had replaced in 1842 because of illness, returned to his long-held post of Secretary of State Finances, fueling suspicions that he had been an active part of the coup against Boyer. The only one to outlive Boyer, Imbert died in 1855 at age seventy-six.[267]

Historical treatments of Haiti tend to place it within the context of slavery and race. However, the amalgam of colonial governors, emperors, and presidents had a singular objective: the concentration of power. Toussaint wanted absolute control of the island, not the island's independence from France, which was ambitious for a man born into slavery, and admirable. However, slavery for him was limited to chains and did not extend to the rights of man, as he was an advocate of forced labor. Dessalines and Christophe were both brilliant military commanders *and* despotic leaders. Rigaud, who was anti-slavery and an early proponent of civil and economic rights, also aspired to dominate, using the absolute power he had in the Sud department as leverage. As for Pétion, his easy manner masqueraded his ambitions. Everyone saw him as a pacifier, a father to all. This was believable because he also practiced laissez-faire where it related to economic livelihoods. However, he seized the first opportunity he got to secure power when he imposed the clauses of a lifetime mandate and the right to choose his successor in the 1816 constitution.

It was out of Rigaud and Pétion's protective shadows and mentorship that Boyer came to the presidency. He remained loyal to his ideological roots of being against forced labor, but he was confronted with challenging social, political, and economic conditions. How was he supposed to manage a country that wasn't meant to exist? How could he incentivize productivity amidst increasing global agricultural mechanization among a people who no longer desired to work the land?

Boyer's own cardinal principles contributed as much to his downfall as to his staying power. His desire to lead led him to take on the role of shepherd—he saw Haitians as sheep that needed protection and guidance, and he believed he knew what was best for them.[268] His revolutionary vision drove him to consolidate the island but also caused him to be inflexible to other forms of governance. That men were inherently equal was a long and tightly held belief, which meant that he would not go down the path of the forced work model. But he did cherish the old world, retaining many of its customs and procedures—he just saw a place for blacks in it.

Boyer's character was best summarized by Bonnet

in his memoirs: "Providence had showered Boyer with favors of a series of events which allowed him to consolidate power ... the pacification of the Grand'Anse Department; the fall of King Christophe; the reunification of the island under one government; the French recognition of Haitian sovereignty." But this made him vain, with a "sense of invulnerability" that only he could make reasonable decisions about the country's welfare. Bonnet argued that the country was well legislated, with competent civil servants and a loyal army. All Boyer had to do was uphold the laws and ensure that they were applied to everyone indiscriminately. Rather, he chose to usurp the institutions created to help him govern and, according to Bonnet, "This engendered a cycle of insubordination and appeasement." Boyer's own indiscipline was replicated throughout the country.

Ardouin offered that it was Boyer's self-imposed isolation that contributed to his downfall. He was affable— as a number of foreign visitors to Haiti attested—but, paradoxically so, as he chose not to socialize with his fellow army officers, nor his cabinet members, and especially not members of Parliament. Instead, he spent the better part of the week at Volant-le-Thort, with his beloved Joutte. His only exposure to the public was on Sundays at the National Palace, during which any citizen had the opportunity to come and be heard. "This isolation eroded his sensibilities about the country's concerns about the economy, about the

French indemnity," Ardouin argued. Bonnet had also referenced these traits, which were coupled with the fact that Boyer was considered highly intelligent and easily absorbed information. This combination made for a dangerous arrogance, with Boyer thinking that all the best decisions were his own.

But was he so socially isolated that he didn't even notice the state of the capital? Insalubrious is how it was described by many travel writers. Its polluted, mosquito-infested shores contributed to the deaths of foreigners by malaria. British abolitionist John Candler, who traveled there in 1841, called Port-au-Prince the "filthiest capital in the world" and described the refuse and standing water throughout the city. [269] This same traveler also visited several schools and found them lacking rigor.

Boyer is not without reproach. Like Louverture, he wanted absolute control over the state. For Louverture, such a goal was ambitious, even admirable, for a man born into slavery. Can we express the same admiration for Boyer? He was born into relative economic and physical security. Recognized by his father, he had access to the French metropole. He was most certainly familiar with the writings of Montesquieu and Robespierre, as well as the global discussions at the time around human rights, the rights of citizens, and nationalism.

The answer is so subtle, it escapes the most scrutinous

of sociologists. Boyer was indeed an abolitionist; he recognized the importance of rules and procedures to govern; he believed in justice and administered it personally. But he was not a democrat. He didn't believe that there was any benefit in letting the public make decisions regarding their welfare. And neither did his predecessors. Ultimately, one can only be a strongman in a sea of fragile, uneducated ones.

The situational irony is that Haiti lies in such proximity to the United States of America, a country that regularly and consistently uses the organization and financing of elections as a diplomatic stick—and only until they are held, does one get the carrots. The vicissitudes of Haitian politics betray these two constants – the society's predilection for strong men and the consolidation of power. Mayoral elections, fiscal decentralization, participatory budgeting, auditing of public expenditures—the vesting of any power at local government level—have never taken root in Haiti. The best example may be found in the most essential of economic instruments, the birth certificate, which still eludes the majority of children born in rural areas. Is the respect for human rights something with which a population must be indoctrinated? Imposed upon? Are some human societies more susceptible to the recognition of the rights of participation and inclusion?

However, Boyer wasn't just a product of his times; he framed the times-to-come, becoming the architect of a modern Haitian political economy characterized by gerontocracy, militarism, and suppression of dissenting opinions. Such times were similarly referred to over a century later by Francois Duvalier, another autocrat, who, along with his son, governed Haiti from 1957 to 1986. During a 1969 interview with British journalist Alan Whicker, Duvalier was asked why he thought that he was increasingly being criticized for his anti-democratic methods. He replied, "Democracy is a word; it is only a word, it is a philosophy, a concept. What is called democracy in one country, another country calls that a dictatorship. To have peace and stability, you should have a strong man in every country. I am the strongest anti-communist man in the Caribbean." From 1818 to 1843, so too was Boyer.

ENDNOTES

[1] All materials in French were translated by the author; hence all errors of interpretation should be attributed to her. Likewise, the author did not use any English translations or interpretations of Haitian or French documents or correspondence.

[2] Johannes Matalius Metellus, *Hispaniola Insula*, 1598, engraving, published in Cologne, 9.5 x 7 inches, https://www.raremaps.com/gallery/detail/74503mp2/hispaniola-insula-metellus.

[3] Ministère de la marine et des colonies, Carte particulière de l'Isle de Saint-Domingue, Paris: 1802. https://memoire-esclavage.org/sites/default/files/2023-06/FME_PD22_029.jpg.

[4] John Luffman, *The Island of St. Domingo*, 1802, published in London, 6.5 x 5 inches, https://www.raremaps.com/gallery/detail/77148/the-island-of-st-domingo-luffman.

[5] Weimar Geographische Institut. Charte von der insel San Domingo oder Hispaniola, Weimar: 1804, 22.5x16.5 inches. https://www.raremaps.com/gallery/detail/86310/haiti-and-santo-domingo-charte-von-der-insel-san-domingo-weimar-geographische-institut.

[6] Lionel Pincus and Princess Firyal Map Division, The New York Public Library, "Carey's general atlas ... [Title page]," The New York Public Library Digital Collections (Philadelphia: M. Carey, 1814), https://digitalcollections.nypl.org/items/254f2a00-c603-012f-2bbf-58d385a7bc34.

[7] Henry Charles Carey and Isaac Lea, *Geographical, Statistical and Historical Map of Hispaniola or St. Domingo*, 1822, published in Philadelphia, 20.5 x 16.5 inches, https://www.raremaps.com/gallery/detail/81525/geographical-statistical-and-historical-map-of-hayti-forme-carey-lea.

[8] The nineteenth century orthography of both the French and English languages has been preserved for authenticity.

[9] Nations Online Project, https://www.nationsonline.org/oneworld/map/Hispaniola-map.htm.

[10] Boyer. Président de la République d'Haïti. A. Maury. Lith de Villain, gravure des portraits, estampe. Publication date 1825, Public domain mark 1.0. Bibliothèque Sainte Genevieve, EST 90 RES (P.5).

[11] Often, former slaves rejected their former owners' surnames, retaining their assigned Christian names. There were also instances in which former slaves renamed themselves to signify their rebirth, as was the case for Toussaint Louverture.

[12] Bonnet, Guy Joseph (1864). Souvenirs historiques de Guy-Joseph Bonnet, général de division des armées de la République d'Haïti, ancien aide de camp de Rigaud. Documents relatifs à toutes les phases de la révolution de Saint-Domingue, recueillis et mis en ordre par Edmond Bonnet. Notice du catalogue : http://catalogue.bnf.fr/ark:/12148/cb30129248p. Identifiant : ark:/12148/bpt6k6135244p. Source : Bibliothèque nationale de France, département Philosophie, histoire, sciences de l'homme, 8-PZ-50. Date de mise en ligne : 04/10/2010

[13] Frank Moya Pons, *History of the Caribbean* (Markus Weiner Publishers, 2007).

[14] An extensive treatment of smallpox may be found here: F. Fenner et al., *The History of Smallpox and its Spread Around the World* (World Health Organization, 1988) 209–243.

[15] Michael Bennett, "Curing and inoculating smallpox: The career of Simeon Worlock in Paris, Brittany and Saint-Domingue in the 1770s," (University of Tasmania, Journal contribution, 2017), https://hdl.handle.net/102.100.100/564117.

[16] Ardouin, Beaubrun (1835). Géographie de l'Isle d'Haïti précédée du précis et de la date des évènements les plus remarquables de son histoire. Imprimerie du gouvernement, Port-au-Prince, 1832.

[17] de la Mardelle, Guillaume-Pierre-François de (1732-1813). Éloge funèbre du comte d'Ennery et réforme judiciaire à Saint-Domingue. Impr. nationale (Paris), 1788. http://catalogue.bnf.fr/ark:/12148/cb307248810. Identifier : ark:/12148/bpt6k5461607w. Source : Bibliothèque nationale de France, département Philosophie, histoire, sciences de l'homme, 4-LK12-222. Provenance : Bibliothèque nationale de France, online date : 11/12/2008

[18] Correspondance secrète des députés de Saint-Domingue avec les comités de cette île. (12 août 1789-9 avril 1790.), 1789-1790. Identifier : ark:/12148/bpt6k5785501k. Source : Bibliothèque nationale de France, département Philosophie, histoire, sciences de l'homme, 8-LK12-267. Provenance : Bibliothèque nationale de France. Online date : 12/01/2010

[19] Title : Précis remis par les députés de Saint-Domingue aux six commissaires du comité d'agriculture et de commerce, chargés de rendre compte à l'Assemblée nationale de l'affaire relative à l'approvisionnement de cette isle. Publisher : (A Versailles, chez Baudouin, imprimeur de l'Assemblée nationale, avenue de Paris, n°. 62 [1789].). Publication date : 1789. Relationship : http://catalogue.bnf.fr/ark:/12148/cb36401137r. Type : text. Type : printed monograph. Language : french. Format : 4 p. ; in-8. Format : Nombre total de vues : 6. Description : Avec mode texte. Rights :

Public domain. Identifier : ark:/12148/bpt6k5786418t. Source : Bibliothèque nationale de France, département Philosophie, histoire, sciences de l'homme, 8-LK12-243. Provenance : Bibliothèque nationale de France. Online date : 12/01/2010

[20] Title : Réponse de M. Duchilleau, ancien gouverneur général de Saint-Domingue, à l'article qui le concerne dans la prétendue justification de M. de La Luzerne, ministre de la Marine, aussi ancien gouverneur de Saint-Domingue, envoyée le 18 juin au comité des rapports de l'Assemblée nationale. Author : Du Chilleau, Marie Charles (1734-1794). Auteur du texte. Publication date : 1790. Relationship : http://catalogue.bnf.fr/ark:/12148/cb303650904. Type : text. Type : monographie imprimée. Language : french. Format : In-4°, 58 p. Format : Nombre total de vues : 60. Description : Avec mode texte. Rights : Public domain. Identifier : ark:/12148/bpt6k57856950. Source : Bibliothèque nationale de France, département Philosophie, histoire, sciences de l'homme, 4-LK12-280. Provenance : Bibliothèque nationale de France. Online date : 12/01/2010

[21] Ward (1978) estimated the profitability of slave-produced sugar in the British colonies of Barbados and Jamaica at 5.3 percent and 6.4 percent, respectively, in the years 1783 and 1791. There are similarly modest estimates from Aufhauser (1974) for Barbados and Louis Joseph (1983) for Guadeloupe, whereas it has been estimated that the Nantes (France) slave traders made between 50 and 120 percent profit annually during the same period (Stein, 1975). J. R. Ward, "The Profitability of Sugar Planting in the British West Indies, 1650–1834," *The Economic History Review*, 31(2), 197, https://doi:10.2307/2594924; James Franklin & Joseph Meredith Toner Collection, *The present state of Hayti Saint Domingo, with remarks on its agriculture, commerce, laws, religion, finances, and population, etc., etc.* (London: J. Murray, 1828) (PDF), https://www.loc.gov/item/02012896/; and Robert Stein, "The Profitability of the Nantes Slave Trade, 1783–1792," *The Journal of Economic History*, 35, no. 4 (Dec. 1975): 779–93, https://doi.org/10.1017/S0022050700073769.

[22] Bonnet, Guy Joseph. Exposé de la conduite du général Rigaud, dans le commandement du département du sud de Saint-Domingue , adressé au Directoire-exécutif, par le citoyen Bonnet, aide-de-camp dudit général. [Paris.] De l'imprimerie de J. F. Sobry, rue du Bacq, n°. 149. [1798]. http://catalogue.bnf.fr/ark:/12148/cb301292460. Bibliothèque nationale de France, département Philosophie, histoire, sciences de l'homme, 8-LK12-542. Identifier : ark:/12148/bpt6k58068847. Online date : 08/02/2010

[23] Title : Concordat, ou Traité de paix entre les citoyens blancs et les citoyens de couleur des quatorze paroisses de la province de l'ouest de la partie française de Saint-Domingue. Publisher : [Paris.] De

l'imprimerie du Patriote françois, place du Théâtre italien. [1791].
Publication date : 1791. Relationship :
http://catalogue.bnf.fr/ark:/12148/cb36401255z. Type : text. Type :
monographie imprimée. Language : french. Format : 15 p. ; in-8.
Format : Nombre total de vues : 18. Description : Avec mode texte.
Rights : Public domain. Identifier : ark:/12148/bpt6k5786576m.
Source : Bibliothèque nationale de France, département Philosophie,
histoire, sciences de l'homme, 8-LK12-356. Provenance : Bibliothèque
nationale de France. Online date : 12/01/2010

[24] Bonnet was a prolific writer and many of his letters have survived
over the years, despite the natural disasters and conflicts in Haiti.
Title : Exposé de la conduite du général Rigaud, dans le
commandement du département du sud de Saint-Domingue , adressé
au Directoire-exécutif, par le citoyen Bonnet, aide-de-camp dudit
général. Author : Bonnet, Guy Joseph (1773-1843). Publisher : [Paris.]
De l'imprimerie de J. F. Sobry, rue du Bacq, n°. 149. [1798]. Publication
date : 1798. Set notice :
http://catalogue.bnf.fr/ark:/12148/cb301292460. Identifier :
ark:/12148/bpt6k58068847. Source : Bibliothèque nationale de France,
département Philosophie, histoire, sciences de l'homme, 8-LK12-542.
Provenance : Bibliothèque nationale de France. Online date :
08/02/2010

Title : Mémorial, ou Journal historique, impartial et anecdotique de la
révolution de France. Tome 3 / , contenant une série exacte des faits
principaux qui ont amené et prolongé cette révolution, depuis 1786,
jusqu'à l'armistice signé dans les derniers jours de l'an VIII... Par P. C.
Lecomte. Author : Lecomte, Pierre Charles (1757-18..). Auteur du
texte. Publisher : A Paris, chez Duponcet, libraire, quai de la Grève,
n°. 34. An IX.-1801 [-An XI.-1803]. Publication date : 1801-1803. Set
notice : http://catalogue.bnf.fr/ark:/12148/cb307677969. Identifier :
ark:/12148/bpt6k3045188x. Source : Bibliothèque nationale de France,
département Philosophie, histoire, sciences de l'homme, 8-LA32-75 (3).
Provenance : Bibliothèque nationale de France. Online date :
17/04/2019

[25] Records indicate he promptly left the island in October 1792.

[26] Saint-Remy, Joseph. Pétion et Haïti. Chez L'Éditeur, 2eme édition,
Port-au-Prince, 1956. In some ways it was very appropriate for Saint-
Remy to have written the biography of Petion. Born in the slave colony
of Guadeloupe in 1816, his parents had heard that Haiti was a land of
free blacks and that all were welcomed. The Saint-Remy family
emigrated to Les Cayes.

[27] Bonnet, Guy Joseph. Exposé de la conduite du général Rigaud, dans
le commandement du département du sud de Saint-Domingue ,
adressé au Directoire-exécutif, par le citoyen Bonnet, aide-de-camp

dudit général. [Paris.] De l'imprimerie de J. F. Sobry, rue du Bacq, n°. 149. [1798]. http://catalogue.bnf.fr/ark:/12148/cb301292460. Bibliothèque nationale de France, département Philosophie, histoire, sciences de l'homme, 8-LK12-542. Identifier : ark:/12148/bpt6k58068847. Online date : 08/02/2010

[28] Madiou, Thomas. Histoire d'Haïti, Tome 1 - VIII. Éditions Henri Deschamps, Port-au-Prince: 1988.

[29] Saint-Remy, Joseph. Pétion et Haïti. Chez L'Éditeur, 2eme édition, Port-au-Prince, 1956.

[30] Title : Paris, le 1er thermidor, an 6 de la République. Léger-Félicité Sonthonax, représentant du peuple, à ses collègues, membres des deux conseils. Author : Sonthonax, Léger-Félicité (1763-1813). Auteur du texte
Publisher : impr. du Journal de l'Amie des lois ((Paris,)). Publication date : 1798. Relationship : http://catalogue.bnf.fr/ark:/12148/cb313842784. Identifier : ark:/12148/bpt6k5812703g. Source : Bibliothèque nationale de France, département Philosophie, histoire, sciences de l'homme, 8-LK12-543 Provenance : Bibliothèque nationale de France. Online date : 22/02/2010

[31] Title : Esquisse historique des principaux événements arrivés à Saint-Domingue depuis l'incendie du Cap jusqu'à l'expulsion de Sonthonax, leurs causes, leurs effets, situation actuelle de cette colonie et moyens d'y rétablir la tranquillité, par François-Frédéric Cotterel. Author : Cotterel, François Frédéric (1767-182.). Auteur du texte. Publisher : impr. de C.-J. Gelé (Paris). Publication date : 1797. Set notice : http://catalogue.bnf.fr/ark:/12148/cb30277246q. Type : text. Type : printed monograph. Language : french. Format : In-8° , X-68 p.Format : Nombre total de vues : 84. Description : Avec mode texte. Rights : Public domain. Identifier : ark:/12148/bpt6k5785732t. Source : Bibliothèque nationale de France, département Philosophie, histoire, sciences de l'homme, 8-LK12-547. Provenance : Bibliothèque nationale de France. Online date : 12/01/2010.

[32] Title : Corps législatif. Conseil des cinq-cents. Discours prononcé par Sonthonax, sur la situation actuelle de Saint-Domingue, & sur les principaux événemens qui se sont passés dans cette île depuis la fin de floréal an 4, jusqu'en messidor de l'an 5 de la République. Séance du 16 pluviôse an 6. Author : Sonthonax, Léger-Félicité. Publication date : 1798. Rights : http://tolosana.univ-toulouse.fr/mentions-legales. Identifier : https://tolosana.univ-toulouse.fr/notice/078039592. Provenance : Tolosana - Université de Toulouse. Online date : 25/09/2019

[33] Title : Quelques éclaircissements sur les troubles survenus dans le département du Sud de Saint-Domingue, en Fructidor an 4eme. (Août

1796, vieux style.). Publisher : A Hambourg, de l'imprimerie de P. F. Fauche. 1797. Publication date : 1797. Relationship : http://catalogue.bnf.fr/ark:/12148/cb47568565f Relation : Appartient à : [Bibliothèque de Moreau de Saint-Méry. T. 51, Pièces concernant les colonies] ; 6 Relationship : http://catalogue.bnf.fr/ark:/12148/cb455456659. Identifier : ark:/12148/bpt6k9788603h Source : Archives nationales d'outre-Mer, 2017-142834. Provenance : Bibliothèque nationale de France Online date : 31/07/2017

[34] The correspondence of this period has been reprinted by both historians Madiou fils and B. Ardouin. Madiou, Thomas. Histoire d'Haïti, Tome 1 - VIII. Éditions Henri Deschamps, Port-au-Prince: 1988. Ardouin, Beaubrun. Étude sur l'Histoire d'Haïti, Vol 1 - 3, 2eme édition, Éditeur Dr. François Dalencour, Port-au-Prince, 1958.

[35] Title : Rapport fait au gouvernement sur Saint-Domingue.. Numéro 10. P. [3]-76. Author : Périchou, François-Marie (1757-1825 ; sieur de Kerversau). Author : Leborgne de Boigne, Claude-Pierre-Joseph (1762-1832). Publisher : A Paris chez Pain, imprimeur-libraire, rue Coquillière, n°. 23. [1797]. Publication date : 1797. Set notice : http://catalogue.bnf.fr/ark:/12148/cb307616550. Set notice : Notice de recueil : http://catalogue.bnf.fr/ark:/12148/cb475285679. Relation : Appartient à : [Bibliothèque de Moreau de Saint-Méry. 2022-61822. T. ..., Pièces concernant] ; Relation : http://catalogue.bnf.fr/ark:/12148/cb47528595j Relation : Appartient à : [Bibliothèque de Moreau de Saint-Méry. 2022-61855. T. ..., Pièces concernant] ; 10-11. Identifier : ark:/12148/bd6t5346232m. Source : Archives nationales d'outre-mer, 2022-61855 Provenance : Bibliothèque nationale de France. Online date : 21/05/2023

[36] Ardouin, Beaubrun. Étude sur l'Histoire d'Haïti, Vol 1 - 3, 2eme édition, Éditeur Dr. François Dalencour, Port-au-Prince, 1958.

[37] Title : Vie de Toussaint-L'Ouverture... par Saint-Remy (des Cayes, Haïti). Author: Saint-Remy, Joseph (1815-1858). Publisher : Moquet (Paris). Publication date: 1850. Relationship: http://catalogue.bnf.fr/ark:/12148/cb312847999. Identifier : ark:/12148/bpt6k5821332s. Source : Bibliothèque nationale de France, département Philosophie, histoire, sciences de l'homme, 8-LN27-19747 Provenance : Bibliothèque nationale de France. Online date : 15/03/2010

[38] Title : Réponse du Général de brigade André Rigaud à la proclamation du citoyen Roume, agent du Directoire Exécutif à Saint-Domingue, en date du 15 Messidor l'an 7ème. Author : Rigaud, André

(1761-1811). Publisher : Aux Cayes : [s.n.]. Publication date : 1799-01-01. Identifier : http://www.manioc.org/patrimon/SCH13107. Source : Collectivité territoriale de Martinique. Bibliothèque Schoelcher. Provenance : Manioc. Online date : 15/01/2014

[39] Correspondence was reprinted by Ardouin, *Etudes sur l'Histoire d'Haiti.*

[40] Some of the exchange between the two generals has survived. Title : Réponse du citoyen Toussaint Louverture, général en chef de l'armée de St-Domingue, aux calomnies et aux écrits mensongers du général de brigade Rigaud, commandant le département du Sud. Author : Toussaint Louverture (1743-1803). Publisher : chez P. Roux, imprimeur du gouvernement (Au Cap-Français) Publication date : 1799. Relationship : http://catalogue.bnf.fr/ark:/12148/cb45205955g. Identifier : ark:/12148/bpt6k9103177w. Source : Bibliothèque Haïtienne des Spiritains. Provenance : Bibliothèque nationale de France. Online date : 06/03/2017. Title : Réponse du général de brigade André Rigaud, à l'écrit calomnieux du général Toussaint Louverture. Author : Rigaud, André (1761-1811). Publisher : Aux Cayes, chez Lemery imprimeur du département du Sud [1799]. Publication date : 1799. Relationship : http://catalogue.bnf.fr/ark:/12148/cb452072869. Identifier : ark:/12148/bpt6k91032725. Source : Bibliothèque Haïtienne des Spiritains. Provenance : Bibliothèque nationale de France. Online date : 27/03/2017

[41] Madiou covers this period extremely well, having amassed all the relevant correspondences. Madiou, Thomas. Histoire d'Haïti, Tome 1 - VIII. Éditions Henri Deschamps, Port-au-Prince: 1988.

[42] Saint-Remy, pg 262

[43] Peter P. Hinks, "'Perfectly proper and conciliating': Jean-Pierre Boyer, Freemasonry, and the revolutionary Atlantic in eastern Connecticut, 1800–1801," *Atlantic Studies*, 16:3 (2019): 364–385, https://doi: 10.1080/14788810.2018.1525649

[44] F. M. Caulkins, *History of Norwich, Connecticut: From Its Possession by the Indians, to the Year 1866* (1866).

[45] *Norwich Courier*, 3 December 1800, Norwich, Connecticut, USA.

[46] This correspondence was reprinted in both Ardouin (1958) and Madiou (1988). Ardouin, Beaubrun. *Etudes Sur l'Histoire d'Haïti*. 2nd ed., vol.1- 3 (1812-1843), Editor Dr. Francois Dalencour, 1958. Madiou, Thomas Histoire d'Haïti, Tome 1 - VIII. Éditions Henri Deschamps, Port-au-Prince: 1988.

[47] James Franklin and Joseph Meredith Toner Collection, *The present state of Hayti.*

[48] Madiou, Histoire d'Haiti

[49] Saint-Remy estimated that Louverture kept thirteen battalions

operational with fifteen hundred men in each. Title : Vie de
Toussaint-L'Ouverture... par Saint-Remy (des Cayes, Haïti)
Author : Saint-Remy, Joseph (1815-1858). Publication date : 1850.
Relationship : http://catalogue.bnf.fr/ark:/12148/cb312847999.
Identifier : ark:/12148/bpt6k5821332s. Source : Bibliothèque
nationale de France, département Philosophie, histoire, sciences de
l'homme, 8-LN27-19747
Provenance : Bibliothèque nationale de France. Online date :
15/03/2010
[50] James Franklin and Joseph Meredith Toner Collection, *The present
state of Hayti.*
[51] Gainot and Mace (2003) compared the two constitutions. Gainot
Bernard and Macé Mayeul. Fin de campagne à Saint-Domingue,
novembre 1802-novembre 1803. In: Outre-mers, tome 90, n°340-341, 2e
semestre 2003. Haïti Première République Noire. pp. 15-40; doi :
https://doi.org/10.3406/outre.2003.4041
[52] The size of the expedition depends on who is furnishing the
information. Saint-Remy (1956) cited a report by General
Rochambeau, who was a division general, that the original expedition
numbered just under 22,000 men on 54 vessels. Guinot and Mace
(2003) concur. Breant de Fontenay (n.d.) estimated 25,000 men on 26
ships. Higher estimates were offered by Metral (1825), of 30,000 men
on 60 ships, and by Moya Pons (2007), with 58,000 on 80 ships—
though the latter may be referring to the entire duration of the
expedition, as reinforcements were sent in three phases. Haitian
historian Thomas Madiou provided an elaborate accounting of forces
sent to the island, by brigade number, ship name, and ship
commander. There were three major waves of forces sent—which
doesn't include additional soldiers dispatched from adjacent French
islands—in February 1802, in June 1802, and in February 1803. In total,
55,609 soldiers were sent to Saint-Domingue. Madiou, Tome 3, pg 133
[53] H. B. L. Hughes, "British Policy Towards Haiti: 1801–1805," *The
Canadian Historical Review*, CHR-025-04-03 (June 2016),
https://www.haiti-now.org/wp-content/uploads/2021/03/british-
policy-towards-haiti-1801-1805.pdf.
[54] Hughes, "British Policy Towards Haiti."
[55] Title : Souvenirs de trente années de voyages à Saint-Domingue,
dans plusieurs colonies étrangères et au continent d'Amérique. T. 2 /
par A. de Laujon. Author : de Laujon, Alexandre Paul Marie de (1766-
18..). Auteur du texte. Publisher : (Paris). Publication date : 1835. Set
notice : http://catalogue.bnf.fr/ark:/12148/cb30749599v. Type : text.
Type : monographie imprimée. Language : french. Format : 2 vol. ;
in-8. Format : Nombre total de vues : 464. Description : Collection
numérique : France-Amérique. Description : Descriptions et voyages.

Rights : Public domain. Identifier : ark:/12148/bpt6k114026g. Source
: Bibliothèque nationale de France, département Philosophie, histoire,
sciences de l'homme, 8-Lk12-201 (2). Provenance : Bibliothèque
nationale de France. Online date : 02/04/2008
[56] A sonnet by William Wordsworth dedicated to Louverture,
published in 1802.
[57] Title : Réponse du général Rochambeau à l'arrêté des agens
particuliers du Directoire exécutif, à St-Domingue. (9 pluviôse an V.).
Author : Rochambeau, Donatien-Marie-Joseph de Vimeur (1750-1813
; vicomte de). Publisher : impr. de Noé (Bordeaux). Publication date :
1797. Relationship : http://catalogue.bnf.fr/ark:/12148/cb31229746p.
Identifier : ark:/12148/bpt6k5803873h
Source : Bibliothèque nationale de France, département Philosophie,
histoire, sciences de l'homme, 4-LK12-518. Provenance : Bibliothèque
nationale de France. Online date : 01/02/2010
[58] Girard (2012) dedicated an article to the role of dogs in the Haitian
Revolution. P. R. Girard, "War Unleashed: The Use of War Dogs
During the Haitian War of Independence," *Napoleonica. La Revue*,
15(3) (2012), 80–105, https://doi.org/10.3917/napo.123.0080.
[59] Seconde campagne de Saint-Domingue du 1er décembre 1803 au 15
juillet 1809; : précédée de Souvenirs historiques & succincts de la
première campagne expédition du général en chef Leclerc, du 14
décembre 1801 au 1er décembre 1803, par M. Lemmonier-Delafosse,
ancien officier de l'armée de Saint-Domingue, lieutenant-colonel en
retraite, officier de la Légion-d'Honneur, chevalier de Saint-Louis, et
de l'Ordre de San-Fernando d'Espagne by Lemonnier-Delafosse, Jean-
Baptiste. Publication date 1846. Topics Imprint 1846
Publisher Havre : imprimerie de H. Brindeau & Compie, rue Saint-
Julies, 16Collection jcbhaiti; JohnCarterBrownLibrary; americana.
Digitizing sponsor John Carter Brown Library
Contributor John Carter Brown Library
[60] Nobi (2015). Similar estimates from Houdaille (1973), who also
suggests that, at embarkation of the remaining soldiers in 1803, there
were only eight thousand.
[61] Métral, Antoine. *Histoire de l'expédition des Français à Saint-
Domingue sous le consulat de Napoléon Bonaparte*, Paris, 1825.
[62] Rigaud's deportation is treated uniformly by several Haitian
historians. See Sanon (2003).
[63] Saint-Remy, Joseph. *Petion et Haiti: etude monographiquee et
historique*. Second edition, Les Editions Fardin, 1956.
[64] For a brief history of the evolution of the French army in the
eighteenth century, see Ross (1965) or Rosen (1981).
[65] Seconde campagne de Saint-Domingue du 1er décembre 1803 au 15
juillet 1809; : précédée de Souvenirs historiques & succincts de la

première campagne expédition du général en chef Leclerc, du 14 décembre 1801 au 1er décembre 1803, par M. Lemmonier-Delafosse, ancien officier de l'armée de Saint-Domingue, lieutenant-colonel en retraite, officier de la Légion-d'Honneur, chevalier de Saint-Louis, et de l'Ordre de San-Fernando d'Espagne by Lemonnier-Delafosse, Jean-Baptiste. Publication date 1846. Topics Imprint 1846 Publisher Havre : imprimerie de H. Brindeau & Compie, rue Saint-Julies, 16Collection jcbhaiti; JohnCarterBrownLibrary; americana. Digitizing sponsor John Carter Brown Library Contributor John Carter Brown Library

[66] Celigni Ardouin (1865), the older brother of Beaubrun Ardouin, present at the siege of Plaisance, described their meetings as civil. Ardouin, C. N. C., and B. Ardouin. *Essais Sur l'histoire d'Haïti*. Chez T. Bouchereau, 1865,

[67] James Franklin and Joseph Meredith Toner Collection, *The present state of Hayti.*

[68] Bonnet, Guy Joseph. Exposé de la conduite du général Rigaud, dans le commandement du département du sud de Saint-Domingue , adressé au Directoire-exécutif, par le citoyen Bonnet, aide-de-camp dudit général. [Paris.] De l'imprimerie de J. F. Sobry, rue du Bacq, n°. 149. [1798]. http://catalogue.bnf.fr/ark:/12148/cb301292460. Bibliothèque nationale de France, département Philosophie, histoire, sciences de l'homme, 8-LK12-542. Identifier : ark:/12148/bpt6k58068847. Online date : 08/02/2010

[69] Saint-Remy, *Pétion et Haïti.*

[70] Gazette Officielle de l'État D'Hayti (04 June 1807).

[71] Essai sur les causes de la révolution et des guerres civiles d'Hayti, faisant suite aux réflexions politiques sur quelques ouvrages et journaux français, concernant Hayti avec différentes pièces by Pompée-Valentin Baron de Vastey. Publication date 1819. Usage Public Domain Mark 1.0 Topics bub_upload. Publisher Imprimerie royale. Collection European libraries. Digitizing sponsor Google Book from the collections of unknown library. Language French. Added date 2014-11-22 00:10:42 Fold out count 0. Google-id 8mRKAAAAcAAJ. Identifier bub_gb_8mRKAAAAcAAJ. Identifier-ark ark:/13960/t1sf5rw48. Ocr ABBYY FineReader 9.0. Pages 438. Scanner google.

[72] William Woods Harvey described the Northerners during his visit to Cap-Haïtien during Christophe's reign as temperate in comportment—petty theft was rare, as was public drunkenness—industrious, and multilingual. W. W. Harvey, *Sketches of Hayti: From the Expulsion of the French, to the Death of Christophe* (L.B. Seeley and Son, 1827).

[73] Saint-Remy, *Pétion et Haïti.*

[74] Madiou, , *Histoire d'Haïti.*

[75] Saint-Remy, Pétion et Haïti.

[76] Madiou, *Histoire d'Haiti.*

[77] There were no birth certificates (in the modern sense) available for non-whites, as they were not considered citizens. However, the baptismal registry has survived, which confirms the names of Boyer's godparents and his mother. The assertion that his name is a combination of his grandfather's and godfather's names is part of the family's oral history. This information was shared with the author during a conversation with Peter Frisch in July 2025.

[78] Conversation with Peter Frisch, a descendant of Charles Jean Pierre Boyer Bazelais, the grandson of Boyer.

[79] James Franklin and Joseph Meredith Toner Collection, *The present state of Hayti*; and Baur, "Mulatto Machiavelli."

[80] Lespinasse, Pierre-Eugène de. Gens d'autrefois... Vieux souvenirs. La "Revue mondiale" (Paris), 1926, http://catalogue.bnf.fr/ark:/12148/cb30803634f. Bibliothèque nationale de France, département Philosophie, histoire, sciences de l'homme, 8-PU-510 (1), Identifier : ark:/12148/bpt6k6148893f. Online date : 25/10/2010

[81] Title : Gazette de France Publisher : Imprimerie de la Gazette de France (Paris). Publication date : 1843-09-27. Contributor : Genoude, Antoine-Eugène (1792-1849). Collaborateur. Relationship : http://catalogue.bnf.fr/ark:/12148/cb41265446t. Description : 27 septembre 1843. Identifier : ark:/12148/bpt6k4490386s. Source : Bibliothèque nationale de France, département Philosophie, histoire, sciences de l'homme, 4-LC2-1. Provenance : Bibliothèque nationale de France. Online date : 28/01/2019. The original article was in the Journal de Rouen, published on 24 September 1843. Reference was also made to Boyer's mother still being alive in the Journal de Lille, 18 October 1843. The family were living together in an apartment on the Rue Neuve de Luxembourg.

[82] According to the memoir written by General Bonnet, Boyer had an unnamed brother who was killed by Christophe, though it is unclear whether this was Souverain. Also, in Candler's memoir of his travel to Haiti, during an interview with Boyer, the latter mentioned having had a brother who was killed by Christophe. Bonnet, Guy Joseph. Exposé de la conduite du général Rigaud, dans le commandement du département du sud de Saint-Domingue , adressé au Directoire-exécutif, par le citoyen Bonnet, aide-de-camp dudit général. [Paris.] De l'imprimerie de J. F. Sobry, rue du Bacq, n°. 149. [1798]. http://catalogue.bnf.fr/ark:/12148/cb301292460. Bibliothèque nationale de France, département Philosophie, histoire, sciences de l'homme, 8-

LK12-542. Identifier : ark:/12148/bpt6k58068847. Online date : 08/02/2010. John Candler, *Brief notices of Hayti* (London: T. Ward & Co., 1842). Library of Congress, item no. 02012376.

[83] Frisch, Peter. "Le président Jean-Pierre BOYER et sa famille" Généalogie et histoire de la Caraïbe, GHC 16, décembre 2003, p.4019-4022

[84] Minutes et répertoires du notaire Louis Benoît BAYARD, 10 août 1839 12 avril 1855 (étude LXXVII) Répertoire numérique détaillé Minutier central des notaires de Paris. Archives Nationales de France. Base Miriad 2 des inventaires après décès, 1801-1850, par Thierry Boudignon, avec le concours de Marie France Nivet et du personnel du Minutier central, 1995-2012 (base de données migrée : voir contexte dans le Plan d'orientation général - Notaires de Paris, guides thématiques du Minutier). Transcribed by Bardin, Pierre. "Le Président Jean Pierre Boyer, une fortune discrète", Généalogie et Histoire de la Caraïbe, bulletin 164, novembre 2023.

[85] Charles Mackenzie, *Notes on Haiti, made during a residence in that republic*, Volumes 1 and 2, (London: Henry Colburn and Richard Bantley, 1830). Accessed through Brown University Library.

[86] Lespinasse, Pierre-Eugène de. Gens d'autrefois... Vieux souvenirs. La "Revue mondiale" (Paris), 1926, http://catalogue.bnf.fr/ark:/12148/cb30803634f. Bibliothèque nationale de France, département Philosophie, histoire, sciences de l'homme, 8-PU-510 (1), Identifier : ark:/12148/bpt6k6148893f. Online date : 25/10/2010

[87] Michael Scott, *Tom Cringle's Log (1789–1835)* (Project Guttenburg E-book, #7281, January 2005).

[88] Minutes et répertoires du notaire Louis Benoît BAYARD, 10 août 1839 12 avril 1855 (étude LXXVII) Répertoire numérique détaillé Minutier central des notaires de Paris. Archives Nationales de France. Base Miriad 2 des inventaires après décès, 1801-1850, par Thierry Boudignon, avec le concours de Marie France Nivet et du personnel du Minutier central, 1995-2012 (base de données migrée : voir contexte dans le Plan d'orientation général - Notaires de Paris, guides thématiques du Minutier). Transcribed by Bardin, Pierre. "Le Président Jean Pierre Boyer, une fortune discrète", Généalogie et Histoire de la Caraïbe, bulletin 164, novembre 2023.

[89] Minutes et répertoires du notaire Louis Benoît BAYARD, 10 août 1839 12 avril 1855 (étude LXXVII) Répertoire numérique détaillé Minutier central des notaires de Paris. Archives Nationales de France. Base Miriad 2 des inventaires après décès, 1801-1850, par Thierry Boudignon, avec le concours de Marie France Nivet et du personnel du Minutier central, 1995-2012 (base de données migrée : voir contexte dans le Plan d'orientation général - Notaires de Paris, guides

thématiques du Minutier). Transcribed by Bardin, Pierre. "Le Président Jean Pierre Boyer, une fortune discrète", Généalogie et Histoire de la Caraïbe, bulletin 164, novembre 2023.

[90] Wallez, Jean Baptiste Guislain (1826). Précis historique des négociations entre la France et Saint-Domingue : suivi de pièces justificatives et d'une notice biographique sur le général Boyer, président de la République d'Haïti. Publisher : Ponthieu (Paris).Publication date : 1826. Set notice : http://catalogue.bnf.fr/ark:/12148/cb31618508t. Identifier : ark:/12148/bpt6k58087158. Source : Bibliothèque nationale de France, département Philosophie, histoire, sciences de l'homme, 8-LK12-636. Online date : 08/02/2010

[91] Title : Biographie des souverains du XIXe siècle, par deux rois de la fève (Paul-Émile Debraux et Ch. Lepage). Author : Debraux, Paul-Émile (1796-1831). Auteur du texte. Publisher : les marchands de nouveautés (Paris). Publication date : 1826. Relationship : http://catalogue.bnf.fr/ark:/12148/cb30307096f. Type : text. Type : monographie imprimée. Language : french. Format : In-32, 191 p. Format : Nombre total de vues : 196. Description : Avec mode texte. Rights : Public domain. Identifier : ark:/12148/bpt6k65831746. Source : Bibliothèque nationale de France, département Philosophie, histoire, sciences de l'homme, G-20011. Provenance : Bibliothèque nationale de France. Online date : 21/03/2014

[92] Bonnet, Guy Joseph. Exposé de la conduite du général Rigaud, dans le commandement du département du sud de Saint-Domingue , adressé au Directoire-exécutif, par le citoyen Bonnet, aide-de-camp dudit général. [Paris.] De l'imprimerie de J. F. Sobry, rue du Bacq, n°. 149. [1798]. http://catalogue.bnf.fr/ark:/12148/cb301292460. Bibliothèque nationale de France, département Philosophie, histoire, sciences de l'homme, 8-LK12-542. Identifier : ark:/12148/bpt6k58068847. Online date : 08/02/2010

[93] Inginac, Joseph Balthazar. *Mémoires de Joseph Balthazar Inginac, Général de Division, Ex-Secrétaire General Pres. S.E. L'Ex-président d'Haïti : Depuis 1797 jusqu'à 1843.* J.R. de Cordova, Kingston, 1843.

[94] Bonnet, Guy Joseph. Exposé de la conduite du général Rigaud, dans le commandement du département du sud de Saint-Domingue , adressé au Directoire-exécutif, par le citoyen Bonnet, aide-de-camp dudit général. [Paris.] De l'imprimerie de J. F. Sobry, rue du Bacq, n°. 149. [1798]. http://catalogue.bnf.fr/ark:/12148/cb301292460. Bibliothèque nationale de France, département Philosophie, histoire, sciences de l'homme, 8-LK12-542. Identifier : ark:/12148/bpt6k58068847. Online date : 08/02/2010

[95] Alcide d'Orbigny, who visited the National Palace includes an elaborate description in his travel memoir. Title : Voyage pittoresque

dans les deux Amériques : résumé général de tous les voyages de Colomb, Las-Casas, Oviedo, Gomara, Garcilazo de La Vega,... etc., etc. / publ. sous la dir. de M. Alcide d'Orbigny,...Author : Orbigny, Alcide d' (1802-1857). Publisher : L. Tenré (Paris). Publication date : 1836. Relationship : http://catalogue.bnf.fr/ark:/12148/cb310389178. Identifier : ark:/12148/btv1b86267486 Source : Bibliothèque nationale de France, département Arsenal, 4-H-291. Provenance : Bibliothèque nationale de France. Online date : 30/07/2012

[96] Scott, *Tom Cringle's Log.*

[97] Fournier-Verneuil, Vincent (1824). Curiosité et Indiscrétion, Paris, Chez Tous les Marchands de Nouveautés, 1824.

[98] Inginac, Joseph Balthazar. *Mémoires de Joseph Balthazar Inginac,* pg 33.

[99] Schmidt, Hans. *The United States Occupation of Haiti, 1915-1934,* Rutgers University Press, New Brunswick: 1995.

[100] Mackenzie, *Notes on Haiti.*

[101] See Janvier for a lengthy discussion of the nature and extent of militarism in Haiti.

[102] C.N.C. Ardouin and B. Ardouin, *Essais Sur l'histoire d'Haïti* (Chez T. Bouchereau, 1865), https://books.google.ht/books?id=d6VDAQAAMAAJ.

[103] Inginac, Joseph Balthazar. *Mémoires de Joseph Balthazar Inginac,* pg 9

[104] Inginac, *Mémoires de Joseph Balthazar Inginac,* pg 25.

[105] Clormeus (2015) describes the extent to which Freemasonry had pervaded Haitian public administration. Clorméus, Lewis Ampidu. "Quelques Aspects Des Rapports Entre La Franc-Maçonnerie et La Sphère Politique En Haïti Au XIX e Siècle:" *Outre-Mers,* vol. N° 386-387, no. 1, June 2015, pp. 183–204. *DOI.org (Crossref),* https://doi.org/10.3917/om.151.0183.

[106] Granier De Cassagnac, A. (1842) Voyage aux Antilles, françaises, anglaises, danoises, espagnoles; à Saint-Domingue et aux États-Unis d'Amérique. Paris, Dauvin et Fontaine, -44. [Pdf] Retrieved from the Library of Congress, item no. 02008513.

[107] Beaubrun Ardouin's multi-volume history of Haiti is also partially a biography of General Borgella, who was also a close friend of his father.

[108] Ardouin's description of Borgella. Ardouin, B. *Études sur l'Histoire d'Haïti*

[109] Mackenzie, *Notes on Haïti.*

[110] Ardouin, B. *Études sur l'Histoire d'Haïti*

[111] Gonzalez, J. (2014). Defiant Haiti: Free-Soil Runaways, Ship Seizures and the Politics of Diplomatic Non-Recognition in the Early

Nineteenth Century. *Slavery & Abolition*, *36*(1), 124–135. https://doi.org/10.1080/0144039X.2014.895508

[112] *Les Plaideurs* was the only comedy written by Jean Racine, who specialized in tragedies. Still staged to this day, it was immensely popular and rivaled Molière. It must have been all the rage when Boyer saw it staged in Paris. Racine, Jean (1697). Les Plaideurs, Publié par Gwénola, Ernest et Paul Fièvre, Septembre 2015.

[113] Simon Henochsberg, *Public Debt and Slavery: the Case of Haiti (1760–1915)* (Paris School of Economics, December 2016).

[114] Henochsberg, *Public Debt and Slavery.*

[115] Pons, *History of the Caribbean.*

[116] Victor Bulmer-Thomas, *The Economic History of the Caribbean Since the Napoleonic Wars* (Cambridge University Press, 2012).

[117] Title : Cours complet d'économie politique pratique, ouvrage destiné à mettre sous les yeux des hommes d'État, des propriétaires fonciers et des capitalistes, des savans, des agriculteurs, des manufacturiers, des négocians et en général de tous les citoyens, l'économie des sociétés, par Jean-Baptiste Say.... Volume 2 Author : Say, Jean-Baptiste (1767-1832). Publisher : Rapilly (Paris). Publication date : 1828-1833. Contributor : Comte, Charles (1782-1837). Éditeur scientifique. Set notice : http://catalogue.bnf.fr/ark:/12148/cb31307081j. Identifier : ark:/12148/bpt6k1516459h. Source : Bibliothèque nationale de France, département Réserve des livres rares, R-21125. Provenance : Bibliothèque nationale de France. Online date : 31/12/2017

[118] Henochsberg, *Public Debt and Slavery.*

[119] Bulmer-Thomas, *The Economic History of the Caribbean.*

[120] Giovanni Frederico and Antonio Tena-Junguito, "American divergence: Lost decades and Emancipation collapse in Latin American and the Caribbean 1820–1870" *European Review of Economic History*, 22, no. 2 (May 2018): 185–209, https://doi.org/10.1093/ereh/hex017.

[121] A. D. Pathak, et al. "Evolution and History of Sugar Beet in the World: An Overview," *Sugar Beet Cultivation, Management and Processing*, Varucha Misra et al., eds. (Singapore: Springer, 2022): 3–10, https://doi.org/10.1007/978-981-19-2730-0_1.

[122] Hector, Michel, and Laennec Hurbon. *Genèse de l'état haïtien (1804-1859)*. Presses Nationales d'Haïti, 2009.

[123] Federico and Tena-Junguito, 2018, "haiti_1820_1938_FTWTHD_201710_v01.xlsx," *Federico-Tena World Trade Historical Database : Haiti*, https://doi.org/10.21950/6SHH8V/QFHVZN, e-cienciaDatos, V1.

[124] Economists Frederico and Tena-Junguito (2018) looked at exports of contemporary independent countries and colonies in the Americas.

Federico and Tena-Junguito, "American divergence."

[125] Federico and Tena-Junguito, "World Trade, 1800–1938: A New Synthesis," *Revista de Historia Económica / Journal of Iberian and Latin American Economic History*, 37, no. 1 (2019):9–41, doi:10.1017/S0212610918000216.

[126] Frederico and Tena-Junguito, "American divergence."

[127] Ibid.

[128] Henochsberg, *Public Debt and Slavery*.

[129] *Le Telegraphe* was the official country newspaper and was widely circulated throughout the world. It is likely that Boyer inflated the size of his army as a deterrent. Ardouin estimated the standing army to be forty thousand. *Le Telegraphe, Gazette Officielle*, No. XXVII, Port-au-Prince, 4 July 1824.

[130] Title : Circulaires du président d'Haïti (Jean-Pierre Boyer) aux commandans d'arrondissement, sur l'agriculture. Author : Boyer, Jean Pierre (1776-1850). Publisher : impr. du Gouvernement (Port-au-Prince). Relationship : http://catalogue.bnf.fr/ark:/12148/cb30152320h. Identifier : ark:/12148/bpt6k57971547. Source : Bibliothèque nationale de France, département Philosophie, histoire, sciences de l'homme, 8-PU-78. Provenance : Bibliothèque nationale de France. Online date : 27/12/2010

[131] Mackenzie, *Notes on Haiti*.

[132] Title : Voyage pittoresque dans les deux Amériques : résumé général de tous les voyages de Colomb, Las-Casas, Oviedo, Gomara, Garcilazo de La Vega,... etc., etc. / publ. sous la dir. de M. Alcide d'Orbigny,... Author : Orbigny, Alcide d' (1802-1857). Publisher : L. Tenré (Paris). Publication date : 1836. Relationship : http://catalogue.bnf.fr/ark:/12148/cb310389178. Identifier : ark:/12148/btv1b86267486. Source : Bibliothèque nationale de France, département Arsenal, 4-H-291. Provenance : Bibliothèque nationale de France. Online date : 30/07/2012

[133] James Franklin and Joseph Meredith Toner Collection, *The present state of Hayti*.

[134] James Logan, *Notes of a journey through Canada, the United States of America, and the West Indies* (Edinburgh: Fraser and Co., 1838) (PDF), https://www.loc.gov/item/01026860/.

[135] Loring Daniel Dewey, *Correspondence Relative to the Emigration to Hayti, of the Free People of Colour, in the United States: Together with Instructions to the Agent Sent Out by President Boyer* (New York: Mahlon Day, 1824.

[136] Granville, Henri (1873). Biographie de Jonathas Granville par son fils, Imprimerie de E. Brière, Paris: 1873.

[137] Le Patriote de la Cote=d'Or on 25 October 1831.

[138] Le Télégraphe, 09 September 1827

[139] Dell Upton, "Lancasterian Schools, Republican Citizenship, and the Spatial Imagination in Early Nineteenth-Century America," *Journal of the Society of Architectural Historians*, 55, no. 3 (Sept. 1996): 238–53, https://doi.org/10.2307/991147.

[140] The Lancaster schools were established in Port-au-Prince, Les Cayes, Cap-Haïtien, San Yago, Jacmel, Jérémie, Saint-Marc, Port-de-Paix, Mirebalais, and Saint-Jean. Ardouin, *Geographie de l'isle d'Haiti*.

[141] Henochsberg, *Public Debt and Slavery*.

[142] St. John, Spencer. Hayti; or, The black republic. United Kingdom: Smith, Elder, & Co, 1884. https://www.gutenberg.org/ebooks/68592. Accessed July 2023

[143] See Le Pers (1730) for a thorough and insightful treatment of the first years of European colonization of Latin America. Title : Histoire de l'Isle espagnole ou de S. Domingue. T2 / , écrite particulièrement sur des mémoires manuscrits du P. Jean-Baptiste Le Pers, jésuite, missionnaire à Saint-Domingue, et sur les pièces originales qui se conservent au Dépôt de la Marine, par le P. Pierre-François-Xavier de Charlevoix,...Author : Le Pers, Jean-Baptiste (1675-1735). Auteur du texte. Author : Charlevoix, Pierre-François-Xavier de (1682-1761). Auteur du texte. Publisher : J. Guérin (Paris). Publication date : 1730-1731. Set notice : http://catalogue.bnf.fr/ark:/12148/cb30224074n. Format : 2 vol. (XXVIII-482-[59], XIV-506-[62] p.) :... Continuation of text. Identifier : ark:/12148/bpt6k113010k. Source : Bibliothèque nationale de France, département Fonds du service reproduction, 4-LK12-187 (A, 2). Provenance : Bibliothèque nationale de France
Online date : 20/10/2008

[144] Carrie Elizabeth Gibson, "The Impact of the Haitian Revolution on the Hispanic Caribbean: 1791–1830" (doctoral dissertation), Cambridge University, 2010.

[145] Gonzalez, J. (2015). *Defiant Haiti: Free-Soil Runaways, Ship Seizures and the Politics of Diplomatic Non-Recognition in the Early Nineteenth Century.* https://doi.org/10.17863/CAM.27859

[146] ibid

[147] Wassell, Peter (n.d.). The "De Facto" Governors of Haiti: The Debate Over US Recognition of Haiti, 1804-1862. https://www.calstatela.edu/sites/default/files/9.%20Pete%26%23039%3Bs%20Article.pdf. Accessed July 2025.

[148] Gales, Joseph, 1761-1841. Register of Debates in Congress, Comprising the Leading Debates and Incidents of the First Session of the Twentieth Congress, book, 1828; Washington D.C. (https://digital.library.unt.edu/ark:/67531/metadc30741/m1/331/?q=Hayti: accessed July 28, 2025), University of North Texas Libraries, UNT

Digital Library, https://digital.library.unt.edu; crediting UNT Libraries Government Documents Department.
[149] John Quincy Adams Digital Diary, diary entry 21 January 1842
[150] United States Congress. House, Martin Van Buren, Martin Van Buren Originator, Publisher United States Government Publishing Office, Author United States Congress. House, United States President, United States Department of State, and Mexico. *United States and Mexico. Message from the President of the United States, transmitting, in compliance with a resolution of the House of Representatives of the 21st ultimo, a report of the Secretary of State upon the existing relations between the United States and Mexico. Referred to the Committee on Foreign Affairs* (Washington, DC: US Government Printing Office, 1838) (PDF). Library of Congress, item no. 2022689171.
[151] Gómez, Alejandro E. « Chapitre VI. Qui craint le "mauvais exemple" de Saint-Domingue ? ». In *Le spectre de la révolution noire*. Rennes: Presses universitaires de Rennes, 2013. https://doi.org/10.4000/books.pur.43713.
[152] Schomburg Center for Research in Black Culture, Manuscripts, Archives and Rare Books Division, The New York Public Library. (1821). *Fugitive Slaves - Turks and Caicos Islands* Retrieved from https://digitalcollections.nypl.org/items/afdc5490-e588-0130-95ee-58d385a7bbd0
[153] Vaur, J.-P. (1849). Précis historique des faits relatifs à l'emprunt d'Haïti et des derniers arrangements financiers conclus entre le gouvernement haïtien et le comité des porteurs de titres dudit emprunt, publié par le Comité. Publisher : impr. de Guiraudet et Jouaust (Paris). Relationship
: http://catalogue.bnf.fr/ark:/12148/cb315497756. Identifier
: ark:/12148/bpt6k5797158w. Source : Bibliothèque nationale de France, département Philosophie, histoire, sciences de l'homme, 8-PU-181. Online date : 03/11/2010.
[154] Louis XVIII (1824). Correspondance et Écrits politiques de S. M. Louis XVIII. Contributeur : Meissonnier de Valcroissant. Éditeur scientifique. Notice du catalogue :
http://catalogue.bnf.fr/ark:/12148/cb30837474q
Identifiant : ark:/12148/bpt6k6138184s. Source : Bibliothèque nationale de France, département Philosophie, histoire, sciences de l'homme, 8-LB45-41. Date de mise en ligne : 06/09/2010
[155] Titre : Copies des pièces des agens du gouvernement français, imprimées et publiées en vertu de la proclamation de Sa Majesté, du 11 novembre 1814, l'an onzième de l'indépendance d'Hayti. Éditeur : (Au Cap-Henry, chez P. Roux, imprimeur du Roi. [1814]). Date d'édition : 1814. Notice du catalogue :
http://catalogue.bnf.fr/ark:/12148/cb34139086f. Identifiant :

ark:/12148/bpt6k318249f. Source : AU, 8-LK12-1279. Conservation numérique : Bibliothèque nationale de France. Date de mise en ligne : 03/12/2017

156 Ardouin,B. Tome 8, chapitre 2

157 Up until this time, French traders were using ships registered in other countries.

158 *Niles' Weekly Register*. Digital, MSA SC 6211, Niles' Register Cumulative Index, 1849 1811.

159 Guillermin de Montpinay, Gilbert de (1819). Colonie de Saint-Domingue, ou Appel à la sollicitude du Roi et de la France, par M. de Guillermin de Montpinay. Publisher : Delaunay (Paris). Relationship : http://catalogue.bnf.fr/ark:/12148/cb305588639. Identifier : ark:/12148/bpt6k58032224. Source : Bibliothèque nationale de France, département Philosophie, histoire, sciences de l'homme, 8-LK12-579. Online date : 08/02/2010

160 *Niles' Weekly Register*. Digital, MSA SC 6211, Niles' Register Cumulative Index, 1849 1811,

161Title : Annuaire historique universel pour ... : avec un appendice contenant les actes publics, traités, notes diplomatiques, papiers d'État, et tableaux statistiques, financiers, administratifs et nécrologiques ; une chronique offrant les événemens les plus piquans, les causes les plus célèbres, etc. ; des extraits de voyages ou de mémoires intéressans, et des notices sur les productions les plus remarquables de l'année, dans les sciences, dans les lettres et dans les arts. Authors : Lesur, Charles-Louis (1770-1849); Tencé, Ulysse; Rosenwald, Victor; Desprez, Hippolyte (1819-1898); Fouquier, Armand (1817-18..?); Publishers : Fantin (Paris); Delaunay (Paris); H. Nicolle (Paris); Treuttel et Wurtz (Paris); Fantin Fantin (Paris); A. Desplaces (Paris); A. Thoisnier-Desplaces (Paris); Lebrun Lebrun (Paris). Publication date : 1822. Contributor : Thoisnier-Desplaces, Adrien-Hippolyte-Augustin (1798-1878). Directeur de publication. Relationship : http://catalogue.bnf.fr/ark:/12148/cb32698157q. Identifier : ark:/12148/bpt6k2003569. Source : Bibliothèque nationale de France.Provenance : Bibliothèque nationale de France. Online date : 15/10/2007

162 Wallez, Jean Baptiste Guislain (1826). Précis historique des négociations entre la France et Saint-Domingue : suivi de pièces justificatives et d'une notice biographique sur le général Boyer, président de la République d'Haïti. Publisher : Ponthieu (Paris). Publication date : 1826. Set notice : http://catalogue.bnf.fr/ark:/12148/cb31618508t. Identifier : ark:/12148/bpt6k58087158. Source : Bibliothèque nationale de France, département Philosophie, histoire, sciences de l'homme, 8-LK12-636. Online date : 08/02/2010

163 Page 7. Title : Le Cri des colons propriétaires à Saint-Domingue, expropriés et réfugiés en France, ou Appel à la nation. Publisher : Goujon (Paris). Publication date : 1822. Relationship : http://catalogue.bnf.fr/ark:/12148/cb36401498s. Identifier : ark:/12148/bpt6k57854173. Source : Bibliothèque nationale de France, département Philosophie, histoire, sciences de l'homme, 8-LK12-592. Provenance : Bibliothèque nationale de France. Online date : 29/12/2009

164 Page 8. Title : Le Cri des colons propriétaires à Saint-Domingue, expropriés et réfugiés en France, ou Appel à la nation. Publisher : Goujon (Paris). Publication date : 1822. Relationship : http://catalogue.bnf.fr/ark:/12148/cb36401498s. Identifier : ark:/12148/bpt6k57854173. Source : Bibliothèque nationale de France, département Philosophie, histoire, sciences de l'homme, 8-LK12-592. Provenance : Bibliothèque nationale de France. Online date : 29/12/2009

165 Page 10. Title : Le Cri des colons propriétaires à Saint-Domingue, expropriés et réfugiés en France, ou Appel à la nation. Publisher : Goujon (Paris). Publication date : 1822. Relationship : http://catalogue.bnf.fr/ark:/12148/cb36401498s. Identifier : ark:/12148/bpt6k57854173. Source : Bibliothèque nationale de France, département Philosophie, histoire, sciences de l'homme, 8-LK12-592. Provenance : Bibliothèque nationale de France. Online date : 29/12/2009

166 An additional article signed by both Great Britain and France on 30 May 1814, annexed to the Treaty of Paris (1814.

167 Discussed at length in Eugène Itazienne. La normalisation des relations franco-haïtiennes (1825-1838). In: *Outre-mers*, tome 90, n°340-341, 2e semestre 2003. Haïti Première République Noire, sous la direction de Marcel Dorigny. pp. 139-154. DOI : https://doi.org/10.3406/outre.2003.4049

168 Madiou, Thomas, Tome Vi, livre 85 On page 461, Madiou lists the ship name and their armaments.

169 Madiou, Thomas. Tome VI, livre 85

170 Madiou, Thomas.Tome VI, livre 85, page 466

171 Gales, Joseph, 1761-1841. Register of Debates in Congress, Comprising the Leading Debates and Incidents of the Second Session of the Twentieth Congress, book, 1830; Washington D.C.. (https://digital.library.unt.edu/ark:/67531/metadc30754/m1/451/?q=Ha yti: accessed July 28, 2025), University of North Texas Libraries, UNT Digital Library, https://digital.library.unt.edu; crediting UNT Libraries Government Documents Department.

172 John Quincy Adams Digital Diary, entry on 20 July 1827

173 John Quincy Adams Digital Diary, entry 27 December 1827

[174] Madiou, Thomas. Tome VI, Livre 85, pg 456.

[175] This consortium included the banking houses of Laffitte, Rothschild, and Paravey.

[176] The benefits realized by Great Britain after recognition of independence of its colonies and the potential economic advantages of doing so for France were discussed in real time by French writers, e.g., Salvandy (1825) and Nonay (1828). Title : De l'Émancipation de Saint-Domingue dans ses rapports avec la politique intérieure et extérieure de la France, par N.-A. de Salvandy. Author : Salvandy, Narcisse-Achille de (1795-1856). Publisher : Ponthieu, Delaunay, Dentu (Paris). Publication date : 1825. Relationship : http://catalogue.bnf.fr/ark:/12148/cb31290689z. Identifier : ark:/12148/bpt6k57744200. Source : Bibliothèque nationale de France, département Philosophie, histoire, sciences de l'homme, 8-LK12-617 Provenance : Bibliothèque nationale de France. Online date : 12/01/2010. Title : La vérité sur Haïti, ses deux emprunts, ses agens, ses finances, son crédit et ses ressources . Réponse à la lettre d'un colon, à l'usage de son exc. le ministre des finances et des capitalistes, par un subrécargue. Author : Nonay, Louis-Jean-Pierre (1793-1867). Publisher : Paris, chez tous les libraires. Imprimerie Moreau, rue Montmartre, n°. 39. 1828. Publication date : 1828. Relationship : http://catalogue.bnf.fr/ark:/12148/cb36491996b. Identifier : ark:/12148/bpt6k5677505b. Source : Bibliothèque nationale de France, département Philosophie, histoire, sciences de l'homme, 8-LK12-895. Provenance : Bibliothèque nationale de France. Online date : 24/08/2009.

[177] Vaur, J.-P. (1849). *Précis historique des faits relatifs à l'emprunt d'Haïti.*

[178] Title : Le National : feuille politique et littéraire / [rédacteurs en chef A. Thiers, Mignet, A. Carrel] Publisher : [s.n.] (Paris). Publication date : 1830-03-25. Contributor : Thiers, Adolphe (1797-1877). Directeur de publication. Contributor : Mignet, François-Auguste Alexis (1796-1884). Directeur de publication Contributor : Carrel, Armand (1800-1836). Directeur de publication. Contributor : Trélat, Ulysse (1795-1879). Directeur de publication. Relationship : http://catalogue.bnf.fr/ark:/12148/cb32822285p. Description : 1830/03/25 (A1,N82). Identifier : ark:/12148/bpt6k1514875c. Source : Bibliothèque et Archives de l'Assemblée nationale, AN sans cote. Provenance : Bibliothèque nationale de France. Online date : 26/06/2017

[179] This subject is treated in Blancpain (2001), Ardouin, Madiou and in many history texts. Blancpain, Francois (2001). Un siècle de relations financières entre Haïti et la France, 1825-1922, L'Harmattan, 2001.

ISBN
2747508528, 9782747508520.
[180] Henochsberg, *Public Debt and Slavery.*
[181] Blancpain, Francois (2001). Un siècle de relations financières entre Haïti et la France, 1825-1922, L'Harmattan, 2001. ISBN 2747508528, 9782747508520.
[182] Bonneau, Alexandre (1862). Haiti: ses progrès, son avenir, E. Dentu Libraire-Editeur, Paris.
[183] François Blancpain et Bernard Gainot, « Les négociations des traités de 1838 », *La Révolution française* [En ligne], 16 | 2019, mis en ligne le 20 juin 2019, consulté le 05 mars 2025. URL : http://journals.openedition.org/lrf/2757 ; DOI : https://doi.org/10.4000/lrf.2757
[184] Henochsberg, *Public Debt and Slavery.*
[185] Ibid.
[186] Bulmer-Thomas, *The Economic History of the Caribbean.*
[187] Ibid.
[188] Federico, and Tena-Junguito, "American divergence."
[189] Discussed in detail by Henochsberg, *Public Debt and Slavery.*
[190] Screenshot of royal decree. L'ordonnance de Charles X du 17 avril 1825. In: Outre-mers, tome 90, n°340-341, 2e semestre 2003. Haïti Première République Noire. p. 249; https://www.persee.fr/doc/outre_1631-0438_2003_num_90_340_4057
[191] Madiou, Tome 3, p 502
[192] These letters were published by famous Haitian doctor, sociologist, historian, and writer Jean Price Mars. Mars, Jean Price. La République d'Haiti et la Republique Dominicaine, Tome 1, Port-au-Prince: 1953. https://ufdcimages.uflib.ufl.edu/UF/00/09/59/32/00001/Mars_RD_Haiti_fr_1.pdf.
[193] *Niles' Weekly Register.* Digital, MSA SC 6211, Niles' Register Cumulative Index, 1849 1811
[194] Madiou, Thomas, Tome V, page 458.
[195] Moral, Paul. *Le Paysan Haïtien : Étude sur la vie rural en Haïti.* Maisonneuve et Larose, Port-au-Prince, 1961. Also discussed in Madiou, *Histoire d'Haïti.*
[196] Discussed in Moral, *Le Paysan Haitien.*
[197] Madiou, Tome II. Romain is introduced to the reader as a capable officer under Christophe's command, and later in the volume his contribution to the revolution against General Leclerc is detailed.
[198] Ardouin, Tome 10, chapitre 2.
[199] Racine, Jean (1697). Les Plaideurs, Publié par Gwénola, Ernest et Paul Fièvre, Septembre 2015.
[200] Dumesle's speech was reprinted in a series by Ardouin, who, in turn, claimed to have been in possession of Boyer's reply to Dumesle.

Ardouin, Beaubrun (1853–1860). Études sur l'histoire d'Haïti ; suivies de la vie du général J.-M. Borgella. Tome 8, pg 332. Dézobry et E. Magdeleine (Paris). Printed monograph, 11 vol. ; in-8. Bibliothèque nationale de France, département Philosophie, histoire, sciences de l'homme, 8-PU-10 (8), Online date : 25/10/2010, Identifier : ark:/12148/bpt6k6148891m

201 Upon annexation, Boyer split Christophe's kingdom into two departments: Nord and Artibonite.

202 Madiou, Thomas. Tome VI, pp 234-239

203 Madiou, Thomas. Tome VI, pp 322-323

204 There is no departure from the official government version, which appeared in a special edition of Le Télégraphe, on 01 September 1822. Le Télégraphe, Port-au-Prince, 1843-03-15. http://catalogue.bnf.fr/ark:/12148/cb32876528p. Identifier : ark:/12148/bpt6k8987039, Source : Bibliothèque nationale de France, département Philosophie, histoire, sciences de l'homme, FOL-PU-233. Online date : 21/11/2016

205 Ardouin, Volume 3, Tome 9, Chapitre 4

206 Madiou, Thomas, Tome VII, livre 92, page 187.

207 Madiou, Thomas, Tome VII, livre 92, page 189

208 Hezekiah Niles, Niles' Weekly Register Volumes 14 and 21. Baltimore: Franklin Press.

209 Mars, Jean Price. La République d'Haïti et la République Dominicaine, Tome 1, Port-au-Prince: 1953. https://ufdcimages.uflib.ufl.edu/UF/00/09/59/32/00001/Mars_RD_Haiti _fr_1.pdf.

210 Racine, Jean (1697). Les Plaideurs, Publié par Gwénola, Ernest et Paul Fièvre, Septembre 2015.

211 Ardouin, Beaubrun (1856). Volume 3, Tome 9, Chapitre IV

212 Dubois (1866), pp 55

213 Details of the earthquake were taken from several accounts by the National Centers for Environmental Information and National Oceanic and Atmospheric Association, https://www.ngdc.noaa.gov/hazel/view/hazards/tsunami/event-more-info/726. J. Scherer, "Great earthquakes in the Island of Haiti," Bulletin of the Seismological Society of America 2, no. 3 (1912): 161–180, https://doi.org/10.1785/BSSA0020030161. Demesvar Delorme and Jean M. Lambert, « 1842 Mil Huit Cent Quarante-deux Au Cap, » (Cap Haïtien, Haiti: Imprimerie du Progrès, 1942), Digital Library of the Caribbean, University of Florida, https://www.dloc.com/UF00100960/00001/citation.

214 Richard Robert. À propos de Saint-Domingue : la monnaie dans l'économie coloniale (1674-1803). In: Revue d'histoire des colonies, tome 41, n°142, premier trimestre 1954. pp. 22-46; doi :

https://doi.org/10.3406/outre.1954.1201
https://www.persee.fr/doc/outre_0399-1385_1954_num_41_142_1201
[215] The first minting was in Mexico in 1535.
[216] Beaulieu, Charles,A. (1987). Le Système Bancaire Haïtien: fonctionnement et perspectives, Tome 1, Banque de la République d'Haïti, Port-au-Prince.
[217] John Maynard Keynes, *The General Theory of Employment, Interest, and Money* (Harcourt, Brace, 1936).
[218] Lacombe Robert. Histoire monétaire de Saint-Domingue et de la République d'Haïti, des origines à 1874. In: Revue d'histoire des colonies, tome 43, n°152-153, troisième et quatrième trimestres 1956. pp. 273-337; doi : https://doi.org/10.3406/outre.1956.1262
https://www.persee.fr/doc/outre_0399-1385_1956_num_43_152_1262
[219] *Le Patriote*, no. 13 (1842). Reprinted in Desquiron, Jean. Haiti à la Une: une anthologie de la presse haitienne de 1724 à 1934, Tome 1, Imprimeur II, Port-au-Prince: 1993.
[220] Lacombe Robert. Histoire monétaire de Saint-Domingue et de la République d'Haïti, des origines à 1874. In: Revue d'histoire des colonies, tome 43, n°152-153, troisième et quatrième trimestres 1956. pp. 273-337; doi : https://doi.org/10.3406/outre.1956.1262
https://www.persee.fr/doc/outre_0399-1385_1956_num_43_152_1262
[221] Madiou, Livre 94, pg 270.
[222] Dubois (1866)
[223] Dubois (1866), pp 63
[224] Inginac, *Mémoires de Joseph Balthazar Inginac*, pg 119.
[225] Baur, "Mulatto Machiavelli."
[226] The Journal des Débats Politiques et Litteraire reported on 01 May 1843 that Rivière Hérard was at the head of 14000 men.
[227] La Presse (Paris), 1843-03-26. Bibliothèque nationale de France, http://catalogue.bnf.fr/ark:/12148/cb34448033b. Identifier : ark:/12148/bpt6k429170g. Online date : 15/10/2007
[228] Ardouin, Tome 2, Chapitre 7
[229] Dubois (1866), pp 55
[230] Title : Coup-d'oeil rétrospectif sur Haïti. Author : Élie, Prosper. Publisher : impr. de Moquet (Paris). Publication date : 1860. Relationship : http://catalogue.bnf.fr/ark:/12148/cb303977905 Identifier : ark:/12148/bpt6k5797114q. Source : Bibliothèque nationale de France. Provenance : Bibliothèque nationale de France. Online date : 25/10/2010
[231] Le Télégraphe, Publisher : [s.n.] (Port-au-Prince),1843-03-15, http://catalogue.bnf.fr/ark:/12148/cb32876528p. Bibliothèque nationale de France, département Philosophie, histoire, sciences de l'homme, FOL-PU-233, Identifier : ark:/12148/bpt6k8987039. Online date : 21/11/2016

[232] They were all eventually offered amnesty and their property rights were restored.

[233] Janvier, Louis Joseph (1883). La République d'Haïti et Ses Visiteurs: 1840-1882, Marpon et Flammarion: Paris, 1883. http://www.manioc.org/gsdl/collect/patrimon/archives/PAP11088.dir/PAP11088.pdf

[234] Title : Du Gouvernement civil en Haïti.Author : Janvier, Louis-Joseph (1855-1911). Publisher : Le Bigot frères (Lille). Publication date : 1905. Relationship : http://catalogue.bnf.fr/ark:/12148/cb30646417h. Identifier : ark:/12148/bpt6k6133568h. Source : Bibliothèque nationale de France, département Philosophie, histoire, sciences de l'homme, 8-PU-445 Provenance : Bibliothèque nationale de France. Online date : 04/10/2010

[235] *The Liberator* (Boston, MA) April 28, 1843, https://www.loc.gov/item/sn84031524/1843-04-28/ed-1/.

[236] Excerpt republished in *The Liberator* on April 20, 1843.

[237] Journal de Toulouse, 26 April 1843. Bibliothèque municipale de Toulouse, P 018, Bibliothèque nationale de France, Online date : 12/01/2020, Collection numérique : BIPFPIG31. Identifier : ark:/12148/bpt6k53638499

[238] *Le Journal des Débats Politiques et Littéraire* , 26 April 1843

[239] Title : Voyage aux Antilles françaises, anglaises, danoises, espagnoles, à St-Domingue et aux Etats-Unis d'Amérique. Antilles anglaises, danoises, espagnoles / par A. Granier de Cassagnac Author : Granier de Cassagnac, Adolphe (1806-1880). Publisher : Dauvin et Fontaine (Paris). Publication date : 1842-1844. Set notice : http://catalogue.bnf.fr/ark:/12148/cb36491882c. Identifier : ark:/12148/bpt6k62974q. Source : Bibliothèque nationale de France, département Philosophie, histoire, sciences de l'homme, 8-LK12-957 (2). Provenance : Bibliothèque nationale de France. Online date : 15/10/2007

[240]

[241] Bonnet, Guy Joseph. Exposé de la conduite du général Rigaud, dans le commandement du département du sud de Saint-Domingue , adressé au Directoire-exécutif, par le citoyen Bonnet, aide-de-camp dudit général. [Paris.] De l'imprimerie de J. F. Sobry, rue du Bacq, n°. 149. [1798]. http://catalogue.bnf.fr/ark:/12148/cb301292460. Bibliothèque nationale de France, département Philosophie, histoire, sciences de l'homme, 8-LK12-542. Identifier : ark:/12148/bpt6k58068847. Online date : 08/02/2010

[242] De Lespinasse, *Les gens d'autrefois.*

[243] Title : Journal de Toulouse : politique et littéraire. Publisher : [s.n.] (Toulouse).Publication date : 1843-09-27. Relationship :

http://catalogue.bnf.fr/ark:/12148/cb345241384. Identifier : ark:/12148/bpt6k5363981v. Source : Bibliothèque municipale de Toulouse, P 018. Provenance : Bibliothèque nationale de France. Online date : 12/01/2020

[244] Gazette de Metz, 1844-05-25. Relationship : http://catalogue.bnf.fr/ark:/12148/cb32780527x. Collection numérique : BIPFPIG57. Identifier : ark:/12148/bpt6k8266258h. Bibliothèque nationale de France, département Droit, économie, politique, JO-8227, Online date : 29/08/2022

[245] De Lespinasse's (1926) p. 78 version appears the most credible. Bazelais, who had accompanied Boyer to meet King Louis Philippe, recounted the exchange to his friend, de Lespinasse's grandfather. Madiou's account is not substantively different: Madiou, Tome XVIII, pg. 63.

[246] Lespinasse, Pierre-Eugène de. Gens d'autrefois... Vieux souvenirs. La "Revue mondiale" (Paris), 1926, http://catalogue.bnf.fr/ark:/12148/cb30803634f. Bibliothèque nationale de France, département Philosophie, histoire, sciences de l'homme, 8-PU-510 (1), Identifier : ark:/12148/bpt6k6148893f. Online date : 25/10/2010

[247] Gazette de France, 04 April, 1844

[248] L'Echo Francais, published on 31 aout 1843, a letter from General Lazare, a letter written in Port-au-Prince and dated 02 July 1843, to the editor-in-chief of Le Globe, Mr. Granier de Cassagnac.

[249] L'Echo Francais, October 9. 1843.

[250] These letters are dated March 9, 1844, December 20, 1844, and February 25, 1845. Madiou Tome XVIII, pp 196-8

[251] Handwritten letter by Boyer, dated 25 February 1845, from Kingston, Jamaica. Reprinted in several texts, including de Lespinasse.

[252] The New York Herald (September 11, 1848), Library of Congress, item no. sn83030313.

[253] Racine, Jean (1697).Les Plaideurs, Publié par Gwénola, Ernest et Paul Fièvre, Septembre 2015.

[254] Title : Gens d'autrefois... Vieux souvenirs...Author : Lespinasse, Pierre-Eugène de. Publisher : la "Revue mondiale" (Paris). Publication date : 1926. Relationship : http://catalogue.bnf.fr/ark:/12148/cb30803634f. Identifier : ark:/12148/bpt6k6148893f. Source : Bibliothèque nationale de France, département Philosophie, histoire, sciences de l'homme, 8-PU-510 (1). Provenance : Bibliothèque nationale de France. Online date : 25/10/2010. The interaction, in a far less dramatic fashion, was also mentioned in *La Gazette de France* on 11 July 1844.

[255] Jamaican Family Search, Genealogy Research Library, Extractions from Roman Catholic Registers. http://www.jamaicanfamilysearch.com/index.htm. Accessed July 2025

[256] Letter from Boyer to Coquierre, dated 6 May 1846 from Kingston, Jamaica, reprinted in de Lespinasse.

[257] Title : Le Moniteur haïtien : journal officiel de la république d'Haïti, paraissant tous les samedis. Publisher : [s.n.] (Port-au-Prince). Publication date : 1847-01-30. Relationship : http://catalogue.bnf.fr/ark:/12148/cb32819449v. Description : 1847/01/30 (A2,N32). Identifier : ark:/12148/bpt6k12639648. Source : Bibliothèque nationale de France, département Droit, économie, politique, JOA-453. Provenance : Bibliothèque nationale de France. Online date : 08/08/2016

[258] Le Courrier français, 1849-09-26. Durrieu, Xavier (1814-1868). Directeur de publication. Relationship : http://catalogue.bnf.fr/ark:/12148/cb32749956z. 26 septembre 1849. Identifier : ark:/12148/bpt6k4710299k Bibliothèque nationale de France, département Droit, économie, politique, JOD-166. Online date : 01/10/2017

[259] La Démocratie pacifique : journal des intérêts des gouvernements et des peuples, École sociétaire (Paris), 1847-07-26. Considérant, Victor (1808-1893). Rédacteur. Relationship : http://catalogue.bnf.fr/ark:/12148/cb32755585p. Identifier : ark:/12148/bpt6k4767498d. Bibliothèque nationale de France, département Arsenal, JOD-1904. Online date : 10/06/2018

[260] Courrier de Marseille : commercial et politique, 1850-07-14. Relationship : http://catalogue.bnf.fr/ark:/12148/cb32750667t. Collection numérique : Bibliographie de la presse... Continuation of text, Description : Collection numérique : BIPFPIG13. Identifier : ark:/12148/bpt6k38081040 Bibliothèque nationale de France, département Droit, économie, politique, JO-2184. Online date : 10/01/2021

[261] De Lespinasse wrote in his memoirs that in the years following Boyer's death, the mausoleum was assigned a guard, with whom he would engage in conversation during visits to the cemetery. The guard mentioned that a "Mr. and Mrs. Boyer" visited the site rather frequently, claiming to be descendants. De Lespinasse, on his visits, claimed to have found cards and flowers signed by the Boyers.

[262] Title : Le Moniteur haïtien : journal officiel de la république d'Haïti, paraissant tous les samedis. Publisher : [s.n.] (Port-au-Prince). Publication date : 1850-07-27. Relationship : http://catalogue.bnf.fr/ark:/12148/cb32819449v. Identifier : ark:/12148/bpt6k12640528.Source : Bibliothèque nationale de France, département Droit, économie, politique, JOA-453. Provenance :

Bibliothèque nationale de France. Online date : 08/08/2016

263 *The New Hampshire Gazette and Republican Union* (Portsmouth, NH), July 30 1850, Library of Congress item no. sn84023141. Also in La Gazette de France, 10 July 1850.

264 Feuille du Commerce, 31 March 1844. Title : Feuille du commerce, petites affiches et annonces du Port-au-Prince. Publisher : [s.n.?] (Port-au-Prince). Publication date : 18??. Relationship : http://catalogue.bnf.fr/ark:/12148/cb327746703. Description : Etat de collection : N° 1 (21/01/1827)-n° 52 (29/12/1860). Identifier : ark:/12148/cb327746703/date. Source : Bibliothèque nationale de France, département Philosophie, histoire, sciences de l'homme, FOL-PU-217. Provenance : Bibliothèque nationale de France. Online date : 14/05/2008

265 Inginac, *Mémoires de Joseph Balthazar Inginac,* pg 120.

266 Feuille du Commerce, 30 juillet 1843. Title : Feuille du commerce, petites affiches et annonces du Port-au-Prince. Publisher : [s.n.?] (Port-au-Prince). Publication date : 18??. Relationship : http://catalogue.bnf.fr/ark:/12148/cb327746703. Description : Etat de collection : N° 1 (21/01/1827)-n° 52 (29/12/1860). Identifier : ark:/12148/cb327746703/date. Source : Bibliothèque nationale de France, département Philosophie, histoire, sciences de l'homme, FOL-PU-217. Provenance : Bibliothèque nationale de France. Online date : 14/05/2008

267 Feuille du Commerce, 03 novembre 1855.Project EAP1024:Beyond the Revolution: Bibliothèque Haïtienne des Frères de l'Instruction Chrétienne Collections, Bringing Nineteenth-Century Haitian History to the World. Collection EAP1024/1: Bibliothèque Haïtienne des Frères de l'Instruction Chrétienne Collection. Collection EAP1024/1/1: Feuille du Commerce. Collection EAP1024/1/1/9: Feuille du Commerce [1855]. File EAP1024/1/1/9/10/1: Feuille du Commerce [3 novembre 1855]

268 Madiou also discussed this in his own analysis of Boyer and his generation. Madiou, Tome VII, Livre 90, pg 112.

269 Candler, *Brief notices of Hayti.*